COMMUNITY PLAYS

How to put them on

ANN JELLICOE

D0319139

A Methuen Paperback

A Methuen Dramabook

First published as a paperback original
in 1987 in Great Britain by Methuen London Ltd
11 New Fetter Lane, London EC4P 4EE
and in the United States of America
by Methuen Inc., 29 West 35th Street, New York, NY 10001

Photographs reproduced by courtesy of Roger Mayne

Printed by Richard Clay Ltd, Bungay, Suffolk

British Library Cataloguing in Publication Data

Jellicoe, Ann
    Community plays: how to put them on.——
    (A Methuen dramabook).
    1. Theatre——Great Britain   2. Theatre
    and society——Great Britain
    I. Title
    792'.022   PN2595

    ISBN 0–413–42150–3

Contents

List of Illustrations

Between pages 174 and 175

Towards Performance
> Constructing a giant puppet.
> Puppets and stilt-walkers in action.
> A set and costume workshop; carpentry – a 'sixteenth-century' door.
> A costume parade.
> Erecting scaffolding; the designer checks costumes.

In Performance
> The fair before *The Garden*; *Ssh!* – Burton Bradstock village play;

Workscenes
> *The Poor Man's Friend* – making rope; *The Tide* – carpet weaving.

Between pages 238 and 239

The Plays
> *Entertaining Strangers* – a father names his son who has died of cholera.
> *The Western Women* – the same scene: boys in rehearsal and performance.
> *The Western Women* – guarding the town perimeter: the same scene in rehearsal and performance.
> *Today of All Days* – a contemporary theme.
> *Colyford Matters* – actors take up position.
> *The Poor Man's Friend*.
> *The Tide* and *The Ballad of Tilly Hake* – audience perching.
> *The Garden* – helping failing memories.
> *The Poor Man's Friend* – a complicated scene.

Possession, imagination, excitement
> *The Western Women* – women demand the right to help defend their town; *Entertaining Strangers* – the people of Dorchester greet their vicar in his hour of triumph.

Acknowledgements

The Calouste Gulbenkian Foundation and the Carnegie United Kingdom Trust, by their early financial priming, made the Colway Theatre Trust possible and so, perhaps, the whole community play movement. The Gulbenkian Foundation first suggested the idea of this book seven years ago; the Carnegie Trust have been our benefactors since 1980. In yet one more helpful and generous gesture both have made financial contributions towards the costs of writing. The Chairman and Council of Management of the Colway Theatre Trust (CTT) greatly helped the preparation of copy by allowing me to share their staff and resources.

I would like to thank Jon Oram, my successor as Director of CTT, and Sally-Anne Lomas, my former assistant and co-director of *The Western Women*, for reading the typescript, sharing their experience and making many useful suggestions. My friend, and former secretary, Sylvia Lee, actress, Chair of Lyme Regis Dramatic Society, member of CTT Council of Management, has been associated with the Colway Theatre Trust since it first started and has typed out the best part of three drafts, correcting my mistakes and making many valuable comments. Peter Hamilton has generously shared with me the results of his questionnaire about the Dorchester community play. I am grateful to the many people who have kindly allowed me to quote from their letters about the work. My daughter, Katkin Mayne, has acted in two community plays and assisted in the design of two more, and I am grateful for her ideas and observations. My son, Tom Mayne, having had experience of computers at school, saved his mother from insanity with her new word processor.

Finally I would like to thank all those who have taken part in these community plays (many of whom, to my continuing pleasure, I still see frequently), for we taught each other how to put the plays on.

Quotations from Writers Unless otherwise attributed are all taken from remarks or presentations made at the Colway Theatre Trust Writer's Seminar held at Monkton Wyld Court, Dorset, in June 1985.

Appendix All documents marked * are reproduced in the Appendix.

Preface

What is a community play like?

Here is a description of a small village community play as it was performed in Colyford, East Devon. Excerpts from an article in *Theatre Ireland* by Baz Kershaw.

The show is performed in the village hall, which is 30 feet wide by 60 feet long and has the ubiquitous proscenium arch stage across one end. However, the initial impression on arriving for the show is one of chaos: there are over 150 people standing and moving everywhere, some in costume, some selling things, some obviously setting up for the performance. The only seating – for older people – is in short rows on rostra scattered round the edge of the space. The rest of us must stand and promenade, following the action round and between the four stages: a large apron extension to the proscenium stage, two smaller ones against the side walls, a tiny one in a corner. So the subdued order of traditional theatre is replaced by a confused hubbub of activity, a re-creation of Colyford's old Goose Fair as many people in nineteenth-century costume try to sell you biscuits, pottery, even badges of the show, from trays. The play, then, does not so much *begin* as *grow out of* the fair, the first scene starting amid the combined chatter of the audience and performers.

Three local nineteenth-century farmers are looking for men. The audience, the men for hire among them, gravitate to the side stage where they stand. As they announce the jobs available the men in the audience make muttering comments. Not everything can be heard, but the general drift of the action is nevertheless clear: there isn't enough work for everybody, and the unemployed must poach to eat. This hinge to the action of the whole play is not explicitly presented – it arrives more as an undertow, a quiet murmur of protest from the men who do not get employed by the farms. This implicit communication is successful because the audience is *in* the action, incorporated into the scene. Similarly, there is a cunning function in the promenade convention: it counteracts the need for theatrical 'projection' and makes the amateur actors seem more natural in performance. A sense of realism then reinforces the very direct communication between performers and audience, so we feel we are not so much looking *at* the nineteenth century, but are still, somehow, a part of it.

The structure of the story-line and the subjects of the scenes reinforce this effect, while making us simultaneously aware of the present. For instance, the second scene has a certain Captain Impey announcing the marriage of his daughter to a Mr John Scarborough. His speech makes direct reference to features of the village which still exist (the reactions of the audience makes this very clear). More fundamentally, the actors among the audience react to the announcement in ways which are still to some extent typical: the women with warm appreciation, the men with a gentle lasciviousness. So the past is brought vividly alive *in* the present, to establish a powerful feeling of historical continuity.

The story concerns a long feud between two village families which was started by a poaching incident, but the story-*line* is only important as an excuse for presenting a wide range of loosely connected scenes, animated by a variety of styles. The chasing and catching of the poacher, Benjamin Appleyard, is done in a near blackout with the actors dashing among the audience, producing an effect more closely allied to sport and fairgrounds than theatres. The problem of what should be done with the deported poacher's children is dealt with in a kitchen setting, which begins and ends with twenty women and girls singing beautiful choric rounds about cooking and lacemaking.

Despite the deportation the poaching continues, particularly of eels from the River Coly. The river is signified through a dance of ten men up and down the length of the hall, which is followed immediately by a wonderful surge through the audience of a brightly coloured twenty-foot-long eel with large jaws that snap at the delighted audience. It is remarkable that such widely different techniques, derived from traditional English May Day celebrations and Chinese New Year festivals, should be so congruent, reinforcing each other's effect by contrast. Similarly, a broadly comic scene in a pub is set against a real game of skittles which is played down the whole length of the hall – a mixture of theatre and sport (Brecht would be delighted) which the audience clearly enjoyed.

This stylistic freedom is possible because the unity of the event derives from a simple shift of focus, away from theatre, towards community. Hence, the typical situations presented provoke an historical awareness that rests on a curious identification between the live actors and the dead people they play. They come from the same community and so it seems, in performance, as if they are the same people. The result is a powerful sense of the mysterious – set within an active celebration of shared meanings. So the explicitly presented development of the community in the past is implicitly animated in the present. The artistic unity consequently derives from the fact that the fundamental event is not the play itself, but the opportunity the play provides for the continuing evolution of Colyford as a community. In other words, community plays *are* a community-forming process. Thus theatre is created *through* community.

Baz Kershaw goes on to consider the nature of community involvement:

> If a community theatre company performs in a village hall, say, the community is inevitably in the role of host because the hall 'belongs' to the village. It opens up its own space for the performers. So at the very least space is exchanged for performance. But usually much more is exchanged: any gesture by the community towards the performers (putting up posters or inviting them to coffee after the show) is the result of animation in the social networks of the community. Virtually all the activities surrounding the setting up of a performance are thus an expression of community: so you might say that performance is exchanged for community, or the community invests itself in performance. I call this type of exchange *implicit* barter. Ann Jellicoe's work obviously depends on it fundamentally: the skills of the professionals are exchanged for performances by the community.

*   *   *

This book seeks to provide a model: you can imitate its practice or create your own. What follows is my experience since I discovered the principle of community plays in 1977 and began to develop it over ten productions and eight years. Community plays are now being produced all over the UK and I myself am now being asked to help set up plays abroad.

At its simplest the process boils down to credibility: can you deliver and convince other people that you can? To discovering how to involve people in creating a work of art, and where to draw the line between the needs of the community and the needs of art.

Community plays:
discovering the principle
and developing the work

When I was four years old I wanted to go into theatre. All through school I got up plays: writing, rehearsing, stage managing, lighting, painting scenery, acting, directing. At drama school I did the same. In 1947 I emerged into a Theatre which, as regards development and growth, had slept since 1939. For ten years the theatre was deeply conventional, almost all energy had been absorbed by the war.

In 1948 my uncle, an architect, a man of infinite imagination and a great influence on my life, aware that I might have lost my sense of direction, commissioned me to make a study of the relationship between theatre architecture and theatre practice. This led to an interest, indeed passion, for the open stage (i.e. a thrusting forestage surrounded by the audience on three sides). My early experience had given me the confidence to do it myself. If a play was wanted I wrote it. I was ready to find means, cast, venue, get the play on and the audience in. This has been a source of strength throughout my work and life. I know that if you want to do something you simply do it.

To explore the open stage I founded a Sunday Club for professional actors; these were mostly working as understudies on the West End stage. There was no television and they were bored out of their minds. Here we mounted a number of experimental productions including an early one-act play which I wrote in the manner of Christopher Fry (and so got that out of my system). These open stage productions were the first to be seen in England since the forestage disappeared in the early nineteenth century; or more truly, as we had no scenery, since Shakespeare's time. In 1953 I was asked back to the Central School, where I had trained, to teach acting. This was a very fertile period for me and for the theatre. You could feel things happening: the Royal Court Theatre was started, Stratford East began to emerge, the centre of artistic balance began to shift from Paris to London, a tide of creative energy began to roll.

One day, while teaching at Central, I watched a student improvising a dream: he was playing a trumpet and it turned into a bird and flew away. I suddenly felt, amidst all the welter of impressions and ideas that were crowding in on me at that time that here was something new and strong: a theatre of images which would be neither literary nor symbolic. So, with the stimulus of the *Observer* Playwriting Competition, I wrote my first play, *The Sport of My Mad Mother*. It won a prize and was immediately accepted by the Royal Court Theatre. Thus began a period when I was closely identified with the Royal Court, won a reputation with my plays, including *The Knack*, and made friendships with people whose work now stretches across the Theatre.

In 1960 I was approached with an irresistible commission: the Girl Guides Association wanted to celebrate the fiftieth anniversary of the founding of their movement with a play in the Empire Pool, Wembley. This is a vast arena surrounded by banked seating. There was to be a guaranteed audience of 5,000 per night, amongst them the Queen, a cast of at least 400 Guides including some foreign contingents, and a few professional actors for the main parts. In the event I wrote a play which involved all the older women in the world supressing men and finally destroying the earth with an atomic bomb, the Empire Pool then turned into a space ship and flew away. This modest, unassuming, optimistic little piece was, perhaps unsurprisingly, turned down by the Girl Guides. It was later produced on a Sunday night, with hundreds of children, at the Royal Court with terrific success.

As a result of *The Rising Generation* I was approached by the County Drama Adviser of Hampshire. The Queen was to open new law courts in Winchester. On the great day the former law courts, housed in the beautiful old Great Hall, would be the venue for a play or happening, which was to involve resources and people from all over the county. I was given a free hand and a budget of £10,000 (probably equal to £60,000 today), and spent two happy months researching the possibilities. It was just at the start of what we then called 'the squeeze' but now recognise as the recession. Suddenly the project was abandoned and the law courts opened without the help of Her Majesty. However, these two projects now seem pointers to my present work.

In 1974, after the birth of my children and two years as Literary Manager of the Royal Court Theatre, we decided to leave London and move permanently to the West Country where we had had a cottage for many years. We disliked the pressures of London and I was dissatisfied with theatre: it's hard to say why except that perhaps it seemed totally unimportant in most people's lives.

We moved to Lyme Regis. I had long wanted to work with schools and schoolchildren but London teachers won't easily let you in, and rightly so. I'm grateful now that my total inexperience was not tested in those tough schools; it would probably have killed all enthusiasm. As part of a small rural community I found things easier. My children were of school age and I went to the headmaster of our local comprehensive, which serves 98 per cent of the area, and asked if he would like me to write a play for them.

The Reckoning
by Ann Jellicoe (Lyme Regis, 1978)

At a meeting with the headmaster, the Head of English and the English teacher who usually produced the school plays, it was agreed that they would indeed like to have a play. Thus began a series of very significant experiences. I wrote a play on a very large scale intending to involve parents and other adults in the older parts. It was about the Monmouth Rebellion which began in Lyme in 1686. When I delivered it, I sensed reservations: it was clear that the teacher/ producer felt threatened. This was my first encounter with what I later came to recognise as the 'siege mentality'. No wise headteacher will go directly against his staff if it can be helped; and so they said the play was too big for them. I withdrew the play and forgot about it. After six months the teacher/producer left to be replaced by a more imaginative and confident man. Meanwhile I had formed a web of contacts through my work on the Drama Panel of South-West Arts (SWA) and was thus able to go to the University of Exeter Drama Department for help with stage management. Medium Fair, our local professional theatre company, was also keen to be involved, as were the Lyme Regis Amateur Dramatic Society, so I went back to the school with a package.

There followed one of the most amazing periods of my life and certainly the most demanding and exhausting. I engaged a young designer, Carmel Collins. She was paid virtually nothing (we both received £250) and lived in my house. The job was so huge that we were forced to look for help. The woman who does costumes for the Lyme Regis Amateur Dramatic Society began to take an interest. She is a true 'gate opener', a key figure in the town, the wife of a publican who is also Lyme Regis Town Crier: 'We'll give all these coats to Mrs

Adams, she's just lost her husband and I know she wants something to do . . . Let's give this hemming to Mary, she doesn't want anything complicated.' So dozens of people began to help make costumes. We set up a wardrobe workshop in the bowels of the school so that kids could help too, running down at lunch-time and after school, enjoying the atmosphere and diversion. There was so little money we had to appeal for materials. The town council allowed us to use their duplicator and the clerks ran the appeal off free; all the kids took a copy home from school and we distributed others wherever we could. People brought material, loads of it, some so good that Carmel couldn't bear to cut it up and, significantly, the people who gave wanted to know what it was all about.

From this it was a very short step to asking for every kind of help. There began to be movement all over the town. The museum loaned a damaged lectern, and the school woodwork department mended it. This was the first contact there had been between them at this level and it went on after the play. The Lifeboat Society lent their street banner and someone else repainted it; a third group asked if they could borrow it later; and so another resource became available to the town. A builder loaned his lorry and someone drove it free. The Town Council lent the elaborately carved chairs from the guild-hall, and the town banner: 'I'm glad to say the vote were unanimous my dear,' said the Mayor in his rolling Dorset accent. Free accommodation was found for the Exeter students. The police loaned truncheons, farmers gave straw. In hundreds of ways people began to help and so made contact with each other; and as they gave their goods and skills, so they became interested in what was happening.

The help was a necessity; the play couldn't have been done on such a scale without the energy and enthusiasm of a very large number of people. One day, Baz Kershaw of Medium Fair said: 'You must have an interval because that means coffee so you'll involve more people.' I suddenly saw that the more we got people to help the more interested they would be, that we should actually be creating opportunities for people to become involved. We decided to have a fair before the play. The school PTA organised it and kept the proceeds: twenty more people a night preparing things to sell and getting their costumes together. The sixth form divided the town up and made publicity door-drops. Shops mounted window displays, the town librarian organised the box office, the Floral Society promised displays.

By involving themselves people were helping create a work of art, giving and sharing towards an idealistic aim. Amazing energy was being released, and people felt good doing it. There was an air of friendliness and supportiveness amongst the cast and helpers. Others began to identify. The play became a topic of conversation in pubs. As you went down Broad Street people would ask 'How's it going then?' or even 'Have you solved that problem in Act 2?' The town was intrigued and gossiping, but not yet committed.

I spent the last few weeks of *The Reckoning* in a haze of exhaustion. It was a very heavy burden doing work which would now be shared between at least six people. The trouble is, until you've done it you can't appreciate how demanding and complex it is, so you can't pace yourself correctly nor organise help as efficiently as you might.

The Reckoning was a promenade production which was still very rare at that time, certainly none had been seen in the south-west. It was done in the school with three banks of seating cradling the action and focusing attention on the floor; there was enough seating for about a third of the audience. Much of the action took place on the floor amongst the promenading audience but there were also three raised stages for important scenes. I think a great deal of the success of *The Reckoning* and of subsequent plays was that we found a physical form which reinforced the idea of involvement. The audience was part of the action, even those who were seated became a backdrop. As a form this is the ultimate expression of theatricality: as far away from television as you can get.

Many years ago I realised that one of the essential characteristics of theatre is that members of the audience influence each other and colour each other's reactions. If you are physically near people your reactions will be affected by theirs. If you are surrounded by people who are wrapped up in a play and excited by it you become excited too. You think you are reacting to the play, but it's not just that: you're being caught up a in a group feeling which is colouring your responses.

So there we were, people of Lyme today watching and identifying with people of Lyme of three hundred years ago. Two women fold washing on a hill above the sea, on the actual spot – just where we are standing – and suddenly, we look out to sea and there are the ships . . . We turn our heads, our attention caught by an incoherent moaning . . . men of Lyme, desperate, dirty, are stumbling back home after the battle of Sedgemoor; they shelter, shuddering and exhausted, amongst the people of Lyme today. . . Seated high above us a corrosive Judge Jeffreys puts on the black cap . . . We stand back to let through the funeral procession of a young man who has been hung, saved from quartering by his sister. Girls and women, dressed in white, hand out sprigs of rosemary, defying the soldiers to stop them. The burial service is read by a real vicar ('Alas! I have read so many'). We are saddened, proud, moved, some are deeply emotional. It is an overwhelming experience, a mixture of us and them and then and now, of pride for what they did and in what we are achieving, of celebration.

It was indeed the first manifestation of what has taken me some years to understand. Howard Barker recently said, in an interview with *Gambit* magazine (No. 41, p. 43), 'Community plays lend tremendous resources to the theatre . . . there is an overpowering emotional state generated which is irresistible.' This overpowering emotion comes partly from scale: 150 actors and an audience of 350 or so are locked into a very powerful imaginative experience. There is, too, a very high standard of work: writing, acting and direction. The actors are either of a degree of natural talent ('a remarkable evening which makes nonsense of the distinction between amateur and professional acting' said the *Guardian*) or they are so openly and unreservedly convinced by what they are doing that you trust yourself to them and are borne alone on a wave of involvement and excitement. After *Entertaining Strangers* in Dorchester, Michael Billington said, 'and when the whole company, after the extirpation of the plague, join forces to sing 'Praise my soul the King of Heaven' it becomes difficult to withhold one's tears.' I have seldom known one of these productions where some members of the audience were not moved to tears, not through sadness but from being touched by overwhelming emotion. That doesn't happen very often in the conventional theatre.

I think it is this extraordinary audience/group experience which finally makes these community plays both triumphantly theatrical and triumphantly community art. The town creates the play, numberless people have either helped in some way, or know someone who has done so. There are links and involvement, however tenuous, which make people feel the play is theirs. The physical arrangement of the hall reinforces the positive aspects of the play. The audience unconsciously, vividly, excitedly and energetically projects its corporate psyche into the play. The audience is a microcosm of the community, they charge each other with feeling that is deep, delicate, exact and very powerful. The production is a catalyst which allows the audience to come together and create or release an extraordinary group experience.

The *Guardian* critic described *The Reckoning*:

The form is three stages, with the audience herded in the centre, surrounded by groups of actors, grumbling, inciting, commenting and pointing up the action. Audience participation is not needed; at any time, a person standing next to you might be involved in a brawl, or suddenly spotlighted to get on with his part in the plot. Dissenters are paraded through the crowd, people rush by you in terror, beg for mercy or confide strange secrets . . . It is a splendid piece of theatre. Dramatic, exciting, bloodthirsty, totally absorbing and above all maintaining an air of spontaneity which must have been organised to the finest detail. (Dec. 16, 1978)

The Reckoning was a solid success of the unmistakable kind. We gave a dress rehearsal for local schools to give the cast some feel of how to work with a promenading audience, followed by four performances. How would this little town take such a new form? During the first performance I heard a delighted voice: 'He said he'd arrest me!' and I knew we were all right. After the first night I was so happy, and probably so exhausted, that I got drunk on half a pint of lager. For all the involvement and interest, the week started slowly and we did not sell out until after the public dress rehearsal and first performance. Then the town became aware of what was happening and wanted to see for themselves. People were clamouring for seats: 'My wife has been three times – she'd come again if she could get a ticket.' In terms of this small and not very lively little town, it was a sensational breakthrough. Standing amongst the audience I breathed in the unfamiliar atmosphere of deep, solid, popular approval.

After the last show, on a Saturday, the stage crew began to take down the lights. We had a delirious party. Over Sunday a team of stage crew, cast and helpers worked on the strike. By eleven o'clock on Monday morning the Exeter team had left. I stood in the school hall: it was clean, quiet, in good order. Every trace of the play had gone except for a coat of arms which had been deliberately left high on a wall. A school of 800 kids and 60 staff had made considerable adjustments to accommodate the play and we had shown that we could deliver and keep our promises.

When the play was over there was great pressure to revive it but it had been such a huge feat of organisation it seemed impossible; I was really too near the experience to think clearly. Its influence flowed on: many of the contacts which had been made survived, parents began to join in and help with school plays, children from the school began to support the LRADS, with the experience of professional stage management technical standards rose, the choice of plays became more adventurous. Sometime later Marylin Fox and her town-crier husband set up an even bigger community play of their own, involving even greater numbers and written, performed and directed by local people. Seated in the sunshine watching this open-air event I felt much satisfaction.

But that was in the future. In the meantime, knocked out, I couldn't imagine reviving the play; could not help when a nearby village asked me to put one on there: 'Do your own,' I said; and they did, directing, writing, acting it down through the village and into the church, with a day-long fair in the church meadows.

Contemplation is a vital part of creation. As I thought about what had happened it seemed to me that we had created a new form of theatre. Nothing like it had ever happened before. The nearest was probably the mediaeval mystery plays and Oberammergau, but there were significant differences.

The Reckoning was, of course, especially written for Lyme Regis. With this play I established the principle of everyone being part of the action all the time: people had their own scenes but then remained in character in the body of the hall reacting to what was happening, sometimes as townspeople or, with small, intimate scenes, acting as an 'ideal audience'. The pace of the play was almost as fast as film with the action whipping from one stage to the next and all over the floor, so that I began to learn techniques of audience control and focus. With this play certain problems isolated themselves and had to be solved for the first time. These included the numbers of women who wanted to take part and the problem of how to clearly identify in the audience's mind the large numbers of characters involved.

With *The Reckoning* I discovered how much talent there is in people if only they can release it. The play could not have been done on such a scale without the energy and enthusiasm of a very large number of people. On the other hand, however supportive and useful Medium Fair had been (and it would have been hard to do the play without them) their professional acting skills were not needed: there was so much amateur talent that the professionals were simply robbing the amateurs of opportunities. In the next play we used Medium Fair in crowd scenes (two or three professionals can really energise a large group) and to help with workshops. With our third play in Bridport the distance was too far from Medium Fair's base and, shortly after, the company disbanded. Perhaps it's a pity that we no longer involve professional groups as such. There is a great deal that amateurs and professionals can learn from each other: the amateurs particularly have much to teach professionals about relating to each other and to communities. However, a professional writer, director and designer are vital since they ensure very high standards which in turn inspire confidence and commitment.

Everything depends upon trust and credibility. I discovered that, with the exception of a few upon whom initially everything depends, people are very cautious to commit themselves until they are certain they won't be made to look foolish; that people will begin tentatively to give – in whatever way is in their nature; that once people are secure they will give and share unstintingly their time, energy, talents, skills and enthusiasm and as they do so they will become more warm and friendly towards each other; that you must perhaps accept that some people seem unable ever to commit themselves; that theatre can use and involve people of virtually every age, background and intelligence – everyone can be involved; that it needs time for this process to grow – you can't suddenly bounce in and expect it to work – the town has to get used to the idea, take it on board, make it their own.

I realised, too, that this was the most demanding work I had ever done, the most exhilarating, exciting and rewarding. For the present, I could not think of returning to conventional theatre with its small, self-regarding world, its audiences whom you don't know and can't relate to, who when they leave the theatre will, if you are lucky, think of the performance a little but then put it out of their minds. Here was art which touched everyone in the community to some degree and by means of which some people changed their attitudes and lives. I have letters to prove it; people tell me it is so; I see it in their faces, attitudes and actions.

Three months after *The Reckoning* I had recovered my bounce. 'Let's do another,' said a friend. 'We'd have to have charitable status,' I said. I had discovered with *The Reckoning* that you need a platform. It's much easier for people to accept you if you appear to be backed by an organisation. A properly constituted body with charitable status is some guarantee that people are not lining their own pockets. Such a body is also able to accept public money. We set up a limited company so that if the unthinkable happened the individual members of the Council of Management would not be liable. Since we didn't know how the work might develop we chose a name which was deliberately bland. The Colway Theatre Trust (CTT) was named after Colway Manor where I live and has proved serviceable.

It was time to think of funding. SWA had given £790 towards the costs of *The Reckoning*. I was Chair of SWA Drama Panel and felt I had to act with the greatest care in asking for money from them. On the other hand I was a mature artist of considerable standing and had just produced, with the greatest artistic and financial success, an innovatory piece of work of exactly the kind that public bodies should be helping. I now asked SWA for money to support a future programme of work. I was beginning to establish our rhythm of working in high profile: workshops, rehearsal, production; while beginning to set up next year's play in another community and meanwhile looking for where we would be in Year 3. SWA gave £1,000 towards the actual costs of the next play, *The Tide*, but refused CTT any money to help with the preliminary work for that play or any other. So I gave up SWA and the chair of the Drama Panel and looked elsewhere.

I turned to the Gulbenkian Foundation. They gave CTT starter funding of £10,000 over about eighteen months, and the Carnegie Trust gave £5,000 towards capital costs to be spent over any period we wished. We thus enjoyed absolutely secure funding for two years. It was adequate and it allowed the work to grow; I was able to focus all my attention on the most creative aspects of the work and there was a terrific sense of energy. It was not until 1981, nearly two years after we had started, that we began to receive money regularly from SWA which with some funding from the Arts Council of Great Britain, came to about £12,000, enough to keep on developing. Had it been left to SWA, the Colway Theatre Trust and possibly the whole community play movement would have died as soon as it was born. In any case I never again had that sense of security which the Trust money gave. From now on it was struggles all the way and I deeply resented diverting time and energy.

The Tide
by Ann Jellicoe (Axe Valley, 1980)

There were now a number of interesting invitations including one from the Northcott Theatre, Exeter, to join them in setting up a play in the cathedral. But for the moment I wanted to concentrate on rural plays. Few townspeople, lost in their fantasies of rural bliss, realise how artistically deprived, indeed dead, the countryside can be. The most interesting invitation came from Axminster. This small market town of about 3,000 inhabitants, bisected by the A35 and hammered by traffic thundering through, has little to distinguish it: 'It's awful here,' people said to me. The town lies on the River Axe which flows on to the sea about twelve miles away, passing the quiet little town of Colyton to reach the sea at Seaton, a fishing village until the beginning of this century when it sprawled into a small resort. Geographically the Axe Valley with its three towns and about twelve villages is a fairly precise area. There was little contact between the three towns but they share two senior schools.

East Devon has not yet gone comprehensive and the Axe Valley is served by Colyton Grammar School and Axminster Secondary Modern. By definition every secondary modern school must feel defensive, embattled; there is an enormous temptation to despair. Such schools are held together only by a staff who refuse to give up. I had friends in the school: Simon Blacksell, deputy head, and Kate Lansbury, drama teacher (and professional actress), who saw the community play as a means to give the school a boost of confidence. Even though the school hall was not large enough they said we could rehearse there and perform the play in Axminster Guildhall. Then we ran into trouble.

The producer of Axminster Dramatic Society had developed his organisation from nothing, building a rehearsal hut virtually with his own hands. He had acted in and produced dozens of plays. He listened to what I had to say but didn't want to come into the community play, would not even let me go and talk to his group, saying, in so many words: 'We know what's best for our town.' It seemed ridiculous to mount a community play without the support of ADS but my teacher friends were outraged: the amateurs didn't own the town! Colyton Grammar School now became very interested and sought to stage the play as an opener for their huge new sports hall. Deeply troubled, Simon Blacksell (who was to be in many more of our productions) told me that such was the sense of bruised inferiority at Axminster Secondary School that if the play went to Colyton he would follow and support me but the rest of the staff would refuse to be involved. Talking it through we hit on the idea of an Axe Valley play, the main rehearsal venue to be in Axminster Secondary School with adjacent costume workshops (so providing the school with stimulus and identification), but, following positive talks with the three other dramatic societies in the valley, the actual production to be in Seaton.

This brought in a third educational establishment: the public school at Allhallows near Seaton. In the event Allhallows gave Medium Fair hospitality and beds during the production. Medium

Fair, who were hardly right wing in their views, found to their dismay that the Allhallows staff and kids were kind, pleasant and really rather likeable. In working on these plays I have been able to penetrate many schools in an exceptionally privileged, worm's-eye kind of way and have never ceased to be pained and amazed at the extraordinary differences in comfort, space and equipment between state and private schools, and the corresponding difference in atmosphere and relationships between staff and pupils that these qualities bring. In the circumstances the work of such state schools as the Woodroffe at Lyme Regis, Beaminster School or indeed Axminster Secondary Modern, are indeed admirable; but it is not too hard to be polite, pleasant, poised and articulate in the conditions which obtain in, for instance, Sherborne School as opposed to Sherborne Secondary Modern.

It was reasonable that I should write the Axe Valley play since I lived only six miles away, and our work was not yet well enough known to attract other major writers. With *The Tide* we began to hold acting workshops in the pre-rehearsal period; we had planned four but they went so well we added a fifth. They were all taken by Keith Palmer, who was then Assistant County Drama Adviser for Devon. *The Tide* was on a larger scale than *The Reckoning*, with about 120 in the cast as opposed to 90 for the earlier play. Three or four hundred people helped to get the play on. It ran for ten performances, spread over two weeks, as opposed to four performances for *The Reckoning*. I chose this number because it made us eligible for certain Arts Council grants, but it turned out to be about right. Few amateur productions run beyond five performances but so much work goes into these plays that the actors need the reward of a really good performance period. In fact we could fill many more performances but there is a limit to how much amateurs, who are also in full-time jobs, can do.

I had a stroke of good fortune when I heard that Joan Mills, with whom I'd worked closely when she was director of the Young People's Theatre at the Royal Court, was leaving her job as director of Theatre Powys and would have six months free. She agreed to come as co-director. This experience later led Joan to produce her own huge community play in Brecon and return to the Colway Theatre Trust in 1984 to direct the Ottery play. Exeter University felt that the current batch of students were not experienced enough to undertake the whole stage-management load so I managed to get Paul Roylance as stage manager. I had directed four or five shows at the Royal Court with Paul, he brought his own efficient and amiable deputy SM. So we had an exceptionally strong production team; which was just was well as *The Tide* was technically a very heavy play.

I had to try and pay something more than the token fees Carmel and I had received with *The Reckoning*. Salaries were still low, indeed Paul gave two weeks free, and again I tried to ease finances by having people live in our house; but instead of just Carmel there was a kitchen full of articulate people coping with crises, and enjoying them. This placed a strain on my family. I saw that in future I would have to try and stop the plays washing right through our home.

I had seen the possibilities of music in *The Reckoning* where we used a little band of schoolchildren organised by the maths master, stiffened by Medium Fair (the school is strong on music but the music teacher did not come in). I had never been lucky enough to work with live music on a large scale in conventional theatre – it's too expensive and complicated. But now I sensed glorious possibilities. A year or so previously I had had a successful collaboration with Steve McNeff. Steve had been Director of Music at the Northcott theatre and lived locally; now I asked him to do the music for *The Tide*. We had the idea of basing the music on local tunes from the area and, partly because of this, but also because much of his time was committed elsewhere, Steve brought in Paul Wilson and Ben van Weede, two West Country folk musicians who led us into a hidden tradition of village music: old village fiddlers and church bands – some of their tunes they found actually in the valley itself.

The Tide confirmed the experience of the first play. If anything it was even more successful. *The Times* said, 'The most consummate display of mass staging since Ariane Mnouchkine's *1789*.' Simon Blacksell wrote a moving letter:

> I want to thank you for involving me in one of the most unforgettable experiences of my life. It is so difficult to say something when all the superlatives have already been used; but *The Tide* was terrific . . . So that's me, personally fulfilled in a way I have not felt for many years. But I must also tell you what it has done for the children of Axminster Secondary School and for the school itself. The children were stretched in a way they have never been stretched before and they came out with flying colours. They have now experienced something excellent and it should last them a lifetime.

Having realised that the more people knew of our work the easier it would be to set up the plays, I had managed to persuade Alan Yentob, then producer of the BBC2 *Arena* programme, to come and see the play. At the end he flung his arms round me and kissed me – not, I fancy, an everyday reaction from such a sophisticated man. There was the same euphoric feeling that something extraordinary had been achieved. 'I usually think it all happens in London,' someone said to me, 'but now it's all happening in Seaton.' Joan Mills isolated a quality I had, until then, taken for granted. She noticed a great friendliness and supportiveness amongst those who took part and said that all the cast were remarking on it as something unusual. There was the same willing help when it came to clearing up after the play; even the local police sergeant weighed in to dismantle the scaffolding on his day off, and teams of men, women and children brought brushes and buckets and scrubbed away in a long line across the hall.

When the play was over there was the same wish to revive it, but I was now committed to the next production. A year later they wanted to get up their own play to help celebrate Maritime '82 – this was to involve the whole valley which certainly would not have been contemplated earlier. It didn't lift off, possibly because it will take more than one play to unite such a sprawling area. The secondary schools did not become noticeably more friendly (as happened later in Sherborne) but now at last in 1986 we hear they are about to merge. We tried to set up a formal organisation, 'The Friends of CTT', but it didn't thrive – perhaps we failed to find the right formula. It confirmed me in my opinion that such initiatives, while we would obviously wish to encourage and give them all the help we can, must come about because local people themselves want them and will support them with local enthusiasm, energy and vision. Probably the most positive follow-up, perhaps inspired to some degree by *The Tide*, was the setting up of a two-day festival in Axminster. Ken Smith, a teacher in the school who took part in the play, became Mayor of Axminster and started up this celebration, with theatre, music, sideshows and stalls, which has flourished ever since.

The Poor Man's Friend
by Howard Barker (Bridport, 1981)

Some actors are so enthusiastic they will follow you from place to place. Such a one was Terry Lunt, a building inspector from Bridport, who had also been in *The Reckoning*. He was keen we should come to his town ('lovely community'). The Secretary of the Bridport Arts Association had taken part in *The Tide* fair dancing with the

Bridport Scottish Dancers (the insane irrelevance seemed good fun). When their feeble gramophone packed in Ben van Weede and Paul Wilson offered to play for them ('You mean you know all the tunes?'). Their flying fiddles and irresistible verve thrust the Scottish dancers into terrific excitement. So there was yet more enthusiasm for us to come to Bridport. With this encouragement I invited town councillors from Bridport and the headmaster of the Colfox School to come and see the Axe Valley play.

Bridport is an old town with few events of national significance in its history. For eight hundred years its chief industry has been rope-making which has literally shaped the town: many of its streets and alleys were built as rope walks with broad pavements. The town's history lies in generation after generation of small, independent families of rope-makers. The town still seems almost classless, or at least without much class differentiation. It's a useful example of how a community keeps its character even though the people who live there come and go. Bridport has such a definite feel that it attracts like people and its layout quite simply ensures that people can stop and chat and keep on meeting and mixing. Everyone who lives in Bridport speaks well of it. A fortunate little town.

Even so we met with one or two tacticians: Bridport has at least five amateur dramatic societies, some devoted to opera and pantomime. I talked to all of them, but the director of one group made it clear to his members that if they joined in the community play they could forget working with him – he produces a play a year and you have to take the long view. The siege mentality cannot be avoided. It may crop up anywhere. In a sense we create it as a wave of energy creates counter energy. Sometimes you can melt the siege mentality with trust, sometimes the siege mentalists themselves will finally decide to join in because of some overriding reason; but most of the time, meeting the siege mentality, you simply have to work round it. Fortunately the most important and relevant group was the Festival Players because they would normally put on a play in the autumn when we had scheduled the community play. The Festival Players were directed by a woman of vision and generosity, and they happily decided to support fully the community play and to cancel their production for autumn 1981.

In Bridport, with the experience of two plays behind us, we really got into our stride. The run-up to the play was the best organised and structured to date. We had a proper public meeting, with people from former plays making the effort to come and say what a good time they'd had. We had tested out the committee system, knew our way around government funding. After the successful workshops in Axminster I set up a much larger series taking some myself but also involving visiting tutors including Keith Johnstone, an old friend and possibly the best and most famous teacher in the world, on a rare visit from Canada.

Contrary to popular belief it takes much more effort to raise money from Regional Arts Associations than from other fundraising bodies. You have to argue, justify and account for money far more punctiliously with RAAs than with trusts, business and even Local Authorities and the Manpower Services Commission. The Regional Arts Associations have the money – it's their job to give it away – but getting your hands on it is no push-over. They really make you sweat for it. At this time South-West Arts were having one of their perennial campaigns to make District and County Councils pay their contributions to SWA. SWA was asking for a contribution of 0.1 per cent of the product of a 1p rate; in the case of West Dorset District Council, who of course did not pay, this was £800. SWA now threatened to cease funding new initiatives in any county not paying their contribution. This would have been disastrous for CTT. I organised a series of meetings with representatives from the larger towns of West Dorset and we drafted a strong letter to the WDDC (this sounds more impressive than it actually was since there are only about six towns with a population of over 3,000). I also lobbied and spoke to every councillor on the relevant committee. This obviously helped, and Dorset actually paid up. These meetings also resulted in the setting up of two community plays: Sherborne and Dorchester. The Dorchester play didn't take place until five years later but they formed a steering committee and over the years contact was maintained.

Administration was increasing and there were more and more calls on my time and energy. I hadn't the time to write a play even if I wanted to. In fact, having shown the idea to be valid, it seemed important that we should have a fresh mind. With our record, the huge cast and other unusual conditions we could offer a writer, it was reasonable to assume we could attract a dramatist of national standing. With *The Tide* I had begun to invite writers with an eye to future productions. One of these was Howard Barker who I regard as one of the great playwrights, a man of exceptional power and talent. It happened that Howard had strong bonds with Bridport where a good friend of his from university days taught English and Drama at the local compehensive school. Howard and his family were frequent visitors. This was the overriding factor in commissioning him to write a play for us.

Although Howard Barker was the firm choice artistically and in terms of his links with the town, he is above all a Socialist: to him his politics justify and fuel his writing. Elsewhere I discuss the problems of politics in community plays; in the meantime this was where it first had to be faced. I had many conversations with Howard, trying to convince him that he must not write a political play, that such a play would divide the town when we were seeking to unite it. In retrospect I am almost surprised that he stuck with the commission. I think he recognised that here was a unique chance to work very closely, even directly, with very large numbers of people. In the end he was very satisfied indeed. Meantime we agreed he should compromise, not write a political play but one which should celebrate resistance.

The writing of *The Poor Man's Friend* had a considerable effect on Howard Barker and its influence can be traced in his subsequent plays. In 1986 he still refers to it; (*Gambit*, no. 41).

> The other example of self-censorship was the acclaimed community play I wrote for Ann Jellicoe's Colway Theatre at Bridport . . . the demand for celebration was such that my natural instincts as a writer went into abeyance – the qualities of cruelty, the extreme power of language, the taking of human relations to the edge of experience – were all inhibited. The result was a very popular success. I learned a great deal from this. I am still learning.

Howard seized upon the rope-making industry, noting with some glee that Bridport rope had been used to hang criminals from all over the British Empire. How my heart sank when he told me this! I was acutely anxious until the script was delivered in case the play should be too much for Bridport. Someone had given Howard a simple fact, not even a story, about a boy of 14 hanged for stealing flax, and from this he built his play. When it came the play was indeed magnificently tough; he is the most masculine writer, rigorous, spare, powerful, but also, less usually for him, this play was extremely funny. From the technical point of view the subject of *The Poor Man's Friend* did not favour women – there were not even enough women's parts. Howard had to write in more and more women's roles which he did with a glint of rebellion: 'I will not go on stuffing in this way.'

Howard fully appreciated the huge possibilities open to the writer

of one of these plays and used them to immense effect. Later in the
same interview he said:

> Community plays . . . can become powerfully ritualistic and
> mythical . . . In those mass images the actual moment of
> celebration was discovered instinctually. It is the release of pity.
> I thought the play was about resistance, and at first glance it is.
> But now it's more about pity, the realisation of the utter
> universality of suffering. That's a very bonding experience.

The play was a huge success: 'an inventive simplicity that makes it
somehow a cross between Peter Brook and a large-scale Bill Bryden,'
said the *Observer*; 'The real feeling you get emerging from a triumphant evening . . . is that a community has been confronted with a
slice of its own past; and that in the process it may have learned
something vital about the turbulent recessive present,' said the
Guardian; 'The production joyously fulfils its basic task as a commu-
nal event, with swift crowds, full-throated choruses and perfectly
staged little scenes cropping up all over the place,' said *The Times*;
'The measured terms of critical appraisal won't do: this is a smashing
night out,' said the *Times Educational Supplement*.

To me there was a rewarding moment when the production was
virtually over. On the last Saturday the weather conditions were
atrocious. Somehow all the audience got there, including a bus-load
from Wales and the double TV crew who came to film parts of the last
performance and selected scenes on the following day. The snow
continued to fall through the night. On the Sunday morning the
actors, band and technical crew struggled back. The Colfox school
hall seethed with cast, cameras, cables and musical instruments. Two
scenes were filmed and then there was a power failure all over the
south-west. For hour after hour it went on. The BBC crew were
powerless, incoherent, wrathful, speechless . . . this couldn't be
happening . . . time and money were melting away and there was
absolutely nothing they could do.

In this crisis the attitude of the cast was amazing: there was no
question of going home: they'd never have made it back. A few
struggled out and fetched bread and packets of soup, others opened
up the school kitchens (and cleared up afterwards). For hour after
hour of waiting for power to be restored there was no boredom or bad
temper but a sense of joy and exhilaration, with an improvised jazz
concert and Christmas carols in four-part harmony. Perhaps it was
due in part to the euphoria of two splendid weeks, to the excitement of

TV (but it wasn't very exciting after four hours of nothing). Essentially these people had worked together closely and creatively over three months, some for much longer through the workshops which had started in May. They had learned to support and react to each other with the greatest speed and sensitivity; in their group feeling they were like a flock of birds or a shoal of fish.

Incidently the weather continued to be so bad that the school was closed on Monday, so we were able to get on with filming. When the *Arena* film was finally shown it was a triumph. Bridport loved it. The BBC gave us copies and I must have shown it hundreds of times. The video demonstrates more effectively than anything what the work is about and the standards reached. Curiously enough what it fails to get over is the extraordinary lift you get from being there – the 'overwhelming emotion' factor.

One way and another our work was becoming much more widely known. Even Dorset County Council was becoming aware of us. I invited various county dignitaries to Bridport and they wrote bemused letters of excited appreciation. It didn't make any difference to our funding, but it gave us credibility and the county now allowed us to use certain resources. People began to ask if they could come and work with us and, since they were usually highly motivated and we had no money, they frequently came for nothing, but somehow seemed to end up on the payroll. This became our chief channel of recruitment.

One of the really positive results of Bridport was the emergence of Norman Saunders-White as a kind of cultural catalyst in the area. Something of a polymath, Norman had just retired from teaching art. He was in the Bridport play, as he has been in many since. He now set up the Improvisational Theatre Company following the workshop model, which has stirred up sleepy old West Dorset quite a bit and led to another such group being started in Dorchester. Norman's wife Pat taught drama at Colfox School. She began to use our techniques in her classes and the school began to stretch its ideas with a promenade production of *Larkrise* but, even more significantly, she and a colleague wrote and directed their own play for schoolchildren which did so well it was published and so lives on. There were minor follow-ups – the youth club began to use drama workshops, the Civic Society took a tip from us and explored the possibility of using MSC schemes for their community work, even the programmes of the amateurs became more original. From our point of view the most significant budding off from Bridport was the Burton Bradstock Village Play.

Ssh!
(Burton Bradstock, 1982)

The initiators were Norman and Pat, who live in the village. Since we were basically funding the play with odds and ends of money left over at the end of the year there wasn't time or staff to do our usual slow build-up and at the public meeting there was a good deal of discussion as to whether the village really wanted a play. It was decided to go ahead with the workshops on the understanding that if it became apparent that the village didn't want the play it would be abandoned. *Ssh!* was directed by Andrew Dickson who had been the composer for *The Poor Man's Friend* but who is also an individual and anarchic theatre director. By this time Andrew, having been captivated by Dorset, had moved down to live there. We couldn't find a local writer for the play, but by this time Andrew was local too so he wrote the play as well as being responsible for the music and direction.

Design and making were by a local girl who had been assistant to the designer of the Bridport play. She had left school at 15, but as a result of her work with us went on to art school to study theatre design. Andrew's assistant was a young man who, when a boy of 15, had been in *The Reckoning* and shown great talent; following this he had a bad patch but we managed to get him onto a YOPS scheme for Bridport. He has since been to drama school and is now, as they say, rich and successful. Two other young people of importance turned up: Sally-Anne Lomas, who wrote a funny and intelligent letter, or rather six letters, each in a different style of approach: subservient, threatening, happy-go-lucky etc., all asking if she could come and work with us. She started helping on the Burton play and after a year or so with us later became co-director of *The Western Women* where she was responsible for initiating a policy of project and video work and especially for encouraging women to take a more assertive role. Elizabeth Katis also joined us. After Burton she became my assistant in Sherborne, later going on to direct her own village play. It is Liz who is now setting up urban community plays in London. These examples, among many, may give some idea of how the work was able to help influence and train young people, and how interest was spreading.

Ssh! was a frolic, a bubble made up mostly from the cast's stories and folk memories strung together on an improbable and lunatic fantasy of Andrew's which made other larger community plays look rather stodgy. It included half the children in the village pretending to be goats and various other things, in the tale of an ex-customs officer, swallowed by a porpoise in the South Seas, who returns to Burton to seek revenge on the lover who betrayed him, who is now a wrecker, disguised as a nun running a shady rest home for shipwrecked sailors. This was just the start. It included the Vicar as a foreign sailor who only spoke Spanish gibberish. The music was very attractive: light-hearted, witty, humorous, but also very beautiful. Of all the plays I loved the music for this one the best. Andrew has written the music for three of our plays: his work is wonderful. The huge and moving choruses of celebration at the end of *The Poor Man's Friend* and *Entertaining Strangers* are celebrated. But with *Ssh!*, having written the play himself, and without losing any of his quality, he was also exceptionally relaxed.

The Garden
by Charles Wood (Sherborne, 1982)

Having done so well we were due for a tumble and in Sherborne we very nearly came a cropper. I was first approached to do a play there by Chris Lea, head of the boys' grammar school who had signed the protest letter to WDDC. Sherborne's local industry is schools: there are ten of them. The senior schools range from the boys' and girls' public schools, a Catholic boarding-school for girls, grammar schools for boys and girls, to a co-educational secondary modern. The schools tended to bunch together in groups: plenty of contact between public schools, who mixed with each other, but not with the grammar schools, who spoke to each other but not to the secondary modern. You can imagine how the kids from the secondary modern felt themselves the bottom of the heap. Fortunately St Aldhelm's had a strong drama teacher and a great many of the pupils joined in.

The community play was to improve relationships between the schools. At the early workshops and rehearsals each school would stick with its own group in a separate part of the hall; by the end they were all mixing and working together. Some groups which were formed for the play, such as the stage management and lighting teams and the band, and which included kids from all the schools, stayed together for subsequent shows. Sherborne's state schools are now trying to go comprehensive. All the schools concerned, their teachers and most of the parents, are behind the change, only the Secretary of State for Education stands in the way. Perhaps the play helped a little in this change of attitude.

Given so many teachers leavening the population Sherborne feels itself to be rather sophisticated in comparison with other towns, and it is certainly humanistic and intelligent. Teachers from the schools play an active part in town politics and while I was working there the three successive mayors all taught at the boys' public school. This made for a more open-minded town council. I was received with very great interest by all these schools. The Amateur Dramatic Society was also enthusiastic. This was important since they are by far the strongest ADS in the area. With their bright audience they can perform much more interesting plays (or perhaps they have the wit to see that good plays are more entertaining anyway) and their actors are correspondingly more widely experienced.

As usual there were a few violent antis, and a meeting with their leader was set up for me. Unfortunately no one warned me, and when he spoke his mind saying that the town knew what it wanted and they didn't need any professionals barging in telling them what to do (this is always the siege line spoken more or less openly), I could not believe that, in intelligent company, he could be serious. I thought he must be testing me. So I answered without my usual cautious diplomacy saying why I thought a community play would be good for the town. I was never forgiven. Call it diplomacy, tact or what you will; I prefer not to provoke the siege mentality out into the open if I can help it. It will be there and will grumble and rumble away in some corner but there is always a chance it will simmer down and be converted. Once the siege mentality has made a stand people have to choose between the play and their friends or acquaintances. By far the greater part will choose the play because they have faith that it's a good thing; but they won't like going against an old friend and they know they will have to work together again when the play is over. However, this was not my most serious error in Sherborne.

Although I had commissioned Howard Barker on the basis of getting him to see a previous production I had not realised how fundamentally important it was that the writer should not only be impressed with the standard and scale of the work, but must also appreciate the faith, indeed vulnerability, of the people taking part. They put themselves on the line. One of the purposes of asking writers to actually come and see a play is to allow them to feel a sense of humility, even awe, at the enthusiasm and trustfulness of those involved. The experience of Sherborne taught me that the writer must be ready to relate whole-heartedly, and with the greatest responsibility to the local community, must fully understand that this work demands a different kind of commitment to most other theatre. The writer must realise that if the work falls short then a whole community will pay, and the writer also runs the risk of exposing their art to contempt. People are not fools: professional artists are on trial with these community plays.

I admire enormously the work of Charles Wood: tough, witty, abrasive, with an element of freedom and fantasy. Although he had written the brilliant film version of my play *The Knack* we had never met, but clearly had the basis of a relationship of mutual respect. Liking his work so much, it was my personal decision to ask him to write the Sherborne play. He wasn't able to see *The Poor Man's Friend* but came and stayed in Sherborne, talked to a great many people and found his subject. This was essentially a somewhat Alice-in-Wonder-land view of the town's history culminating in the bombing of Sherborne in 1942. But then Charles was overwhelmed by work, presumably had to select priorities, and delivered a play which, as he admitted himself, was unfinished, and which also had a tone which some Sherborne people found offhand. The play had flashes of brilliance but didn't seem to hang together. Charles was too busy to rewrite and asked me to do it for him, but the better the writer the more difficult it is to reproduce their particular voice and frame of thought; you can only try and botch it about. It must be said that Charles Wood was so unhappy about the situation that he refused all payment and gave us the script free. But that was not quite the point.

I made every effort to present my usual front of optimism and enthusiasm. At this time we still distributed copies of the script through the library and when the script was ready for reading (possibly the worse for my 'improvements') there was some difficulty in holding the production together. A number of people became disillusioned and dropped out. Others complained at the image presented of their forbears (it was indeed our first experience of image sensitivity). I considered giving up the project altogether, but the Organising Committee held steady as usual. I saw that to abandon the play would be to betray all those people who had already given so much, and might also lead to cynicism at the failure. It would also have been dishonest toward SWA who were now giving us year-round funding.

I started rehearsals with a heavy heart. There were compensations: we were forced into intensely demanding group improvisations. *The Garden* was as near a devised play as we have ever got. Thankfully the music, by Nick Bye, was excellent; so good it almost held the

production together by itself. The play was still an enormous success
in community terms. The performances were borne along on the
usual tremendous enthusiasm, the play's administrator saw his opportunity to harness all the goodwill and energy generated by the play and
set up the Sherborne Association for Craft and Arts which was
ambitious and successful. But people knew.

Fortunately there was the support of a strong production team,
almost all of whom were highly motivated having asked to come and
work with me. These included Jon Oram who, for some reason, didn't
impress me when we first met but came and gave a workshop in
Sherborne and was so successful that I got him onto the team. In a
very short time it was obvious he was being under-used, so we took a
vote on it and made him co-director. When the production was over I
tried to persuade him to come on the permanent staff of CTT, but
people who have been successfully trained by us develop certain skills
and experience not widely found elsewhere. SWA appointed Jon their
first Theatre Worker in Cornwall where he extended his experience
and produced a community play, *The Earth Turned Inside Out*, by
Nick Darke, followed later by another community play, of his own
writing, in Gainsborough.

The workload began to increase dramatically. Previous to starting
rehearsals in Sherborne the Arts Council had agreed to fund Marilyn
Floyde as Associate Director of the CTT. Mal was to set up a branch
of the Trust in Crediton, her home town in mid-Devon. We wanted to
spread the workload so that I should not be solely responsible for the
very heavy burden of setting up and producing a play a year as well as
running the CTT, raising all its funding, and coping with the many
queries regarding community play practice which were beginning to
come in from all over the country. There was also a village play which
we had promised to help mount in Colyford and which was to be
directed by Liz Katis. Liz was giving workshops and setting up the
Colyford play even while we were rehearsing *The Garden*. Naturally I
was overseeing all this work as well as directing *The Garden* and at the
same time attending discussions and meetings in Lyme Regis and
Dorchester about their community plays.

The venue for the Dorchester play was to be St Mary's Church as
this was the only building big enough. The Vicar told me that the
churches themselves now planned to put on a very large 'inter-church'
play in the open air over Easter 1984. Hearing this the Dorchester
Steering Committee agreed that they would mount the Dorchester
play in March 1985. The church now decided that Easter was too

chilly for an open air play (they were right) and that they too would perform in the church. We were delighted that this big local effort should be going forward and decided that my assistant, Sally-Anne Lomas would take part in the church play to generally demonstrate support and as a good way of making contacts.

SWA never really understood this continuous and demanding process of constantly talking to local people, gathering opinions, establishing local taste and requirements and shaping plans according to local need. There was always the question, 'What on earth are they doing with all that money we give them and only producing one play a year?' To answer the implied accusation I kept a diary for a few weeks which showed I was working fourteen hours a day, seven days a week. Like most other pieces of paper produced for SWA one had the impression that it was filed away in some limbo and forgotten if ever read at all. I thoroughly enjoyed all this work, but it was certainly at the expense of creativity and the Sherborne play was no better for all the distractions.

Colyford Matters
by Denis Warner, (Colyford, 1983)

Colyford is a very lively, friendly little community with its own annual Goose Fair. The village nestles in the middle of the Axe Valley and has a population of about 350, a third of which took part in the play. The Mayor of Colyford and his family had been in *The Tide* and wanted a play of their own. It was written by a local writer, Denis Warner, who was encouraged and revitalised by the experience, and gave the village a very pleasant, straightforward little piece about the setting up of two great houses in the village. Nick Bye wrote the music again and it was designed by Norman Saunders-White who, having just attended a Welfare State summer school, was bursting with their ideas. He produced a Welfare-State-type eel, supported by about fifteen people, which lashed around taking up most of the available space in the hall. Publicity promised, 'This is the play where you will eat!' Cooking was part of the action. Colyford women baked over 200 pies (i.e. 1600 slices): venison, rabbit, fruit. There was also a wedding where the audience toasted the bride and groom with wedding cake and cider, and a reconstruction of the traditional Goose Fair with pancakes and meringues.

The village hall, where we did the play, was run by a committee (not the play's Organising Committee) which displayed its spirit and determination in a number of dramatic ways. Half way through rehearsal the Fire Officer discovered that the hall licence had lapsed; he demanded extensive alterations which would cost £2,000. He wouldn't believe they could do the work ('They're very slow down here, you know.'). But the Village Hall Committee was determined and threw itself into the conversion and fundraising. When they realised how keen people were and how firmly the village was tackling the problem, the Devon County Authority, though not abating a single inch of fireproof skirting, got caught up in the spirit of the thing and were totally unbureaucratic, standing by the telephone, accepting verbal assurances from the Fire Officer and passing on messages so as to rush the licence through eight hours before the performance. So apart from the other benefits of the play, which included much increased theatrical activity, the village now has one of the best-equipped halls in the area.

The strength of will of the Village Hall Committee then taught us another salutary lesson in community sensitivity. An inexperienced helper invited CND to take part in the fair before the play without consulting the Fair Committee. CND didn't just carry their stuff around on a tray but rigged up a table to display all their books, badges and pamphlets. Suddenly we touched basic sensitivities: the Village Hall Committee reared up and said if CND came again the play would be thrown out of the hall. To some of us it seemed like censorship and extremely provocative. CND were themselves upset since they were trying to get Axminster declared a nuclear-free zone and didn't want to antagonise people. There was confrontation, forthright speaking and bitterness. Even after all this time I never fail to be startled at how savage otherwise reasonable people can be.

Fortunately there was also plenty of low comedy: the young stage-management team hated knuckling under to what they considered right-wing authoritarianism and took to teasing the Village Hall Committee by sticking up postage-stamp-sized CND signs for the Committee to find on their nightly tour of inspection. Enraged and upset, a committee member would thrust in my face a finger with a CND sign stuck on the tip: 'We found this in the gents' toilet!' A bright assistant stage manager baked cheese straws in the shape of CND signs and sold them in the fair. . . Between them I felt I was riding the Grand Rapids on a plank, but the Play Organising Committee remained steady and balanced and, with a great deal of restraint and diplomacy, the matter was smoothed over. Some would say the issue should have been faced: it was a point of naked confrontation when you had to choose. It seemed to us more valuable to have people working together than provoking bitter argument.

Under my direction, and now under Jon Oram's, CTT sees its role as relating to the whole community. We do not see our role as telling people what they should think politically, or in any other way. We consider this would be arrogant; it would also alienate half the community. We are trying to help build communities, not divide them. We feel that co-operating with other people is in itself a political and humanising experience.

We work within the system. The plays would be impossible, financially, and in terms of general support, if we set out to destroy the framework in which we live. No school or town council would help, the very people we seek would draw back. If you are a community theatre worker you have to make a choice: in or out of the system. If you cannot work within the system then the CTT form of community theatre is probably not for you.

During the course of the Colyford play we came under attack from SWA Community Arts Sub-Panel who had inherited us from the Arts Council and wanted to cut our funding. The term 'Community Artist' covers a very wide spectrum of philosophy and belief. The Panel was belligerent, defensive, and incredibly naïve: not a comfortable lot to have to deal with over money. They loathed what we were doing because it was extremely close to their own work, yet significantly different and, at the same time, extremely successful. The extreme community artist deeply distrusts artistic success, or indeed any other kind. To them it's a contradiction in terms; they also dislike success because it implies inequality and poses the question that one artist may be better than another. To the true community artist all work is of equal value, the process is of prime importance, the product is irrelevant. To even aim for success may be damaging.

The extreme community artist aims to involve everyone in everything: whatever the quality of the work produced it must all be used. If someone wants to design and paint part of a set, no matter how inappropriate or unskilful, it must be used; and there that image will hang, fighting the play and the actors. Quality is irrelevant, joining in is all: the philosophy of the infant school painting class. I have a good deal of sympathy with these ideas, particularly at an individual and workshop level, but I think it's dodgy to use them in theatre unless the audience is of the most partial and indulgent kind, e.g. parents at a junior school play.

It took protests, discussions, paperwork and many meetings and telephone calls, but finally SWA Management Committee overrode the decision of the Community Arts Sub-Panel and made us wholly a client of the Drama Panel. While helping us with one hand SWA socked us with the other, refusing to fund Marilyn Floyde and the Crediton branch. I think it was really a matter of personalities but SWA rationalised the decision by saying they already paid too much into Devon and weren't going to give any more. Devon receives so much because it gives so much. Mid Devon District Council gave £500 to Crediton, and that was just a beginning. (But even Devon's relative generosity should be compared with what happens elsewhere. The little Danish town of Holbæk, population 30,000, slightly larger than Yeovil, slightly smaller than Clacton, give the Arts 356 kroner per head of its population, i.e. just under a million pounds per annum. Figures like this will make any English Arts Administrator reel.)

We were damned if we were going to give up. Under Arts Council funding Marilyn had already done a great deal of very successful work in the town, being the catalyst in forming an Arts Festival (which still goes on), setting up a Playwrights' Group with its own performances, together with workshops of all kinds. At this moment the balance was tipped by Television South-West which takes its responsibilities to the Arts seriously and gave us £3,000. We managed to float the Crediton play with some of this money, sponsorship from Lloyds Bank, a grant from Devon County Council and an MSC scheme. However, none of these would promise support for more than the one project.

In fact TSW also gave us £2,000 in 1984 and 1985. This money was of great significance. Apart from the funding we had initially received from the Carnegie Trust and the Gulbenkian Foundation, this was the beginning of our efforts to look elsewhere than SWA for our central funding. It meant too that an important TV company, based in the south-west, was involved in what we were doing and gave us valuable coverage. It is not altogether usual for a public company to continually fund a single organisation, and I was always afraid that next year TSW would take its money elsewhere. Not the least of my reasons for feeling grateful to TSW was that when the great SWA cut came in 1985, which could have been a negative signal to funding bodies, TSW remained steady and continued to fund us.

It is one of the prime advantages of government funding that once a company is accepted as a revenue client they are considered to be working throughout the year and their grant will not be cut off without a year's notice. This allows some stability and the possibility of growth: you can see one year ahead. (France works in three-year cycles.) In practice SWA treated CTT as a revenue client, and verbal assurances had been given to that effect. The SWA Management Committee had even minuted that they supported our year round programme of work, yet we were not officially a revenue client. The difference in status is crucial and with a future change of SWA Director was to justify hard, bitter and cruel treatment of CTT. In the meantime SWA's refusal to fund Crediton meant that, instead of the initiative growing and becoming established with the prospect of more CTT branches beginning to bud off, when the play was over and Marilyn's fourteen months of funding from the Arts Council finished, the Crediton initiative had to shut down.

SWA then took the line that since they were not funding Crediton it did not exist and so, in their books, CTT was mounting no production that year. We had hurriedly to get another play together. They lightly suggested that we bring forward the Dorchester play, but you can't just impose a play upon a town. Dorchester had its own plans: the church play was to be produced in that period. After five years of working with SWA it was nauseating and disheartening that they still did not appreciate how we worked and with what care we related to the various communities.

It was now autumn 1983. The second Lyme Regis play was scheduled for July 1984. Dorchester was to be March 1985. With some inconvenience to the town, which had a full programme celebrating the 700th anniversary of its charter, we managed to move the Lyme Regis play forward four months so that it should fall within the previous financial year of 1983. This arranged, there was then a bombshell from the Dorchester vicar who said that his church play was proving traumatic and his parishioners would not stand for 'losing' their church in Lent two years running (High Church, you see). So Dorchester had to be put back to November 1985. To those with the tenacity to follow this saga it will be clear that CTT now had no play within the financial year of 1984. I had to act fast and find a community already so together and cohesive that it would be able to mount a community play in an exceptionally short time: fourteen months as opposed to the usual two years. We were already involved with discussions over two strong invitations and, talking it over, it seemed that Ottery St Mary was best equipped to cope. Ottery, however, is in Devon (remember Crediton?), but a phone call to the new Director of SWA revealed that they had no objection to our going there . . . Ho Hum . . .

Today of All Days
by John Downie (Crediton, 1983)

Since it takes an hour and a half to drive from Lyme to Crediton and I
was also so occupied with setting up Lyme, Ottery and Dorchester, I
didn't help as much as I would have liked in Crediton; but this may
actually have built up Mal's confidence and capacity since she's a girl
who responds to a challenge. I took some hand in working through the
script. Determined not to repeat past errors we commissioned John
Downie, a West-Country writer of standing who had previously been
Crediton's writer-in-residence. The play dealt with how Crediton
celebrated the Coronation Day of King George VI in 1937, the
festivities joyful, rural and friendly, with an undertone of the rising
threat of Fascism.

With this particular play the problem was cutting: Mal was torn
between her wish to do a good production and her determination to
keep the individual parts as meaty as possible. The play should have
been cut more in order to make a better evening, for John Downie,
though sparky, is often a discursive writer. If a play is too long then
the audience will get bored and that is not going to help the actors,
who will have correspondingly less satisfaction. Provided the major
cutting is done before the play is cast there is little harm. We came up
against the problem in a rather different way in Dorchester where the
play was so rich and powerful it was extremely difficult to cut.
Fortunately, in Crediton, most of the audience was seated and so were
just that bit more tolerant than a standing audience. John Downie was
conscientious, particularly towards women, providing plenty of interesting 'baskets' (see p. 129) – farmers wives, girls from the jam
factory, etc.

After the play the Crediton Arts Festival continued to flourish, as
did the town band, which had been revived for the play; the
Playwrights Group got up a further programme of its own plays. As
generally happens, an exceptional individual harnessed the energy of
the community play: here it was the co-director, Peter Hamilton,
drama teacher at the school, who went on to direct a number of very
large productions, almost community plays in themselves. Peter was
then attached to Exeter University for a year, researching into
community plays. Marilyn Floyde became Director of the new Exeter
& Devon Arts Centre with plans to do a number of community plays
in the area.

The Western Women
by Ann Jellicoe, based on a story by Fay Weldon, with historical
advice from John Fowles (Lyme Regis, 1984)

In one sense this was a high point of our work. The squabbles with
SWA seemed to be over. The idea of community plays had taken off
and they were being performed all over the country. We felt terrific
confidence: we were building on six years' successful experience and
felt ourselves the spearhead of a new movement in the theatre. It was
also an important development that, after pressing invitations, we
were returning to Lyme for the second time. Some people had
doubted whether it would work twice over. This production showed
that not merely was a second production much easier but that it would
be entirely feasible to do a succession of community plays in the same
town.

The difference between working on the first and second productions was astonishing. *The Reckoning* had done our work for us. With
The Western Women we had no trouble in persuading people that the
play would be exciting, successful and a good experience. Far more
people from a much wider social spectrum were eager to join in and
the town raised substantial amounts of money. I had the help of a
strong and relatively large production team. For the first time we sold
out almost as soon as we opened and our reputation was such that we
now had coach parties coming from as far away as Canterbury and
Manchester.

The Western Women derived from a piece of hidden history. No one
can fail to be struck by how many more parts there are for men than
women throughout the whole of drama. Shakespeare may have five
women to twenty-five men and, though there may be historical
reasons for this, the proportion is far from uncommon; there are
always fewer womens' parts than mens' unless the dramatist has a
special reason or has made a particular effort. I used to think that this
was so because men tend to initiate action while women stay at home
and look after the children. Up to a point this is true. But in
researching for community plays I have found too many examples of
what women did in the past being suppressed, ignored or disregarded
because history is usually written by men. Men select what we shall
know and remember and where emphasis will lie.

John Fowles, in addition to being a famous novelist, is also curator
of our local museum. One day he showed me *Joaneridos or The Western
Women*, a contemporary poem, written by a local vicar, to celebrate

the part played by women in the Siege of Lyme in 1644. Once you have been alerted you can find in other contemporary accounts tiny, glancing references to the part played by women in the siege. The little Parliamentary town, lying in a dip and without natural defences, held out against a Royalist army for six weeks and at the end of that time all the besieging army could do was shuffle away. That the siege was successfully resisted was due just as much to the women as the men.

Joaneridos is not a poem of great quality and it probably only survived because a group of Royalists later felt sufficiently strongly to compose some extremely clever and scathing lampoons including cod-Anglo-Saxon, dog-Latin, spurious Spanish and fractured French: 'Vous avey ici (Mastres) verses scaches/Des tres grand faits de nostre Western lasses.' The whole lot was published together with the original poem and reading their jolly verbal japes it is clear that they sought to pulverise *Joaneridos* because its author was praising and elevating women. One is grateful for such a transparent example of the scorn which might fall upon a man who didn't toe the line.

I asked Fay Weldon, who lives not far away in Somerset, to write the play. Fay is an author of great reputation and talent, a generous and charming person but, unfortunately, it was not a successful commission. The problem was mainly technical: how to coherently organise and cope with 150 characters. As David Edgar said later, speaking of his own play:

> It's murderously difficult to handle 150 people . . . 150 is a nightmare. I was asked to do something which I assumed would take no effort, would be a doddle . . . I made a mistake. I said: 'I think I'll get it done by Christmas.' . . . I delivered it in June.

This was basically Fay's problem. But David Edgar has written over 47 stage plays, including his adaptation of *Nicholas Nickleby* which to some extent faces the problem of large casts. The first script of *The Western Women* did not have the depth and power the subject demanded. I organised workshops and tried to help Fay rewrite, but her method, I am told, is to write a bubble: if it doesn't work she throws it away. So, with the hard experience of Sherborne, I regretfully decided to write the play myself.

Of the three community plays I have written perhaps *The Western Women* causes me least pain. Chiefly because, apart from my growing experience and confidence, the power and drive of the play come not from the adventures of a single hero or heroine but from the testing, courage and steadfastness of every single person in the community. It was a terrifically exciting story about the valour and endurance of ordinary people defending their principles against great odds. It was also, at a time when the Greenham women were making their greatest impact, inescapably relevant. 'Could scarcely have found a more topical subject for their play,' said the *Guardian*:

> Are laws to be obeyed? Oaths taken? *The Western Women* comes straight to the point: Tom Seeley cannot in conscience swear fealty to the Crown, only to the King in Parliament. Therefore he cannot be Mayor, nor can any of the other burghers who all join in this crucial and communal declaration for the parliamentary cause. Lyme puts itself on the line and is called to famous account. (April 2, 1984)

Thus the story gave the cast tremendous emotional force and commitment and grabbed the audience in the gut. It was the ideal subject for a community play.

With *The Western Women* we were able to improvise from strength. The atmosphere at rehearsal was so good and the cast so confident that if something was not working we felt no despair but simply looked for a better way. One of the finest scenes did not arrive until very late in the rehearsal period. At an important moment in the story where the women begin to take over and help the exhausted men, I had written a number of small, simultaneous scenes hoping to give as many people as possible more to do. The actors had worked hard improvising and rehearsing, the whole atmosphere was very creative, but it was clear the scenes weren't making the point with enough force. One morning I woke up, took a pencil and in two minutes had sketched a new scene in which the women of Lyme, improvising, speaking randomly, began to find a rhythm and purpose. The bones of this scene we worked up in rehearsal. It was an amazing creative experience and fascinating to see how unselfishly the individual scenes were given up amid the growing excitement when this new scene so triumphantly worked. As we rehearsed the women began to find a voice and, drawing together finally, with thrilling force, gathered the whole community to resist the enemy. The episode was shattering in its intensity of feeling. The sense of fulfilment amongst these women, both as characters in the play and as real people was deeply moving.

With a view to Dorchester I asked David Edgar to come and see *The Western Women*. He later said:

> I was seduced into doing a community play by the simple

expedient of being invited to the last one, and I think it is worth saying that the experience you sense from the closing song in *The Poor Man's Friend* [in the BBC *Arena* programme] is really extraordinary, overwhelming . . . I think the only recent experience I find remotely akin to it was that of seeing the National Theatre *Mysteries* cycle.

The Ballad of Tilly Hake
by Sheila Yeger (Ottery St Mary, 1985)

As has been seen, SWA's bureacratic writhings meant that we somehow had to put on a play in fourteen months. It couldn't have been done in a 'bad' community, but Ottery is close-knit, confident and has a clear sense of its own identity. It's a balanced little town of about 7,000, with a much larger catchment area; indeed, the Organising Committee decided that the official title should be 'The Ottery St Mary and District Community Play' which displays their concern for each other.

In an attempt to let the community help choose the playwright, and also to allow the author to see the terrain, we invited two writers to visit the town. We finally commissioned Sheila Yeger because she is a woman and because her previous experience as a community worker would, we felt, be very valuable in relating to the town. The other writer was extremely generous and withdrew, leaving the friendship intact; he was in fact possibly a more experienced and prestigious writer than Sheila, but the decision to commission her was supremely justified. Sheila taught us a great deal about how a writer may interact with a community and, under her guidance, we began to structure the author's involvement far more carefully than hitherto. We would continue to build on and develop her methods first in Dorchester and later in Beaminster.

There was time and energy to develop the work firstly because I decided not to direct Ottery myself – with three plays onstream I was too committed – but I maintained a very close relationship with Ottery, filling the role of producer/manager. Thus Joan Mills, who came back to direct the play, enjoyed the luxury of working without a thousand distractions. The second reason we were able to take a fresh look at our methods was that the Carnegie Trust, in a characteristically imaginative and supportive gesture, guaranteed us three years' funding for development work. Thus we were able, for the first time, to create the post of Play Officer.

Until now we had never had the resources to allow a representative of CTT to actually live in the town in the long period before production; I myself was the only full-time, year-round employee (other staff were a secretary for three mornings a week and a part-time book-keeper). Now we were able to have a continuing physical presence. The play officer began to know the town extremely well, and they him. It was his job to think exclusively of the community play and to advance interest and involvement in every possible way. The scale and organisation of events leading up to the play was far more effective in Ottery, and it was the play officer who did much of the work in setting up Sheila's encounters with the town. There was time to consider certain problems which previously we had simply had to ignore: how to involve younger children; increased work with schools, e.g. through Play Packs, Art, History and even Computer Studies. We could also think about whether it would be useful to reserve seating places on the scaffolding, and a new structure for ticket-pricing, and many other small but important matters. Ottery marked a significant stage in our work because for once there was a little surplus energy to think and cope.

Sheila's play, *The Ballad of Tilly Hake*, grew out of the town. It concerned two families, one poor, the other comfortably off, which highlighted each other. The play showed how the poorer family endured and survived, totally unable to comprehend national events (the Crimean War, the coming of the railway) which did in fact touch their lives with great immediacy, and how even momentous Ottery happenings (the restoration of the church, the crucial cricket match) meant little to them until they were swept up in the all-consuming conflagration of the cholera epidemic and the Great Fire of Ottery.

MARCH 1985: SWA ANNOUNCES A 50% CUT IN ITS GRANT TO CTT.

It was fortunate that I was not directing Ottery when SWA delivered its depth-charge. I found out about the proposed cut by chance five days before it was to come up for final ratification at the SWA Executive Committee. There was no time for the vapours; I had to act quickly and methodically. Day 1 was spent getting out a duplicated appeal for people to write to SWA, and particularly any town or district councillors who might be sitting on the Executive Committee. Day 2 was spent lobbying the Committee by phone. Here I was extraordinarily hampered by the fact that the south-west is such a huge geographical area stretching over distances as great as from London to Aberystwyth. Very few of the Committee members had

seen our work. The SWA Executive Committee is easy to lead from
the centre because each member knows only about their own corner.
Day 3 I contacted the local and national press and local TV. Day 4 was
spent lobbying miscellaneous 'influential' people and generally plug-
ging gaps. (I was delighted when our MP managed to find the private
phone number of the Director of SWA and ring him up on a Sunday
morning.) Each night, during the performance of *The Ballad of Tilly
Hake*, we asked people to sign a petition. As a result SWA received
over 160 letters and telegrams of protest and I was able to present a
petition signed by more than 1,800 people. There was, too, considerable coverage in the media including TSW and the *Sunday Times*. Not
bad for five days.

I also carefully considered my personal position. No explanation
was (or has ever) been given for the cut. It outraged every funding
principle of SWA and the ACGB; it was made without notice (four
SWA officers came to see *The Ballad of Tilly Hake* and failed to warn
me). I was now raising twice as much money elsewhere as we asked
from SWA and, at the same time, creating innovative work and
employment of very high social value in a poor rural area with few
resources. (Indeed in the previous year I had been awarded the OBE.)
Yet we were also achieving artistic standards worthy of national
comparison. If this was the support I could expect I had had enough,
and announced that if the cut went through I would resign as Director
of CTT once I had fulfilled my commitment to Dorchester.

The upshot was a stay of execution: the Executive Committee
referred the decision back for further discussion. It was beautifully
handled: three months is a long time in public life; there was no way
we could sustain a campaign for that time and get on with our work.
After a while, the decision finally slid through. Many people rushed to
plug the gap and stand by us. Jon Oram had been awarded £8,000 by
SWA to produce a community play in Cornwall (a sum which
corresponded roughly with our cut). He gave up the play and dumped
the money back in SWA's lap. TSW, who might reasonably have been
expected to cease funding us after three years, held firm; the ACGB let
us know they were against the decision and have since supported us
with training and other grants wherever possible.

The whole controversy revived with the production of the Dorchester play and virtually every critic and interview referred to the cut.
Benedict Nightingale in the *New Statesman* (November 9, 1985)
summed it up:

It's sickeningly sad that Ann Jellicoe should have been driven by the parsimony of South West Arts to resign as director of the pioneering organisation she founded; but at least she can be sure that her last production for the Colway Theatre Trust is as little likely to be forgotten in Wessex as (let's say) the celebrations after the Battle of Trafalgar. . . It's exhilarating fun, yet socially also so obviously worthy as to make South West Arts' decision to halve Colway's tiny grant quite inexplicable. This is no posh and stylised civic pageant, but history graphically relived. Isn't it good that a community should learn more, much more about the past that has shaped its present, the roots that have determined its identity? Isn't it good that it should deepen its understanding of itself? And isn't it good that it should so skilfully entertain itself, as well as any outsider willing to pay a few bob for a ticket, as it goes about the business of auto-instruction? If only your average or even your above-average subsidised theatre could claim remotely as much.

Although this support was gratifying for me it also may have had a practical effect of raising sympathy and so making my successor's job of fundraising a little easier. SWA were decent enough to let me have photocopies of the letters of support which had been written and they make moving reading as a testimonial to the last eight years; some are quoted in this book.

Entertaining Strangers
by David Edgar (Dorchester, 1985)

Every community play is unique. Dorchester, in contrast to Ottery, was in our minds for five years, and was twice postponed. The play was greatly influenced by the fact that we had a powerful sponsor within the town. For the first time we performed in a church. David Edgar began to be fascinated by the opportunities for research.

Dorchester is the slumbering county town of sleepy Dorset; a delightful place to live in, but it's hard to get things moving. The town was rebuilt by the Romans on top of something earlier, after they had stormed nearby Maiden Castle. By that time its liveliest period was probably already past.

David Edgar and I had a couple of haunting and reverberative experiences. A friend from the museum took us on an archeological circuit which, while never going further than ten miles from Dorches-

ter, showed us hillforts, field systems, burial mounds. This part of
Dorset has over 2,000 tumuli. It is the largest burial site in Europe
which, paradoxically, must have made it one of the liveliest places in
prehistory. As the sun set we were standing on top of a vast grave
where a great man had once been buried wearing his gold breastplate.
The second, almost visionary, experience was when we saw the site of
an archeological dig in the heart of the town. You could visibly see the
layers of history: the marks of a water tank of 1942; the floor of the
Greyhound brewery where Sarah Eldridge had her first pub (the
diggers swore that when they reached it they could smell beer); a
fourteenth-century dovecote; the Roman roadways and buildings
and, below everything else, huge pits 8 × 4 feet, set on a slow curve
where once had stood the massive posts of a great wooden henge, 600
feet in diameter, over which the town has grown.

Sarah Eldridge founded her brewery in the 1830s and now her
successors Eldridge, Pope & Co., the largest employers in the town,
offered £5,000 sponsorship. They asked in return that the play
should, in however small a way, show the firm as part of the
Dorchester community. David and I met Christopher Pope, the
Chairman, and it was made clear that there would be no wish to
interfere with the play once it was written. Christopher Pope asked
merely that the play 'should not knock the product', and expressed
himself satisfied that David was 'not out to ride any hobby-horses', by
which he clearly meant political hobby-horses, but nobody raised the
question. This meeting was so important that I took notes and gave
copies to both parties.

The meeting did not altogether prevent misunderstanding but it
meant that David and I at least were able to be very open with each
other. The conditions did not seem to me particularly arduous but
David chafed a good deal about what he called 'imposing requirements on the text which add up to free advertising', as indeed they
did. The sponsors were fortunate to get the services of David Edgar,
amongst other things, for £5,000. David was well aware of this and
though he was too generous and honourable to say so, probably felt
that he was being used, bought cheap and pushed into a situation of
dealing with 'paternalistic capitalism' as he described the attitude of
Eldridge, Pope. How on earth had it come about that he, one of the
most successful and important writers on the international scene, was
messing about with this mingy little *galère* where £5,000 meant so
much?

However, under pressure to provide a strong female element,

David began to be interested in Sarah Eldridge. I rang the Rector and asked if the church would mind a play featuring beer. 'Not at all,' he said, 'I drink it myself. Did you know there was a nineteenth-century vicar who was strongly teetotal?' So David began to perceive a story where one set of entrenched ideas confronted another and the experience of the cholera epidemic of 1854 challenged these ideas and led to the possibility of a more humanistic view. Interestingly it was set in the same period and dealt with a similar subject to Ottery, yet produced an utterly different play.

Meanwhile a local journalist, having interviewed David and superimposed his own fantasies, printed a piece about Sarah Eldridge describing her as a brothel-keeper and using such phrases as 'private vice', 'pleasures of the flesh', 'boozy tavern' and, finally, 'a church may not be the most suitable setting for Sarah Eldridge'. The temperature began to rise. Some parishioners became restive; the Rector, Vicar and churchwardens began to feel the boat rocking. But they had given their word and meticulously protected the play while, I imagine, praying that when the script arrived it would not be offensive. Eldridge, Pope & Co., clearly began to feel very nervous: Christopher Pope had laid his neck on the line, was the firm going to be made to look foolish? A quiet voice with a distinct edge indicated that if the play was really going to be like this we should perhaps look elsewhere for sponsorship. David refused to commit himself, insisting simply that he would show the truth. The only thing to do was take a deep breath and ask everyone to be patient until the script arrived.

In arriving at the truth (which, in my opinion, is always subjective and selective) David had the help of six people who set up a research group and turned up a vast amount of new information. David had only to lift an eyebrow and they dived into the Public Record Office or the museum emerging with the names of real people of the age, social class and address which David required. He became obsessed with the real possibility of only using people who had actually existed. The more he asked for, the more they found. Finally there was so much information it couldn't possibly all be used. It spilled over into a book, *Dorchester 1854*, which the Research Group produced and published themselves and an exhibition in the Museum which included a rare, if not unique, example of one of Revd Henry Moule's inventions, the Moule Patent Earth Closet.

When the script arrived it removed all fears. I was breathless with excitement. Christopher Pope said he read it with tears in his eyes. David gave a triumphant public reading and all the difficulties connected with the town's acceptance of the script, which had seemed so threatening, melted away.

Certain parishioners continued to protest at the use of the church its disorganisation and change of use: 'The mess went on for months, and drove us all mad – and so did the howls of anguish from a few members of the congregation,' wrote the Vicar in a letter to the town of Monmouth who had asked for a report/reference. The Rector, a vicar and two churchwardens all took part in the play and so gave it their blessing; it was they who took the flak, it affected us very little. We had a really conscientious stage manager who took the greatest care to leave the church in as orderly as state as possible. One small side chapel was never used for anything to do with the play, unless a member of the cast wished to simply sit there and be absolutely quiet. At the start of one of our later rehearsals the Vicar led a short service. In his report he sums up: 'Yes. We would do it again. For two months the church was a real centre and real life went on in it. We had contact with many people we would otherwise never have touched – and they were so grateful and co-operative.' Incidentally, I am always touched by the fact that, in almost every town, in churches of all denominations, prayers are offered up for the success of the community play.

Eldridge, Pope were delighted with the sponsorship. During a period when, as High Sheriff of Dorset, his time was at a premium, Christopher Pope, no mean actor, played the role of his own great-grandfather's business partner, and clearly had much fun doing it. The firm received a lot of exposure on TV and, with some trepidation, invited dozens of their tough, tied-house publicans to see the show; they erupted with delight. Sometime later Pope's involvement was further recognised when, nominated by CTT, they received the prestigious award for Best First Time Sponsor from the Association for Business Sponsorship of the Arts.

Christopher Pope wrote:

> A business is the life-blood of the community in that it generates the new wealth which through taxation can pay for the community's social needs. It is part of the community in that its suppliers, employees and customers are the community. It needs to be active and to be seen to be active in the community.
>
> Eldridge, Pope's sponsorship of the Dorchester Community Play in 1985 was intended to be active participation, nothing more. It turned out to be one of the most effective promotional exercises ever undertaken: giving satisfaction and pleasure to employees and customers and generating enormous publicity.

Credit for this must go to the superb standards of the concept
and the production and to the organisers for strenuously gaining
publicity for us. We intend to sponsor another community play,
given the chance.

I felt that once more we had delivered what we had promised. There is
a little coda to this story which can be interpreted in several ways. A
member of the cast who worked in Eldridge, Pope's warehouse came
up to me late in rehearsal with tears in his eyes. 'I've worked for Pope's
for fourteen years,' he said, 'and this is the first time that Christopher
Pope has called me by my Christian name.'

The Dorchester Community Plays Association (note the plural) was
formed to continue the work. As always the cast felt a greatly
increased warmth and friendliness towards other people: 'Anyday I go
down South Street and say "hello" to six people I didn't know before.'
Another put it even more precisely: 'We greet each other in a different
way,' she said. 'We touch each other.'

On 31 December 1985 I ceased to be Director of the Colway
Theatre Trust and Jon Oram took over. The Trust is now working on
the Beaminster community play to be written by David Cregan, with a
Research Group and strong MSC team working alongside. Training
schemes are being set up, invitations considered for future plays. All
over the country community plays are being produced. Now they are
beginning to be set up abroad. The movement is flourishing.

2

Communities and art

WHICH COMMUNITY?

How to define a community? By class? By age? By common interest?
CTT does so geographically in the widest possible sense by taking the
school catchment area which will include a large, clearly defined
section of countryside beyond the actual small towns in which it
works. The town itself may have a population of 3,000–15,000, but
the catchment area may be as large as 80,000–100,000, covering
possibly 200–300 square miles. Distance is a great problem in rural
areas, bringing isolation and poor resources. Beaminster, where CTT
will mount its next play in 1987, seems idyllic enough but is actually
designated an area of Rural Deprivation by the EEC because it has so
few cultural and social resources. Getting about in the countryside
costs time, energy and money. It's probably most oppressive for the
unemployed and for young mothers: stimulation falls and people just
stagnate.

Paradoxically, however far the distance, in a rural area people can't
escape from hearing about a community play. Even with such a sparse
population schoolchildren will bring home news of the play and some
will be in it. The area becomes a sounding-box: news of the play
bounces about and is amplified so that nobody can quite escape.

Much larger communities, such as London, have defined the
community politically and geographically by boroughs: Ham-
mersmith, Islington and so on; but that presents difficulties. Stephen
Clerk, the writer of the Islington community play, said:

> We started it as the Islington community play – but Islington's
> much too big. It then became the South Islington community
> play – still too big. It then became the Islington Green com-
> munity play. Islington Green is about the size of a large room
> . . . So we ended up with just two little areas, two parishes; and
> the definition of who could take part in it was: anyone who lived,
> worked or did their shopping in the area or was in some way
> associated with it. There were still too many and it didn't have a

nice clean edge to it . . . and this did cause resentment, for instance: 'Why are they joining in when they're from Clerkenwell? I live in Hackney and it's two miles nearer.'

Unlike the sounding-box effect of rural areas the population of large towns and cities is so enormous, the distractions so many, the geographical area so vague, that it is only too easy for the impetus of the play to trickle away and get lost. However, there are compensations in working in large communities: they have correspondingly greater resources.

In defining communities you must also consider class-mixing. In rural areas, since everyone more or less knows everyone else, you will get a very wide cross-section of all classes. If you take a geographical patch in a big city you will probably get a narrowish class band. One example is the Newcastle suburb of Cowgate, where a community play is planned for 1987. This is mostly working-class with a high proportion of unemployed. The St Paul's district of Bristol is another area suggesting itself as fairly definite in terms of geography and class.

There is also the consideration of change and turnover. We tend to think of communities, particularly rural ones, as static and unchanging. But the village of Blewberry in Oxfordshire, where I recently saw a community opera, turns over 80 per cent of its population every four years. Most of this prosperous little community of 1,400 work for Harwell or Esso, or any of the number of huge multinational companies within easy distance, and they are constantly changing jobs and moving on. This is a continuing process with families coming and going all the time. I was introduced to one member of the production team with awe, being told that his grandfather had actually lived in the village. The change in population is so rapid that people hardly have time to get to know each other using the old, slow ways.

Some people in Blewberry became so upset living in a place which seemed literally disturbed that they turned to drama. There is no formal Blewberry Amateur Dramatic Society, but there's lots of drama. Anyone can come to auditions and will be used somehow. Drama is a year-round activity. Every so often they commission a community opera especially for the village. In 1986 it was *The Adjudicator* by Jonathan Lloyd, involving about 160 people between the ages of 7 and 70. One man when asked why he did it said it was so boring if you didn't take part, because everyone in the shops and pubs was talking about the opera.

In the rural south-west the changeover is only slightly less dramatic than Blewberry. My family and I have been in Lyme Regis for fourteen years and in that time there have been four librarians, three town clerks, three vicars, three headmasters; pubs have changed hands, shops opened and closed, there have been endless changes of staff at the school, children have grown up and left home. People have moved in and moved on. One of the difficulties of my work has been that as soon as I get someone interested and supportive, e.g. a chief education officer, they change jobs and move on. We have become a very mobile society, and not just in cities. A community is like a pond: water flows in at one end and out the other, but the pond remains the same. The fresh water prevents the pond from becoming stagnant. So communities are refreshed by constant renewal, but this can mean that people don't get to know, or speak, to each other. It can lead to rifts and division, coldness and lack of support.

In Lyme Regis, where I live, there are indeed families who have lived here generation after generation. There are also many retired people to whom generous pension schemes, coming well before they are worn out, have allowed a new start. There are numbers of people with young families who have left London looking for a more fulfilling lifestyle. These people have terrific energy and have probably been stimulated by the move. They often take an active part in local affairs. This can lead to resentment and divisions. The better-off live up the hill, away from the council estate. It becomes easy to rationalise all sorts of resentments as 'us' and 'them'. The impulse to claim 'our' territory is enormously strong. It may be possible to say that a community 'belongs' to some more than others, but where do you draw the line? And who is to judge? If the town becomes divided into cliques of 'old' families and newcomers, wealthy and poor, young and elderly, working and unemployed, or whatever, then the community will become sour and unsupportive. In a good community people talk to each other.

'GOOD' AND 'BAD' COMMUNITIES

A 'good' community depends upon people who are lively, energetic, caring and in touch with each other. Ideas will emerge without being blocked, stifled and put down; they will be thought about and tossed around. In a 'bad' community, people are afraid to stick their necks out. They think that if they have ideas, people will think they are silly or pushy.

Although a good community depends first of all upon people, a town plan which encourages communication can help. Bridport has a really cohesive, energetic, vital community, greatly helped by its very wide pavements, which are ideal for sauntering. You are always seeing people you know and having a chat. Broad streets are a natural club. Market Day draws everyone. Sometimes they close the great wide road altogether for the Christmas Meet of the Hunt, or a Pram Race. Sherborne, a much larger town, with a good deal of local pride, has one long narrow street where everybody does their shopping and so are encouraged to meet. Axminster, on the other hand, is less lively. It has a tiny narrow pavement, edging the violent A35, where huge lorries lumber past, inches from your shoulder. Not so easy to stop and chat. The town plan doesn't encourage communication.

It's very well worth listening to what people say about their own community. They are usually surprisingly honest and accurate. 'This is a great place to live,' they say, 'smashing people'; or 'This is a dreary sort of place – nothing goes on here.'

It's far easier to mount a community play in a good community. There are more energetic and enthusiastic people, who know how to work together without fuss. Lines of communication are already open. They will know who can do a particular job: who can be relied on; has money, time, or special skills. However, bad communities *need* a community play. It offers an opportunity for communication across ages and backgrounds. Time and again, people say they love doing these plays because 'I made lots of new friends'; 'I met people I wouldn't have met otherwise.' This opportunity for friendly co-operation over a long period stimulates and helps to unite a community. It will give them something to celebrate together and be proud of. Communities need community events to continually refresh them. Community plays can't draw everyone in and can't change everyone, but they are one of the most successful and all-embracing community events.

ART

CTT wants to help communities create a work of art. Others might simply wish to produce a community event. Why the insistence on art? If I am an artist trying to help people share my vision, or even just asking for money, I find I frequently have to justify myself.

Art is a means to the still centre, the moment of balance, the unchanging truth. Amidst all the triviality, muddle and distracting

Public Meeting. ▲ Ann Jellicoe describes the work. Supporting the play, ready to say a few words and answer questions are a youth leader, the school music master, a leading member of the Amateur Dramatic Society, the Mayor, headmaster, and three actors who took part in previous plays.
▼ Lively discussions follow the formal meeting.

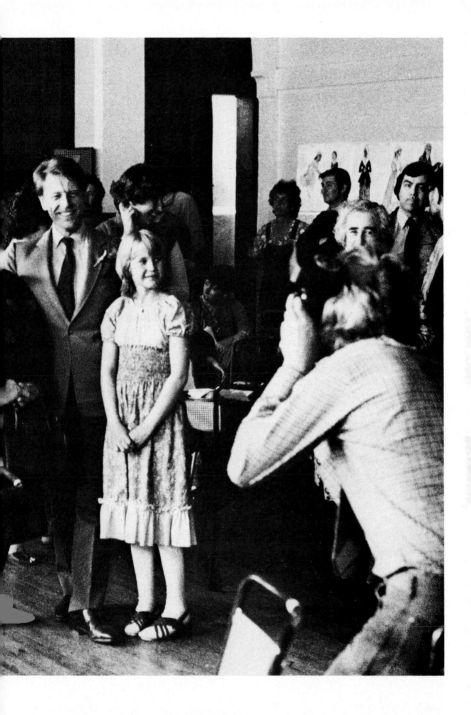

A less formal alternative to a public meeting: Edward Fox is guest of honour at a giant tea party held just before rehearsals start for the *The Tide*. Since this was unusually late in the process costume designs were available for display.

Raising Consciousness and Funds. ▲ A local amateur string quartet performs in the library of Chanters House, Ottery St. Mary. ▼ A carnival float: fifty people were involved in its preparation.

▲ (*left*) In an old folks' home: the lady (*right*) is demonstrating how to use a posse tub 'dolly' (*see p.90*). ▲ (*right*) A street event in Dorchester. ▼ Garland King parade in Beaminster.

Workshops. ◀ Learning circus skills; including stilt-walking, juggling, monocycling, clowning, tumbling and acrobatics.

▼ The start of a workshop held in a school hall where the play was to be performed. A large circle means that everyone commits themselves and all are equal. (see p.192)

A mask allows us to experience, with great purity and intensity, the actor's feeling of being possessed (*see p.189*). A young actress has made her own mask in a workshop and gazes into it for the first time.

▲ A movement workshop. Free and confident use of the body may be the amateur actor's greatest problem. ▼ When the energy is flowing then people are ready for a large group improvisation.

chaos of our lives we can open ourselves to art and sense a breathing tranquillity. Not dead, not fixed, but not moving. Art is the centred being 'I am here now'. This is where art and religion meet.

Through sensitivity, expressiveness and economy of line, words or musical phrase art can ravish and delight us. The organisation of matter and form can lead us through tension and relaxation to a emotional ecstasy and intense pleasure.

Art shapes our perceptions and opens our eyes: an artist can enable us to see something freshly–a pile of bricks, given significance by an artist, will mean that we never see bricks in the same way again. It follows from this that art, which strips away everything unnecessary and focuses on the essence of an event, makes it an ideal means to help people, or as in this case a community, perceive some aspect of themselves and celebrate their particular nature.

Art can reassure: our problems are not abnormal, they are shared, we are like other people. Art can be a rehearsal for life. It can educate us in social and moral behaviour.

Art refines and strengthens and enriches: through enjoying and understanding art our eyes and ears can learn to distinguish the true from the meretricious, the strong from the inflated, the sensual from the lifeless.

Everyone can enjoy art, its demands, disciplines, rewards all the more vividly if they create, or help create it. But people benefit from experienced and sympathetic help, particularly with objective standards and technical know-how. Self-expression is all very well. Art is tougher, more purposeful, dangerous, and ultimately a means of change.

A few days ago I received a letter from Margeret Ansell who took part in the Dorchester play:

> The incredible feeling of being part of something much bigger than self, and seeing it, other people, yourself, grow and improve and reach great heights. For many of the participants a one-off experience never to be forgotten.
> For some a stepping stone.

Does anyone come out of a community play the same person? I know I am changed, certainly my outlook on many things.

I say!

BEWARE – getting involved with a community play: it can disturb, disrupt, exhaust, uplift, make despair, it is a physical and mental stretcher.

It is the most enjoyable experience I have ever had and I wish it were all to come again.

To feel that you have the power to release such a response is both a reward and temptation.

3
Setting up:
the first 18 months

Timetable for a community play production over 2 years (Table 1)

CTT generally allows 2 years, but the process can be condensed into 18 months. The governing factor is the amount of time needed for the writer to research and write the play so that it will be ready in good time to make script changes and be ready for casting by June of Year 2.

Approx. date	Main event	Action to be taken
Year 1		
Early months	Initiator talks to a few sympathetic and enthusiastic friends Steering Committee formed	Basic decisions: how much professional involvement?; outline budget; initial fundraising discussions; key people/patrons; possible venues for performance and rehearsal; timetable; possible subjects for play; sub-committees etc.
	Contact school head	Begin card index for mailing list; start thanks list for later inclusion in programme; headed writing paper produced; possible logo
		The Steering Committee may consider appointing a professional director before the writer is commissioned
June–Sept.	Play commissioned	Writer will need at least 3 months for research and relating to community; 3–4 months for writing; 2

Approx. date	Main event	Action to be taken
		months for script alterations and reproduction, holidays and mishaps (this is the tightest possible schedule)
		You will probably want publicity for writer and this may be perhaps best handled by the Steering Committee at this stage, unless you want to form your Publicity Committee early
	First talks with fire officer (if venue unlicensed)	First step to getting a licence: talk to fire officer and see what numbers he will allow (so that you can fine up budgeting) and any conditions he will impose, e.g. more 'Exit' lights, doors to be kept open at performances etc., which may affect writing and design of production
Sept.–Oct.	Fundraising Committee formed	First approach to sponsors
		Steering Committee begin to look for wet and dry costume workshops; venue for play office; consider appointing play officer to start work after Christmas
		Begin design of play leaflets
Year 2 Jan.	Play officer appointed Play office opens	Phone/answerphone; coffee things etc.; hopefully someone there during office hours. Best of all: full-time play officer
		Start tentative discussions to see if art teacher and others are interested in involving children
	Possible MSC Team	Based at play office; starts

Approx. date	Main event	Action to be taken
		work in community; these schemes are set up for a year and this means the MSC Team can work in the community right through the period of production
	Publicity Committee formed	(See separate publicity notes)
		Big publicity push for Public Meeting
		Steering Committee starts to consider arrangements for reproducing, collating and binding scripts
Mar.–Apr.	Public meeting	Steering Committee becomes Organising Committee. Begin distributing play leaflets
	Project Committee formed	Begin to make plans for fund and consciousness-raising events which will support the play and keep it in the public eye from the Public Meeting to the start of rehearsals
		Big increase in card index
		Start Newsletter
	Play delivered	Optimistic, often much later than this
	Play director appointed	(But see early months of Year 1)
	Other professionals appointed: designer, musical director, stage manager, etc.	Big publicity push for workshops
May	Workshops start	Publicity push for reading of play
Late May	Scripts ready for cast to read, or:	

Approx. date	Main event	Action to be taken
Early June	Play is read by writer	Big publicity push for casting
Late June–early July	Casting	Scripts available; rehearsal availability and measurement forms distributed and filled in; identity photos taken and fixed to rehearsal availability forms
July–Aug.	Apply for theatre licence	Fire officer may require second meeting; have prepared detailed plans of production; showing space, stages, etc.
	First rehearsal schedules	Prepare and distribute
	Leaflet asking for materials	Ready to be distributed at beginning of school term
	Order AA signs	
	Organising Committee sets up a group to make tea and coffee for rehearsals and possibly later for the production	Possible basis for later Fair Committee
	Organising Committee looks for box-office and front-of-house managers.	Box office may need separate telephone booking number plus answerphone
	Production meeting	Professionals: writer, director, co-director, designer, musical director, plus any unpaid volunteer production assistants and any amateurs who will be heavily involved on the technical side. Very important to define roles and areas of responsibility
		You may prefer to make this into 2 meetings: (i) professionals (ii) professionals and amateurs
Aug.	Holiday	
Sept.	Fundraising events	Except raffle and

Approx. date	Main event	Action to be taken
	completed	merchandising
	Designer moves into costume workshop	
	Rehearsals start	Distribute 'materials wanted' list as early as possible
	Programme design	Organising Committee considers whether this is the job of Publicity Committee or other
		The Organising Committee may now find that they are heavily involved as individuals in the play and have a less active role as committee members; the chairperson, however, needs to maintain close liaison with all committees and a high profile, so that original structure is not lost
Early Oct.	Cast check names in programme	They then take responsibility for any errors in spelling, etc.
Late Oct.	Booking for cast and helpers opens one week before general public	
	Box office opens one month before production	
Late Oct.–early Nov.	Take over venue 1–2 weeks before production	Scaffolding/stages erected, lighting hung, etc.
Week before production	Costume parade	
	Technical rehearsals	
1st week of performance	Previews (Monday/Tuesday) Civic Night/official opening (Wednesday)	
2nd week of performance	Sunday/Monday no performance	
	Circulate questionnaire if desired	

Approx. date	Main event	Action to be taken
	Last performance	
	Party	
	Cleaning up and return of borrowed or hired items	
	Washing and cleaning of costumes	
	Audited accounts drawn up	This is a slow business, as bills will continue to come in at least 2 months after the show
Within one month of last performance	Organising Committee meets to sum up and consider what next?	The play will have thrown up people of particular energy who were not originally involved and who were therefore not on the Organising Committee; they should of course come to this meeting

PRIMARY DECISIONS AND FIRST STEPS

Anyone can initiate a community play. What's needed is the drive to get on with it and to go ahead one step at a time. Housewife, bookseller, arts enthusiast, farmer, postman, shopkeeper: all these people have started plays in the past. The chances are they've seen a production and thought: 'Why shouldn't we have one?' Even as they start thinking of the possibility of a community play there are questions to be asked and the answers will fundamentally affect the whole enterprise.

A community play will help the community, but in what way? Should the town do everything itself with the local drama teacher or amateur director directing the play, and a local writer writing it? Or should it bring in professionals? The notion of taking on this work is fantastically attractive and tempting: think of controlling and using 150 people, hundreds of helpers and all their resources. We all delude ourselves as to our creative merits. Are locals really good/experienced enough to cope with an event of this size and complexity? Does it matter if they are not? After all, it's 'their' community.

If local people do everything, it's axiomatic that the artistic standard will be lower than if professionals are called in. No community of manageable size has enough experienced and talented theatre/community workers and artists to provide a totally satisfying work of art. Nor am I convinced that if a community does it all itself that community involvement or satisfaction will be proportionately higher. I have found that if professionals commit themselves unstintingly, over a period of time, they themselves become part of the community. Some even stay on and put down roots: this has happened in four cases. If the professionals are not experienced at community work – drawing people in as I hope to describe in this book – then they will need help, and that means more community involvement. However, professionals bring fresh ideas, attitudes, values and standards which are useful and stimulating in themselves. Another advantage in using professionals is that they are above local politics and are perceived as being free and uncluttered; professionals can maintain a degree of objectivity which will make it easier for all sorts of disparate factors and people to come and work together towards the common goal. There is one final consideration with professionals: they must be good at their job and take it seriously. It's no use using mediocre people simply because they call themselves professionals; in such a case it's far better to use locals. (See p. 147)

There may well be one or two good local professionals and it may be possible to compromise. The example of Peter Hamilton, drama teacher at Queen Elizabeth Community College in Crediton has already been quoted. The Worcester community play was directed by Richard Hayhow, drama director of Worcester Arts Centre, who had previously spent several months seconded to CTT, as assistant director of the Ottery play, so as to gain experience before setting up Worcester. He is now directing the Lincoln play.

When people approach me at CTT it is usually assumed that I (or Jon Oram, who has taken over from me as Director), or another professional director, whom we will find, will direct the play. The point of asking CTT is to take advantage of our experience and professional expertise. With its record, CTT is now able to tell people, in general terms, what the process will be, what they can expect, and even to guarantee results. CTT, in consultation with local people, will draw up a budget, advise and help in setting up committees, organising events and projects, fundraising and research. CTT will set up pre-rehearsal workshops and find people to run them; commission other professionals, including the writer. At a certain point in the process, CTT personnel will move into the town on a semi-permanent basis, for a year or more, and will relate to the community at every level. They will be followed by other professionals who will share skills, guide and help the local community with the production. In a sense, CTT has developed to the point where it can offer a package. Up to now CTT has made no charge for this service. On the contrary, we have been funded from other sources and our input represents a considerable cash injection into the town.

What has happened in the past is that someone has said to me, 'Could you come and help us do a play in my town?' No one can issue an invitation on behalf of a whole community; at this stage the most they can say is: 'I know the school/arts society/amateur dramatics society/youth club would be interested.' If the invitation seems a good idea we meet and talk. At this first meeting I suppose we are watching each other, trying to sum up personality and clout. The initiator is going to be a key figure in the production, whether s/he realises it at this stage or not. Going back to the town and proselytising about the play, they will convince themselves irrevocably. The initiator will certainly be on the Steering Committee and possibly be its Chair.

At this first meeting we would have a fairly wide discussion. Probably the initiator would have little idea of what might be involved, so we would try and cover the process and what it demands. I would give concrete points and information to take back: in what way the town is likely to gain; a rough timetable of the process; information about previous productions. We might touch on possible venues and dates; discuss the town's resources. I would warn that the town itself would need to raise money but would make it clear that far from making a profit CTT would commit its resources over a long period and I might attempt to translate this into cash terms. At this stage nobody would commit themselves: the points of discussion will probably be talked over again at future meetings, but I would try to help the initiator clear his or her mind and have something to take back to talk about.

Following this first meeting, I would ask the initiator to discuss the idea around town and then arrange for a second meeting with a few other people who are also enthusiastic. In Ottery St Mary, the original proposal came from a man who (having just moved into the town) had opened a bookshop and was sufficiently interested in theatre to write drama notices of amateur productions for the local paper. He came back with the school drama teacher and a local bank manager: in effect we had cultural, financial and educational representatives from the town. These three later became respectively Chair of the Publicity, Finance and Organising Committees. At this meeting all the points were discussed in greater detail, together with who might possibly be invited to form a steering committee.

Whether s/he decides to approach me or not, the process for the initiator would be much the same: sorting out his or her ideas a little, then discussing the project with a few other people. This group in turn clarifies and structures the proposals a good deal more carefully in order to set them before a steering committee.

Key meeting: headteacher

Before the idea goes any further, and certainly before any final decisions are made, someone should arrange to see the headteacher of the school. (If CTT were setting up the play, as Director I would do this job myself.) If the play is going to want to use the school, or seek its co-operation, the headteacher must not, in any way, be made to feel that decisions involving school territory are being taken without reference to him or her.

IMAGE

Anyone whom you are meeting for the first time and whom you want to win over to the idea of the Play, will judge you by two things: your track record – (perhaps you are known as a person who gets things done, or have some influence in the town, or a particular skill) and the image you present at the first meeting. The less impressive the track record, the more important the image.

People are going to deliver themselves up to you on trust. They are being asked for time, energy, enthusiasm, commitment, imagination, cash. At first they will be worried about associating themselves with such a crazy and, perhaps, foolish idea as a community play. Will the school's routine he disrupted or the teachers' authority be eroded? Image can subtly reassure. Will town councillors lose votes? Image must somehow demonstrate that you are honest, efficient, good at organising, skilful at your job, really will deliver the goods. If you are the director of the play, then you will have to reassure people that you will make it possible for other talents to operate, will not be arrogant or destructive; that if you get into a position of power, as at rehearsal, you will not be cruel and will not try to make people look foolish. At the same time, you want to reassure everyone that they are going to have a fantastic experience and that it's all going to work. Your

appearance announces your intention. You mustn't project a dishonest image, but if you are hoping for co-operation from a school, it's
no use going to see a headteacher looking a mess.

If you are a town councillor, then it's likely you will already have
studied your image, but if you are an artist be careful. You will be
straining your listener's trust if your image seems to say, 'I'll be
blowed if I'm going to dress like a penguin. What the hell business is it
of their's what I look like?' An arrogance over image may just possibly
proclaim an arrogance over other things – or your observer may think
so. Neither should you look too conformist and dull. A slightly
unconventional appearance gives a small warning that you are an
independent person, should not be thought of as a teacher and that
you will be asking for room to manoeuvre. Somehow your appearance
should proclaim both trustworthiness and flair. If you are going to talk
to the amateur dramatics society (always a difficult occasion) or youth
club, your appearance should likewise be suitable. You may need to
emphasise some physical aspect of your personality which will appeal
to the person to whom you are talking. Just as you will select what you
say so as to present the attractions of the idea for them.

Writing paper Once the steering committee is set up, headed writing
paper gives an air of confidence. It can be produced quite cheaply and
simply with a Letraset heading, e.g. 'Dorchester Community Play',
and photocopied. If you have a good typeface and a sharp black
carbon ribbon, you can also type in the patrons' names. In a larger
town, you might find a design studio or printer willing to lay out paper
for you. Such printed paper can also be very useful for small
handwritten signs advertising workshops, coffee mornings, projects,
etc.

Logo Be very careful with amateur-designed logos. Don't trust your
judgement unless you know you have an eye. Your logo will be reproduced thousands of times: it will be the emblem of the play and it
must be good. If you can't get a good design early, far better wait until
you find the right person to do it.

Early leaflets It's helpful in the early stages, using your headed paper,
to have a brief outline of what a community play is all about. You
won't need many copies, since these are to give to key people, not for
general distribution, and of course you can photocopy them as you
want them.

Telephone manner The telephone is very much part of your image. Whenever the phone rings, however bad you are feeling, however evil-tempered or low, remember that the person at the other end of the line is going to receive an impression of you and your work. It helps to try and smile as you talk: it affects the timbre of your voice. Always try and sound cheerful as you answer the telephone; you should also be quite clear, saying: 'Community Play Office', or 'Beaminster community play'. It sounds efficient and welcoming and it trains you to be the same.

Patrons This is a job for the steering committee. Patrons can be part of the image. Names which people recognise and trust will guarantee the work you do. For Colway Theatre Trust I wanted to project our professional and theatrical background and our links with education and business. People being what they are, I included a few titles, thus doing double service, e.g. Dame Peggy Ashcroft DBE, and the late Lord Robbins, who was not only Chairman of the Robbins Report on Education, but also lived locally. Mrs Lois Sieff (Marks & Spencer), an acquaintance from the Royal Court Theatre, who gave us some money for *The Reckoning*, the writers John Fowles and Tom Sharpe (because they are artists and live nearby), the Bishop of Salisbury (a great help in our relationship with vicars and their churches). Private individuals who have contributed fairly substantial sums in covenants have also been invited to become patrons.

For each individual play, the steering committee invite local patrons and these will join ranks with CTT. Thus, the Mayor of Colyford, Mr Pady, found to his mild satisfaction, that his name was printed next to that of Laurence Olivier. Local patrons will guarantee your standing and good faith in the community. It's important that the steering committee should decide who to ask. They will know who has the real clout and who will be offended if not asked.

Keep a record Apart from your own personal achievements, if you are hoping to do further plays it's important to try and keep a detailed record. If you want to work ahead it will be extremely useful to have notices, photographs, etc. to explain the work. Theatre is so ephemeral that you must try and keep the fullest records you can. With *The Tide* we began to make albums, at least two per show, because one was always out on loan. These were basic photograph albums in which the material is laid under Cellophane. The albums contain photographs, press cuttings, anything which may give some idea of the work. Extremely useful, light and portable, they can be taken out at a moment's notice. We now encourage each town to make its own book of the play.

Video The BBC2 *Arena* video, 'A Play for Bridport', has been of immense value to CTT. Skilful and attractive in itself, easy to watch, the video gives a very good idea of the whole process of putting on a community play. All of the plays have been videoed by amateurs, and we also have useful, short extracts which have been made by local television companies. But it's difficult for amateurs to achieve really finished results which will give an image of the play as it actually happened. Amateur videos are great for those who took part in the work, since it will remind them of the fun they had, but they are not usually valuable for showing to people who don't know what it's all about. With professional work, remember the rules of copyright. If necessary, you must get an agreement that you can copy the film for non-profit-making purposes. This should not be too difficult, particularly if you are paid little or nothing by the TV company for the privilege of making the film. Try and get a really good master copy, a Umatic if possible, since you can continuously make high-grade copies from it.

Slide projections I am now making a collection of colour slides, showing every aspect of the work, to use as another visual aid. Slides have the advantage over video that the length of the talk can be varied and you can select the emphasis according to need.

COMMITTEES

Committees are magical. You get a few people together, they commit themselves by actually turning up and then volunteering for jobs – out of interest or community sense or sheer shame at not doing something. What this means is that the process reaches out. There is no way that I myself, a single, unknown individual, could reach 300 businesspeople and ask them for a donation and get it. But a committee of local businesspeople can do so. At the same time, why should 40 ladies make cakes and tea for me when I ask them? If there is a representative of the Ladies Circle on the committee, she will approach her friends and the job is as good as done. Multiply this by 8 or 10 people representing different groups in the community. Suppose each group averaged a number of 40 people and out of these 3 people in turn become interested and themselves involve more people . . . think about it. This is basically how the whole job is done. You will know you are on your way at the point when people stop saying, 'You should do this' and instead say, 'I will do this.'

Ideal committees

It might be useful to study the notes of Dr Meredith Belbin and his Industrial Training Research Unit at Cambridge. What Belbin basically says is that the least successful team is that which is exclusively composed of very clever people. The ideal team consists of 8 types who share 4 principle traits which have been isolated by Belbin. They are (1) intelligence (2) dominance (3) extrovert/introvert (4) stability/anxiety. Belbin apportions these traits so that he gets a mixture of originators, good team people, good communicators and people with a high anxiety to get a job done. I have never been able to form a team exactly along Belbin's lines because no situation is ever clinically flexible enough, but it's useful to keep his ideas in mind. Basically you need people who have ideas and personality and who will actually do the job. I rather dislike too many ideas people myself. I prefer doers. Brilliant people are sometimes too apt to be full of bright ideas which they expect others to carry out.

Steering/Organising Committee

In the productions which Colway Theatre Trust helps set up, the Organising Committee supervises and decides upon an enormous amount of work, apart from the actual artistic side of the production.

This first committee may prefer to call itself a steering committee until the public meeting when they should receive a vote to transform themselves into the Organising Committee.

The Organising Committee is at the heart of the venture. It goes right through the process – very busy in the early and middle stages, perhaps dormant during rehearsal, they emerge at the end, strengthened perhaps with fresh blood thrown up by the process, to wind up the play and hopefully to direct the energy that has been released forward to something else.

Who is on the Organising Committee?

The people who first approach Colway Theatre Trust really form the nucleus. They start to look for representatives of key organisations and social groups:

School drama teacher, or teacher responsible for drama This person should be very close to the whole centre of the production. If they don't want to join in the community play this may mean trouble. I also look for a close and direct contact with the head and deputy head of the school. Headteachers themselves are often too busy to serve on committees, although in Sherborne the grammar school head was both the initiator of the play and chair of the Organising Committee.

Town council Try and have at least one town councillor. S/he will act as your liaison with the town council and will help find you accommodation, money and general town support.

Local amateurs You must have the local drama group supporting the play. Hopefully, they will give up their seasonal production to join in.

Local arts society

Press You may prefer to have a press representative on your Publicity Committee, but take care: you may find that a local reporter favours his or her own paper and starves the rest – who will be annoyed.

Gate openers/social groups (1) youth leaders/welfare officers (2) businesspeople (3) the culturally deprived (this last is a difficult area to reach as they are seldom organised into groups like the middle class and you will have to make a special effort).

You will find you have plenty of teachers, doctors' wives, etc. They are always the most alert to new ideas in the community and the most willing, and trained, to help. They will suggest areas where a committee should be seeking representation.

I prefer committees of not more than 10 or 12 people, otherwise they may start to polarise. You can always take on more people by forming sub-committees. I am also much aware that committee members are not working for me but for their community, for each

Play Officer If you have a play officer s/he relates very closely to the Organising Committee, otherwise the committee itself must take on the tasks which would be done by the play officer.

What does the Organising Committee do?
The job of the Organising Committee falls into two sections: before
and after the public meeting. Up to the public meeting you will not
have a mass of names; individuals must be sought out and groups
approached.

Basic decisions In CTT productions, certain basic decisions are
already made, e.g. that professionals will be involved. If not the CTT,
then someone, probably the Organising Committee, will have to make
these decisions. If you are going to use professionals, including a play
officer, director, writer, designer, composer, stage manager, etc.,
then it will be the job of the Organising Committee to find and appoint
them.

Draw up a budget All basic decisions are also finally budgeting
decisions. The Organising Committee will budget to cover any
deficit, i.e. agree to raise a certain amount of money from within the
town and from other sources.

Represent and reach the town 'Contact trees' may structure this effort.
Each member of the committee contacts four people: (1) someone
with money (2) gate-openers/the disadvantaged (3) history (4) technical. In turn these people are invited to give four more names.

Decide on and book performance venue Because schools and halls are
booked up sometimes years in advance, it's important that a provi-
sional booking is made as early as possible. The Organising Committee usually makes the final choice and they can be very effective. In
Sherborne we could have used the hall of the secondary modern
school on the edge of town, but Sherborne has six senior schools of
every complexion. The Organising Committee wanted neutral
ground; they were determined to get the use of the Digby Hall, the
community centre, but as is usual with such halls, it had a full
programme for the period of the production nearly two years ahead.
The Sherborne Organising Committee, which included the Mayor,
found alternative venues for all the bookings and persuaded them to
vacate the hall, except for a rabbit show on an unvital day. The
committee ran into trouble here: the local council officer responsible
for bookings was very obstructive. I think she feared that if the
bookings were turned away, they might not come back (this did not
happen), but it took the combined weight of mayor, ex-mayor and

deputy mayor to shift her. Fortunately this officer left shortly afterwards and her successor was very helpful.

There was no way that I myself could have overcome the objections
of that officer. Only a committee with a degree of clout could do it, not
only in terms of bringing pressure to bear but also having the capacity
to find alternative accommodation.

Appoint sub-committees Find people capable of serving on sub-committees: those with special aptitudes and relating to other sections of
the community, etc. The Chair of each sub-committee should also sit
on the Organising Committee.

Organise public meeting The first big practical test.

Support the dramatist in the town Arranging meetings, etc.

Card index/mailing list This will form the basis of a mailing list for a
later newsletter, appeals for materials, etc. If you also cross-reference,
you will be able to find an engineer, sanitary inspector, offer of
accommodation, etc. if and when you want them. It's important that
somebody keeps this card index continuously up to date, if not the
Play Officer, then someone on the Organising Committee. You
should also be thinking of a postal mailing list.

Thanks list From the very beginning, a list should be kept recording
help given. It will later be printed in the programme. This is
important because not only is it pleasant to acknowledge people's
help, but it will demonstrate the enormous degree of support the play
has accumulated.

Invite patrons to support the play

Find play office and costume workshops In the course of time, the
Organising Committee will need to find a play office and costume
workshops (wet and dry).

Appoint box-office manager This is often done surprisingly late,
perhaps only two or three months before production and it's as well to
wait until you find the right person.

Entertainment base When I am doing a play near my own home in

Lyme Regis, it's most helpful to be able to say to people: 'Come to supper' or 'Come and stay in my house.' When I am too far away for this to be easy and convenient, it has never failed that some good-natured family fills the gap. They begin to be the natural hospitality focus for the play, providing a meal, a bed, a cup of coffee, or somewhere to meet, and these generous people are always very near the centre of the play, i.e. on the Organising Committee. It may indeed be that when I am not in a position to offer this relaxed hospitality myself it draws someone else forward. There is a lesson to be learned here.

Executive committee If you think for political reasons you need to have a large Organising Committee which is therefore slow and cumbersome, it may be a good idea to form a much smaller executive committee, responsible to the Organising Committee, who will actually do the work.

Sub-committees

Sub Committees mean that people may work more precisely towards a target, according to their talents, and not too much is asked of any one person. The chair of the Organising Committee, the director of the play and the play officer are ex-officio members of all committees, but in practice none of these attend all of them, except possibly the play officer. The Fair Committee particularly is an opportunity for an energetic assistant to learn and develop.

Fundraising Committee

The Organising Committee has already promised to raise an agreed sum of money within the town. This now becomes the responsibility of a Fundraising Committee which will explore ways of finding the money. You will hope to find a banker and perhaps a few influential businesspeople. In Ottery St Mary, the chair of the Fundraising Committee, a banker, who was at the original meeting with me, brought in two more bank managers and the chief of the local office of a credit-card firm. In Dorchester, the chair of the Organising Committee, himself a town councillor and ex-mayor, brought in the county treasurer and four businesspeople. The primary job of the Fundraising Committee is an appeal to local businesses. Coming from such a heavyweight group this is usually very effective. Thereafter, the Fundraising Committee relates very closely to the Projects Committee (one of whose jobs is to set up events which will raise money). The Fundraising Committee checks that targets are being met and warns that more must be raised if necessary. Controlling and disbursing the money raised is not usually the responsibility of the Fundraising Committee. This is a job which requires experience, flexibility, easy availability (authority may be needed at very short notice) and an iron grip. CTT would normally undertake organising the disbursement and control of money. Failing this, a treasurer should be appointed. The town contribution is only part of the money which will need to be raised. Approaches will probably have to be made to three other groups: (1) the local Regional Arts Association and Arts Council of Great Britain (2) trusts and business sponsorship (3) local authorities.

The Fundraising Committee needs to be formed early. Quite a lot of finance takes time to come through the pipeline and you must be sure that your budget target is met before you go into rehearsal.

There is sometimes the danger that if you get too experienced and high-powered a Fundraising Committee you are going to create a conflict of loyalties with their other appeals and divide their interests. For example, if someone usually raises money for the Red Cross, they will feel that any penny they raise for the play has been taken from their own charity. This is an area to watch because the good and experienced fundraisers you want are probably helping other charities anyway.

Projects Committee

This committee will organise events which will (1) raise consciousness and publicity for the play (2) maintain and increase interest from the Public Meeting to the start of rehearsals (3) raise money from events (4) reach and involve the disadvantaged (5) try out the quality of helpers: discover how much they can achieve and how well they work together (6) provide focus and goals for new skills. It will organise everything from coffee mornings and 'diminishing tea parties' to 'poets & pints', talent shows, carnival floats and maybe a prestigious evening at the local great house; it will also organise general fun/culture events, such as midsummer festivals, etc. The Projects Committee generally ceases work as soon as rehearsals start because no energy can then be spared for outside events.

Publicity Committee

As with most committees, you need people who are willing to cope with methodical work and some who have flair. A great deal of publicity is simply method. When it comes to journalists, TV, etc., personal contact helps. For dealing with major publicity, such as television, you need somebody who has a wide knowledge of the subject, who can talk easily and with confidence.

Production Committee

We set up a Production Committee for *The Western Women* because it seemed appropriate: technical people representing different parts of the town were looking for a niche. It didn't function all that well as a working committee, although the chair, a postman with a talent for carpentry, did an enormous amount of work. However, the committee did serve as a lead into various organisations when it came to borrowing resources, etc. If you have a Production Committee, it probably runs more or less over the period of rehearsal with of course greatly increased activity near to performance. But a good stage manager will probably organise the technical side. This is an area where very large numbers of people may be involved – over 90 in Dorchester.

Research Group

This formed itself spontaneously in Dorchester when a group of about six people who were interested in local history offered to help David Edgar. They stayed on working together after the play and now, a year later, are helping the museum prepare another large exhibition about the play in retrospect. A research group is thus extremely useful not only in helping the writer but as a general source of information and for finding material for exhibitions and displays. The idea has been used again in Beaminster.

Fair Committee

There is little need to form this committee until after rehearsals start. Its job is to approach all organisations in the town and invite them to join in the fair. We prepare a duplicated sheet*, saying in some detail what the fair is, how it supports the play and how it will be organised. The Fair Committee decides which group or charity will have which night in the fair. It's extremely important that they take the lead here: they know their town, e.g. one community will welcome CND, another won't. When it comes to the actual fair itself, the in and out, etc. will be organised by the stage manager.

Hospitality Committee

This is likely to be simply an *ad hoc* group of people who may be asked to take on the job quite late in rehearsal, perhaps three or four weeks before production. There is always a need for free hospitality for interested impecunious and important guests, such as visiting dramatists, etc. The committee may well find that those who filled in the play leaflets many months previously, saying they could help with hospitality, have now left town, or are using their spare room in other ways, and so fresh accommodation has to be found. The other group of people who will be coming (newspaper critics, representatives of the Arts Council, etc.), who are on business expenses, may need help in booking hotels, etc.

Misfits

It's really not hard to find people who will work on committees. Sometimes mistakes are made and people come on for the wrong reason: they want power, or they are out of sympathy with the rest. If they don't get what they want, such people generally quietly drop away provided the committee in question is strong and not divided.

Minutes

The job is so sprawling and complicated that we always take careful minutes. It's worth reminding yourself of the obvious: if the committee decides upon a certain action someone must undertake responsibility otherwise there's a danger it won't happen or will get dumped back onto the play officer. In drawing up minutes we generally have an 'action' column with initials of whoever has taken it on. You can run your eye down the list and see what's for you – and it will come back to you at the next meeting. I have also formed the habit of making notes on any important conversation or meeting but this may be simply because I distrust my bad memory.

VENUES

Size In order to make productions commercially viable, CTT needs a hall holding at least 450, i.e. 150 in the cast and 300 audience. With a larger cast it's possible to juggle so that not all are in the hall at the same time. I would prefer a space holding at least 600 people, i.e. approximately 150 cast plus the audience, but venues of this size are not easy to find in the rural south-west. Bear in mind that (1) the larger the audience, the more money or the lower the ticket prices (2) an enormous effort will go into the play and you will want the cast to feel that the effort was worth it. (3) a great many people are going to want to see the play.

Geography The Organising Committee will always want a venue in the middle of town, but the large schools of the fifties were usually built on new land on the edge of town. People fear that the audience will never go up the hill, but they do. When we have presented plays in one of these outlying schools, we have sometimes talked of laying on buses or ferry services, but it generally comes down to everyone making their own arrangements and we help with difficult cases.

Politics In both the Axe Valley and Sherborne there was tension between schools and a neutral venue had to be found. In Dorchester, a considerable factor in deciding not to go to the larger Eldridge, Pope Warehouse was the fact that Pope's was already giving so much support that the play might have well become the Eldridge, Pope Show rather than the Dorchester Community Play.

Possible alternatives The south-west is a dispersed rural area with no big towns. We have the following alternatives: (1) *school halls*: seldom more than 450 people allowed (2) *community and town halls*: seldom more than 450 people allowed (3) *churches*: possibly 600 or more may be allowed (4) *school sports halls* (5) *barns and industrial warehouses* (6) *the open air*.

Schools
Advantages
1 There is one central authority immediately available: the head teacher. You can get quick decisions which other people will respect.
2 Usually free of charge if you are involving numbers of children.
3 Plenty of rehearsal and dressing-room space and many other resources.

Disadvantages
1 Take care that the project is not looked upon as a glorified school play.
2 The decoration of school halls is usually a bit dreary.

Community and town halls

Advantages

Recognised as a community centre and neutral ground.

Disadvantages

1 Possible difficulties of authority structure. Town and community halls are generally looked after by a caretaker who is responsible to some fairly remote official who is himself controlled by a committee. Unconventional use of the hall may make the caretaker nervous. At Seaton we had provided the authorities with full plans of the stages and scaffolding we intended to erect. Nonetheless, when all the scaffolding came in and was laid out on an enormous piece of old carpet, the caretaker was so nervous that there would be damage and he would get the blame that he called in the district surveyor. In self-defence we had to make our own survey of the state of the hall (fortunately, we had a building inspector in the cast who brought in a surveyor friend). In the end, the only damage done was when we came to dismantle the scaffolding and a friendly neighbourhood police sergeant, who was helping, dropped his end of a large steel pole and gouged the floor. I was terrified of a large bill but the play was in fact so successful and popular that it dissolved bad feeling and no more was heard of the matter. On the other hand, at Colfox School when the scaffolding was going up and the school hall looked, as they always do, like a builder's yard, the headteacher merely nodded and all was well.

2 Possible cost: town halls vary in price. Seaton Town Hall (Devon) is run as a community amenity and cost £75 for three weeks in 1980. Sherborne's Digby Hall (Dorset) cost £600 for the same period in 1982.

3 Possible lack of dressing-room space. This is usually limited to two or three dressing-rooms in community halls. We have successfully solved the problem with remarkably little trouble by having people dress at home. We have also used empty shops, etc., and in Dorchester the Vicar was extremely helpful, allowing use of part of his house nearby.

4 Hard to get three weeks clear of bookings: town halls are for the use of the town and are heavily booked. Many organisations have regular annual dates.

Churches

We used a church for the first time when we mounted *Entertaining Strangers* in St Mary's Church, Dorchester.

Advantages

1 Numbers: there is no other available space in Dorchester which can accommodate 600 people.

2 Relative cheapness: the church authorities recognised the play as being for the good of the community. We were charged for electricity and heating and also for our use of the parish hall, but this was infinitely less than we would have had to pay for the Corn Exchange which is the Dorchester community centre and which only holds 200 people.

3 An attractive space. The carving and decorations, the soaring arches looming up into the darkness added greatly to the Dorchester play. *Entertaining Strangers* deals with the story of the Reverend Henry Moule, Vicar of Fordington, a suburb of Dorchester. Unfortunately, Moule's own church has fixed pews, so we settled on St Mary's because the whole area could be cleared. Likewise, Worcester community play, *Woodbine Willy*, about the Reverend Studdert-Kennedy, gained immeasurably by being set in his own church.

Disadvantages

1 Sightlines and layout: pillars, pews, etc. may be permanent fixtures.

2 Acoustics: sometimes difficult and demanding for inexperienced actors (though music can sound very good).

3 Mild form of censorship: at Dorchester, the Vicar, Churchwardens, etc., once convinced of our goodwill, did not in any way try to impose censorship, but there was a great deal of pressure on them from some sections of their congregation and they were anxious. Out of consideration we showed them the script as soon as it was ready. Had they asked for changes the situation might have been difficult, but they did not.

4 The church's need to hold services: in Worcester, the community play was given total use of the church. In Dorchester, we had to work round services. There was no real problem about this, except for a small area of misunderstanding, when we had to stop work at some weekend rehearsals because of christen-

ings. Fortunately, we could go into the parish hall. This needs to be discussed beforehand.

5 Lack of toilets: in Dorchester, we arranged minimum toilet accommodation for the cast but the audience had to take their chance. I heard of no complaints. Perhaps people don't expect to go to the loo when attending church.

6 Fire exits, etc. in Dorchester, the fire officer demanded that two outer doors be kept locked open during the freezing December nights. Eldridge, Pope lent huge industrial heaters to help warm the church before the show but they were too noisy to use once warm-ups started. The heat of the lights and the audience were then just sufficient to keep the temperature comfortable. (A conventional school hall can become appallingly hot.)

7 Possible damage to delicate church fabric: check that you are insured.

8 Lack of dressing-room space.

9 Possible objections from people who may have deep convictions: in Dorchester, there was a small group of people, members of the congregation, who were disturbed that the actors should drink and smoke during the play. They could not accept that a community play may be a valid means of achieving good. It really did not amount to much until the play was over when there was a sharp little correspondence in the local paper which was so blinkered in tone it probably influenced people towards the play.

Similarly, I had a few uncomfortable moments when I heard that a group of people were going to force themselves into the play on the grounds that entrance to a church should be free. Fortunately, the Rector was taking part in the play and said firmly that he had the right to ban anyone from coming to church. We gathered a few heavies from the cast to support him if necessary, but the party never materialised.

Warehouses
Advantages
1 Large uncluttered space.
2 Possible low cost.

Disadvantages
1 The space may indeed be vast; too big. At Stratford-upon-Avon, a performance of *Mary after the Queen*, the RSC's so-

called community play, was lost in the middle of Flower's vast modern warehouse. Had we used Pope's warehouse in Dorchester, we would have had to create a smaller space, probably built up out of scaffolding, so as to achieve some intimacy.

2 Fire regulations: there may be difficulties over insufficient exits, etc.
3 Heating and acoustical problems, including rain on tin roofs.
4 Lack of dressing-room space, toilets, etc.

Open air
Advantages
1 Size.
2 Little or no cost.
3 Sometimes the settings can be very beautiful, e.g. the gardens of country houses.

Disadvantages
1 Weather.
2 Acoustics: normally, in the open air, the voice flies straight upwards and it's hard to hear anyone, let alone somebody young and inexperienced. But I have seen amateur productions in country gardens, where the house itself, or some feature of the garden, has served to bounce the sound back to the audience. My own feeling about open space is that the things that come across best are masks and brass bands.
3 Possible interference from traffic and other noises.
4 Possible problems of controlling access. Either a country house is miles out of town, or the area may only be enclosed by the lightest of railings.
5 Lack of dressing-rooms, toilets, etc.

I have never dared work in the open air because of questions of weather and acoustics, but two years ago I saw a community play in Newbury, in summertime, where they elegantly solved both problems.

Newbury were presented with a derelict, rubbish-filled site, which stood in the heart of the town just behind the church. At one side was a long, old barn with one wall missing. They bulldozed the site and pushed the rubbish into three huge heaps, which they wrapped around with wooden industrial pallets, bound with industrial packing tape. These were flattened and smoothed on the top and were then used as stages for groups performing all day long and taking part in the fair, which swirled round them.

The venue for the performance was the barn, which became the acting area (and thus provided a good sounding-board). The audience sat on tiered seating (borrowed), enclosed in a simple scaffolding structure, wrapped round with tarpaulins: in effect, a rough tent. This structure certainly kept out the weather (it rained while I was there), but there were rather charming gaps through which you could see life outside, e.g. the little fires over which the fair people were cooking.

THE SCHOOL

The school hall may be the largest available hall in your community, but even if you are not using it for the actual production, you will almost certainly want to use the school for rehearsal space and other resources.

It's probably undesirable to do a community play if you don't have the school's active, enthusiastic co-operation. You are trying to reach into the community and find people who have little or no contact with art. A school reaches directly into at least a third of the homes in the community: it is the most broad-based of all community organisations, and the kids and teachers probably form the largest and most active group in the community.

The headteacher will welcome the play for the following reasons:

1 Providing the school curriculum is not too disturbed, the play will immensely stimulate and enrich school life. There is direct contact with working artists and the experience of aiming for excellence. There is also an atmosphere of freshness and excitement: the routine is being broken.

2 By means of the community play, the school is demonstrably allying itself with the community. Schools see their role in the community as very important, particularly perhaps as artistic and intellectual leaders. It is not easy for them to find the means to do it: a community play offers the opportunity.

3 A really good and prestigious production will draw attention to the school. It may even help them to attract better teachers if they gain a reputation for this sort of successful venture. Certainly, more than one drama teacher, recently

arrived in the area, has told me that they came here because of the chance of working with us.

Resources

Schools have very large and diverse resources, most of which are in constant use. These include space for rehearsal and possibly perform-ance, stage lighting, photocopying, duplicating and lithoing machines, art rooms, sewing rooms, including sewing machines, metal and woodwork workshops, etc. The list is long. Up to a point, you may be allowed to share these resources, but be very tactful in your approach: don't snatch, ask for one thing at a time, go from the top, through the head or deputy head. The school may be afraid that if they let you use resources without charge or at preferential cost other groups in the town may ask why they can't enjoy the same privileges. The answer is educational involvement: you are after all giving the school considerable free service. Whether you will be able to use a particular resource is generally up to the teacher who actually controls it. Headteachers are not all-powerful and can't *make* other teachers co-operate with you (but can certainly stop them co-operating). Remem-ber that the free use of the school hall will itself be worth several hundred pounds.

How much is the school affected?

A headteacher recently said to me that the community play had interrupted the school routine considerably less than a conventional school play. There should indeed be no disruption of classes: none should be planned for and none needed. Television excerpts are the only exception to this rule. You will want to get local TV to give you a boost. Local companies will never, in my experience, come outside normal working hours. You may need to ask for a few of the kids/teachers for a short period for TV extracts, probably very near production.

Educational pyramid

At the top is the *Chair of the Education Committee* and the *Chief Education Officer*. Try and get on some sort of terms with them. Invite them to your shows. Demonstrate how much work you are doing for the educational system and the community. I was introduced to the Chair of the Dorset Education Committee by Lady Digby, who is a member of the West Dorset District Council and of South-West Arts Management Committee, and who has since become a member of the

Arts Council. She is thus a power in Dorset. Twenty minutes'
conversation with Dione Digby, Jeanne Bisgood, Chair of DEA, and
myself cemented the connection and from then onwards Jeanne
Bisgood came to virtually all our shows until she resigned from the
Education Committee and, though we have never had any money
from the DEA, we received a good deal of support in kind. There were
other results, e.g. one headteacher gave a small drinks party every
night and said to me on the night Miss Bisgood came: 'That's the first
time we've been Jeanne and Alistair.' [Not his real name.]

School governors

In theory, governors control the school. In practice, they listen very
much to what the head says.

Headteacher

Within their limited area, headteachers really do have a great deal of
effective power, certainly in terms of resources. While only the
Education Committee can give you blanket authority to allow you to
use all their halls free of charge (which may well include youth clubs
and other useful centres), when it comes to an individual school it is
the headteacher who will decide which classification you will come
under and what scale of charge is applicable. Although, if you are near
a bureaucratic base as we were in Dorchester, the head may be more
comfortable if you get authority from the chief education officer. It is
my experience that, so long as the head is convinced that large
numbers of kids will be involved in what is essentially an educational
experience, they appear able to take the project on board as a school
activity and will allow you the use of the hall and other rooms free of
charge.

The head is leader of a team and not a dictator. Teachers are
independent to a degree and it's an unwise headteacher who rides
across the wishes of the staff. S/he cannot deliver the teachers to you
ready, willing and enthusiastic. Even so, the head's actual authority is
paramount and no one else has the same clout.

If the head is satisfied both from talking to you, looking at your
background material, absorbing the image you project and from
personal enquiry, then it is very seldom that s/he will not welcome
you. Best of all is when s/he has seen a previous production. Heads
like community plays. They are very good for the school. David
Butterworth, who until recently was headteacher of the Woodroffe
School in Lyme Regis and one of our most dedicated supporters, said;

'It's very good for us, but it's more than that, it's not just the artistic experience: the whole moral ethos of the school is being improved.' When, subsequently, heads of other schools telephoned David to see if we could deliver, he would always say: 'You'd be mad to miss it.'

I like headteachers (though deputy heads are more fun), but they are headteachers because they appreciate power and authority. *Always go and see the head first.* Never let things develop too far before you go and talk to them. The school is the head's kingdom. S/he runs it and won't like it if assumptions are made about its use which s/he has not directly sanctioned. I recently forgot my own golden rule. The drama teacher had been so positive, assured, enthusiastic and welcoming that I never actually went to see the headteacher until after the basic decision to do the play in the school had been taken. I then had a rather disastrous interview with him when I felt I had totally failed to gain his confidence. I could get no undertaking regarding full and free use of the hall, indeed we only ever had it three or four times a week, a serious matter with a play of that size. Fortunately, the school also possessed a large drama studio (controlled by the drama teacher) and a sixth-form common room. This was too the only time when we have had to pay for a school, although it was only a token payment of £300 and this was probably a tenth of what we could reasonably have been charged.

Had I gone to the headteacher first, I am sure there would have been no trouble at all, for the story has a happy ending which is entirely due to him: he and his wife came regularly to the workshops before the play and became deeply interested; both took part in the production (he even went through the misery of growing a beard); both became my friends and amongst the most sensitive and sure supporters of the play. It was a near thing and that the situation resolved itself was due to the headmaster's generosity in attending the workshops after our unsuccessful meeting, and so allowing his interest to grow.

Apart from this one episode we have never had to pay for a school hall, and have had few problems about getting space for rehearsal once a headteacher has put his or her authority behind the idea.

Talking to the headteacher
If you get the confidence of the headteacher s/he will be your strongest ally. At the first meeting dress the part and try and relate to the head as an equal, neither subservient nor patronising. If you feel uncertain of yourself it might be helpful first to read Keith Johnstone's *Impro* (Methuen London, 1981) and then set up a few simulations so that

you could experiment with relating to different kinds of people. Try and get on Christian-name terms, but in private only. Few members of staff ever call their headteachers by their first names. Actually, in rehearsal, with the head's agreement, I break this rule. Everybody in rehearsal is called by their first names. On the other hand, in talking to a third party, I would still probably refer to 'the head'.

You should aim to set up the sort of relationship where you can talk absolutely frankly. Try and sense where their strengths and weaknesses lie. You may find in talking to a headteacher that s/he begins to throw out interesting suggestions and to develop your ideas. You should welcome this with enthusiasm – s/he is taking the idea on board. One headteacher I dealt with liked to handle publicity. Others acted in the plays. You shouldn't bother heads with trivial things, but you need to have the sort of relationship where you have reasonably free access to them. Remember the names of their secretaries. Above all, never look as if you are challenging, questioning, or eroding their authority.

What to ask for at the first meeting

If you want to use the school hall for the production of the play, you should try to get decisions on the main points at the very first meeting: dates of performance; dates when the school hall will be needed almost exclusively for the production weeks alone; date by which the play will be out and the hall clean and usable by the school; use of hall for rehearsals; possible alternative large and small rehearsal areas if the large hall is not available.

You have to foresee, plan, and stick to your plan. If you want the school hall, you should be absolutely concrete about when you will want it. To begin with, I ask for every evening from 4.0 p.m. to 10.0 p.m. and on Saturdays and Sundays from 2.0 p.m. You won't get all you ask. Some days will be impossible, but the school will probably be able to let you use some other large space or spaces. Also, ask if you can use clasrooms for small rehearsals. The main thing is to be reasonable, co-operative, understanding and clear. The head wants you in the school but they want to know where they are and they may have some difficult negotiating ahead of them.

I also explain exactly when we shall need the hall for production and what this will mean, i.e. a school hall full of stages and scaffolding. We generally need the hall for three full weeks: one week setting up and two weeks for performance, when the hall will be almost entirely out of action for the school unless they can work amongst the stages. But sometimes, with a complicated production, we might try and get a longer setting-up period. This is at least one quarter of the school term when the hall may be needed for games, etc. in bad weather; in addition to its usual purpose for assemblies, classes, after-school activities and possibly even meals.

You may also want to use the hall for workshops once or twice a week and maybe the odd weekend before the rehearsal period starts. The school may also have possible space for costume workshops, etc. (and it's rewarding for the school to have such a lively activity going on with people coming and going and the kids able to join in during their free time). It's probably unwise to make too many pernickety and possibly confusing requests at the first meeting, e.g. asking if you can use the school litho machine. In any case such details may be better dealt with through the deputy head.

Apart from asking the head to commit the school in various ways, you also need to sense what they think about certain aspects of the school's nature and its relationship with the town. There are all sorts of questions to which it would be useful to find an answer. What are the relations between the headteacher and the staff? Are the staff likely to co-operate? Who of the staff are most likely to be enthusiastic about the play? Who may prefer to remain uninvolved? What is the general atmosphere of the school? What is the head's relationship with parents? I would be interested if any head agreed immediately to involve the school without at least making a show of consulting teachers. It may indicate a bad relationship and a dodgy school. It would be useful to ask if you might speak to the teachers, the governors and the PTA. This has to be done with a good deal of tact. I doubt if any head would speak freely at a first meeting. Even so, you can gain a great deal of information.

Head's questionnaire*

I generally have a form listing all the things I need to know which I sometimes use at the first meeting with the head. I wouldn't show it and often don't fill it in at all, but it reminds me of the questions I ought to ask and gives a structure to the discussion.

Take the head into your confidence about cost

Usually, so very early in the project, I would in general be wary of talking money in too much detail. Most people are accustomed to amateur shows which cost virtually nothing and money can be upsetting and scary. But headteachers are administrators and businesspeople. They understand money and the need to pay people. Even though it is a very long time before production, try and have some sort of outline budget when you first speak to the head. In the past, I used to ask schools for a contribution of about £150 per school. In Bridport the school gave £500, but we had to put quite a lot of this back in ways we had not anticipated, e.g. paying the caretaker for some overtime. In the Axe Valley, three schools gave £150 each. In Sherborne, five schools raised £900 between them. But we no longer ask schools for a contribution. Money is now too tight and it's enough that they share their resources. Private schools are another matter.

Visibility
If the head asks you to some function, e.g. Speech Day, where you will be seen as part of the acknowledged structure of the school, i.e. an honoured guest, it is wise to accept. I have been at a Speech Day where the headteacher has slipped a paragraph about the community play into his speech, which I am convinced he would have quietly cut had I not been there. You may also have an opportunity to meet school governors and other influential people. I had a very easy introduction to the Mayor of Sherborne and other dignitaries through being asked to sit on the stage at Speech Day at Foster's School and to dinner afterwards with the head and his guests. Invite the head to be a patron of the play. They like it and it demonstrates that a key member of the community supports the project.

PTA
The PTA is a different problem and not an easy one. It is astonishing what a narrow view parents take of education; teachers are far more outward-looking. You may meet with some resistance from the PTA. It won't be great because, if the head and teachers have given their blessing, the PTA will not struggle too much. You have to slowly win them over. Perhaps you won't gain their confidence until they experience the play themselves. In the meantime try and talk to them: explain the play, the ideas behind it, and answer questions. Their main worry is how much time it will take from lessons and whether it will disturb exams. The answer is: 'No' – no child who is soon to take O or A levels will take part in the play unless they and the teachers consider it is vital for their good (e.g. they are going into the theatre) and they can cope. On the other hand, an intelligent, well-organised, talented young person, who longs to be in the play can do so; the child

simply says: 'I can't come during weeks 4, 5 and 6' or whatever, and you work round this.

The PTA will probably be the mainstay of one or two evenings of the fair. Remember also that they may have their own dates during the period of production, the Christmas fair and so on, when they have a regular booking for the hall. Leave the head to sort this one out, but be tactful. Don't insist. It may be far better public relations to let the PTA have the hall.

Deputy headteachers

Heads make strategic decisions: they give the broad, general approval. Deputy heads make things work. I don't really see how you could do a play, using the school, without the deputy head on your side. It's s/he who will get kids to carry the desks from the hall, borrow tables from another room, arrange with the caretaker that he will unlock at a certain time. In a thousand ways, the deputy head will help and smooth your way. Deputy heads are overworked people and, as a race, I like them very much. They are all in a Mafia-like league against headteachers. Once they trust you – to be discreet, not arrogant, tactful, dependable – deputy heads will feed you all kinds of information and warnings which will make your path smoother. Just as one head will vouch for you to another, so deputy heads will pass the word along that you're OK. They sometimes have a highly developed sense of the dramatic. I've had a deputy head catch my eye meaning, 'I want a word with you,' and discreetly tell me that I ought to phone the deputy head of another school where I was thinking of working, because there was trouble and my friend had told his opposite number to let me know what was happening and how to handle it. Likewise, I have had very private drinks in back rooms of pubs with deputy heads ('This meeting never took place'), which really gave me the practical, inside picture of what made a particular school tick.

Teachers

Teachers are a mixed bunch. At their best they are idealists, working like mad for the kids; in a sense a school is an under-used source of idealism. Never believe you'll get all the teachers on your side. With the majority, the best you can hope for is negative support: they are not actually against the play. If you're going to work closely with the school, however, you really must have the positive help of the English teachers, or at least the teacher responsible for drama. It's also enormously useful to have the art and music teachers on your side.

I don't know how to win over teachers (or anyone else) who is not enthusiastic. I don't think it's possible to do it all at once. I think you have to regard it as part of your central job: drawing people in who have no interest in art and who, possibly, are actively against it. I use various methods. I try and talk to them and enthuse them. Sometimes I distribute an explanatory leaflet amongst teachers, but this really has a negative purpose – they check to see that their province won't be interfered with. I think that perhaps the best way to get someone to join in, or at least to involve them modestly, is to follow the golden rule: try and involve them through their work. Thus I have asked physics and chemistry masters for their advice about how to make artificial smoke, and a history master to accompany a group visiting a local museum (this was not a success, as he didn't know enough about the subject; I should have warned and protected him). A metalwork teacher helped to cast badges for soldiers in our first play and thereafter his family joined in later plays and became heavily involved in various offshoots of the work in Bridport. If you don't get teachers' support you will find that not many children join in. At one school, even though the head was very supportive, the English teacher would have nothing to do with the play and so we had only about 14 children from that school. Fortunately, the production was not based there.

English/Drama

The drama teacher may well become the co-director. This has happened in five out of ten Colway Theatre Trust productions. What you hope for is a really enthusiastic, gifted drama teacher, who sees the play as an opportunity to improve his or her basic skills and is clever and confident enough not to see the production as a threat. I have been fortunate enough to find several such. The English teacher at the Woodroffe School was co-director of the play. At Axminster, the drama teacher, who was an ex-professional actress, later joined me as associate director of the Colway Theatre Trust and co-director of the Bridport Play. The drama teacher in Ottery St Mary was one of the initiators of the play and became the Chair of the Organising Committee. These are a few examples amongst several of teachers' enthusiasm and dedication putting all their weight behind the work. They make a crucial difference.

The drama teacher is usually happy to let you come and observe school workshops and I very often join in alongside the children. Sometimes I take a few school workshops myself. It's all part of getting to know people and trying to build a bridge between the school and the play.

Some drama teachers may be ambitious to become playwrights. It's unlikely that their work is yet good enough. They are usually quite satisfied to develop their work in small productions: they well appreciate that there may be too great a risk with a very large community play.

Art

Art teachers usually feel less threatened than others when it comes to helping the community play. They will enjoy the idea of designing scenery and costumes, but may not be overconfident about the technicalities of stagework. A good art teacher will see a tremendous opportunity for involving children, but they need plenty of notice because they must draw up work schedules well ahead. Art teachers may also help in producing artwork for leaflets, posters etc. Professional theatre designers are not always good at this and in any case they may not be around early enough in the process. In Dorchester, the art master prepared charming drawings to illustrate the play leaflet. In *The Western Women* the art teacher of the Woodroffe School, Sue Dart, joined in with wholehearted enthusiasm, organising kids to make props, decorating the approaches to the hall, taking on responsibility for decorating the fair. Most of this work was done by children under her guidance. She herself also produced designs for the programme, etc. She showed such enthusiasm, talent and dedication, and furthermore was so interested in the idea of becoming a designer that we invited her to design the whole of the next production at Ottery St Mary and she managed to get a term off school to do it.

Sue made an enormous success of the project, but was more or less shattered by the experience and is still digesting it. (Design is probably the heaviest burden of all.) Speaking to Sue Dart recently it's clear that it was a shock to discover the degree to which she was required to compromise her own ideas and work with the director (which she did very successfully). This is acutely interesting since it pinpoints a key problem for individual artists in taking on theatre design. Likewise, Norman Saunders-White, an art teacher in Dorchester, who joined in many of our plays, did much of the design work for posters and programmes and also took on the design of a village play in Colyford. These two examples seemed to be absolutely

justified demonstrations of the way that professionals in another field
can be taught to develop their theatrical skills.

Music

Music teachers are often composers in their own right, but they may
not write the sort of music you need. Some community plays have
certainly used local music teachers, but I myself prefer to use
professional composers with an experience of music theatre. This may
be why some music teachers have not joined in my productions, but
there is, too, a tradition of non-co-operation between arts departments in schools and elsewhere. Even at Dartington College of Arts I
found almost no support or contact between theatre, music and art
departments.

Auxiliary staff

Caretaker and cleaners The caretaker is so important that you need to
find out very early what sort of a person he is. On the whole, we have
found them helpful. You shouldn't have too much trouble since the
caretaker isn't openly going to go against the head but he can make life
pretty miserable if he's not on your side. You will probably need him
to open and close the school, turn the heating on, etc. Also cleaners
come within his orbit and they mustn't be upset. Treat them carefully. Get out of the room without fuss if they need to clean it; if you're
on good terms with the caretaker he'll find you somewhere else. Put
desks and tables back as you find them. Don't drop ash on the floor:
make people bring their own tins to put their ash in if they smoke (or if
sufficient people object, take a vote and see if they want to ban
smoking altogether in rehearsal). Pick up sweet papers and rubbish. I
sometimes tip a difficult caretaker a few pounds at the beginning,
middle and end of the production and I'm afraid this usually works a
treat.

Secretaries and clerical staff Learn their names. Be warm and friendly
on the phone. Sometimes there is a particular member of the auxiliary
staff in charge of photocopying, duplicating and lithoing. Make any
initial request for photocopying, etc. through the deputy head. You
should not have to pay more than the teaching staff. Always see that
the staff and auxiliary staff are thanked in the programme for their
help.

School Key

At first schools will be very fussy about letting you in and locking up after you and this is a great bore for them and for you. Once they are sure they can trust you they will very likely let you have a key; this is fantastic trust if you think about it. Early on in my work, to my horror and dismay, a school key was lost. Since then it has been our unbreakable rule, probably the only inflexible rule we have, that the school key is threaded on a tape which is *always* round someone's neck or hanging in a designated safe place. I impressed this rule upon all concerned and since then CTT has not lost a key.

Morals

It hardly needs saying that the professionals and others working in the school have to behave with total moral scrupulousness towards the kids. I only once had any breath of trouble in this area in the very first production, whose venue was a state boarding school. We used professional actors and one of them was attracted to an extremely beautiful, blonde, bold boarder. The actor concerned should have known better, for he was a member of a community theatre company. It was the deputy head who first spotted what was going on and we agreed that we would have to quietly slow things down. Happily the parties concerned both caught 'flu and by the time they recovered the play was over.

THE AMATEUR DRAMATIC SOCIETY

The amateur movement, though only slightly organised at national level, is in reasonable shape. In a single year in the Axe Valley, where we produced *The Tide*, there were two light opera productions, eight straight plays ranging from Coward to Anouilh and including an interesting production of a play by André Obey, at least four pantomimes and many variety shows; there were also numerous school plays. In terms of quantity this provided a year-round theatre service in a rural area hardly touched by professional theatre: amateur theatre is all the theatre most people ever see.

To demonstrate the range of amateur theatre: I have seen a bad production, thinly attended, by a company with a poor record, of Coward's *Nude with Violin* (an unpleasant play about how avant-garde artists deceive the public). By contrast, Lyme Regis Amateur Dramatic Society, with a good record and a conventional play, can sell out for five performances to a hundred and fifty people per night.

Dorchester ADS have, for some years, given performances of classic plays in country house gardens: one year it will be *The Servant of Two Masters*, another *Twelfth Night*. The unique pleasure of these performances is the magical and beautiful setting – but the company is actually also, perhaps due to our influence, becoming a little more adventurous in the way it stages the plays, placing the audience in the middle of the action, etc. At the very head of the amateur movement is a company such as the Questors Theatre, Ealing with its own theatre complex and a policy which is adventurous by any standards. However, companies like the Questors are rare.

Historically, the amateur movement had a moment of great glory in the 1890s and showed its potential. Antoine founded the *Théâtre Libre* which was quickly copied in Germany and England by the *Freie Bühne* and the Independent Theatre. These amateur companies hoisted the flag, each giving Ibsen's *Ghosts* its first production in their respective countries, following it with other key and innovatory plays. Thus they helped break the mould of nineteenth century theatre; you can hardly be more adventurous than that. There are enormous possibilities in the amateur theatre if only the standards of direction and choice of play could be raised, for it is weakness in these departments which make the amateur theatre look feeble and old-fashioned. Just occasionally amateur dramatics societies do find sparky, intelligent directors, and then the work leaps forward. There are plenty of good actors. Acting is not a rare talent, and every ADS has one or two really good actors and several more of an acceptable level of talent. Good actors are not only to be found in the ADS – you may find them anywhere – if you look.

As regards choice: reading a play is a skill, as difficult to learn as reading music but, beyond this, surprisingly few people actually understand how theatre works. If an amateur company decides to take the plunge and do something 'good' they all too often choose a work which is literary and symbolic in the manner of the poetic drama of the 30s and 40s: such plays are felt to be worthy and good for you. More common is the depressing choice of tired old West End successes. The reason generally given is that that is what audiences like. But I think this lack of vision is really due to the fact that the amateur moment is essentially controlled by actors. Actors, professionals included, are seldom innovatory. In my experience, audiences are far more intelligent than they are given credit for. Contrary to popular belief amateurs cannot automatically fill their houses though of course they have a head start over unknown visiting professionals.

The community play needs the amateur dramatic society

In addition to being a focus for good actors the ADS will be seen as guardians of the community's theatrical tradition. The danger is that directors may fear that professionals will show up their skills, and actors may be worried that they will not get their customary large parts. They need to be reassured that the play will add to their satisfaction: it will bring greater interest and more members for the society. It may also raise their standards, but it's probably wise not to stress this too early on for it implies that current standards are low and such a suggestion will not be popular.

Interface between professionals and amateurs

This can be quite dodgy. Professionals sometimes apparently fear that they may be lowering themselves and their standards by working with amateurs. There is certainly a feeling that the amateur may be taking a great deal out of the professionals' mouths by working for free. I have known an instance where the agent of a professional actress who was working with us (unpaid and alongside the amateurs) refused to represent her because she was working with amateurs, and yet she was probably giving the performance of her career.

Some amateurs resent professionals because either they suspect that their own work will be shown up, or that the professionals will barge in and boss everybody around. These attitudes are both understandable, but the attitudes of both amateurs and professionals only betray their basic insecurity. The trouble may arise at any level or in any field of activity.

CHILDREN

Until Dorchester we tended not to use children under 14 in the play itself. The practice began with *The Reckoning* when the school made it a condition of doing a play, probably because we were an unproven organisation. But under-14s do bring problems of concentration and discipline. At 14 and over, children are sufficiently mature to sympathise with normal, adult, emotional situations, i.e. they can identify with the subject of the play. Parents worry about under-14s coming home after dark, whereas older children are their own masters and easier to get to rehearsal if they are keen.

In Axminster, the drama teacher was co-director and an enormous number of young children wanted to join in. They came to the workshops in numbers and were very excitable. So we had to give them separate workshops. We solved the problem in casting and rehearsal to some extent by doubling: two children playing one part and performing on alternate nights (toss up for which night, everyone wants the last performance). Doubling certainly reduces the strain on young children as eleven performances plus all the technical rehearsals are really too much; it also allows more of them to have good parts. We do try and use young children a great deal in the fair before the play, with circus skills, sideshows, etc.

After *The Tide* we reinstated the 'No under-14s' rule, partly I suspect for our own protection as so many kids wanted to join in we felt we had to draw the line somewhere. We kept up this rule more or less without question until Dorchester. However, some under-14s are so keen that nothing will keep them out, they somehow seep in through the edges, coming to all the workshops. They have a grave, totally determined air and don't draw attention to themselves. Such children who are clearly dedicated we try and give a good little part – they've earned it.

However, in Sherborne the balance went the other way. With six schools involved, the play seemed swamped by enormous numbers of young men and women, some of whom got very excitable at being together (but not the secondary modern or grammar schools who were exceptionally well behaved). Finally, in Dorchester, we used numbers of very young children, mostly alongside their families, and I now feel that this is probably the best way.

You may well run into The Children and Young Persons Act 1963. This only caught up with us in Dorchester, possibly because we were performing in a church, not a school, but more likely because we were actually involving the daughter of the local government officer concerned. What it meant in practice was that while we were granted an exemption from the Act, it still meant that every child under 16 without a family in the show had to have a 'guardian' or chaperon (12 children per guardian), with different dressing-rooms for boys and girls and all children to be out of the theatre by an agreed time. These were not particularly arduous conditions, although they appeared irritating at the time, and they actually offered another way of involving more people. One good lady organised the whole thing and set up a rosta. It was an advantage in that it meant that any child who preferred to stay in the Green Room, i.e. the parish hall, when not performing, was supervised. Since it was a long play and young children can get very restless, we were grateful for this help.

There is such terrific enthusiasm for theatre and acting amongst young children that CTT is now considering a special children's community play. This presents a fascinating opportunity: to try and recognise and use the children's particular capacities and turn their apparent weaknesses into strengths.

THE CULTURALLY AND SOCIALLY DISADVANTAGED

The middle class will volunteer themselves but the working class and culturally disadvantaged may need to be searched for and gently persuaded in. The unemployed, elderly, one-parent families, house-bound mothers and all those people who think that art is not for them and is none of their business, need more time and specific encouragement. You'll make some contact through projects, street events and market stalls, indeed that's partly why you set up such projects, and you'll involve others through their children. If you're going to be more than superficial the whole matter needs special thought.

One of the best ways is to try and get some gate-openers onto your committees. That way they will bring in their friends to help do a job. Beyond this you may need to woo the disadvantaged on their own ground, perhaps even indirectly. We managed to get about six teams from different pubs to compete in a tug o'war contest. (It was one of the most dramatic things I have ever seen: those men were ready to die rather than be beaten.) By having the friendliest helpers relate to them we got some of them into the play. A subtly different approach was when a cricket team was conned in by calling at each house to say that everyone else was on their way to rehearsal and they weren't going to let down their mates, were they?

With many disadvantaged the problem is finding and meeting them. Old people are often in homes and that has the advantage that they are easily contacted and the matron generally welcomes diversions and stimulation. However, in spite of drop-in centres and the like, unemployment is often a lonely and individual misery, particularly in rural areas where the unemployed may be stranded out in some village, ashamed to be unemployed and lacking the means to get into town. Once you can make contact with the unemployed the very real contribution they can make in terms of time, energy, skill and commitment gives them confidence. Likewise young mothers may be stuck at home, but if you can contact them at the clinic or wherever, and catch their notice by setting up something which will include the babies or keep them safe and occupied, then you may be able to help the mothers join in by arranging mutual babysitting, crèches, etc. Half the battle is reassuring people who may lack confidence that they will be welcome, that they have an important contribution to make.

CTT is feeling its way towards structuring an approach to the disadvantaged. We are aware that we are not trained and that we are very short of cash and labour. We have taken advice from Dr Langley of Exeter University, and others. This is a field I had planned to develop – probably through our practice of first teaching ourselves, and anyone else who is interested, by means of workshops and visiting tutors and then passing the knowledge on. In the meantime we set up a pilot scheme in Dorchester, funded by the MSC, to work alongside the community play and try to reach out to people who might not otherwise be touched by it. We kept the first scheme small and very modest, so as to gain experience and experiment without taking on too much. At first we worked on reminiscence sessions with old people with a view to their actually helping research for the play. The enthusiasm and willingness of the old folks to talk about the past was almost overwhelming – we couldn't hear ourselves speak.

We began to use video, and this was a big step forward: it meant that only one person was speaking at a time and, like everyone else, the old people loved seeing themselves on TV. These sessions led the Dorchester research team, which was formed to help David Edgar, to begin recording these reminiscences. We also set up music and singing sessions of old favourites, and here we were able to bring in young people on 'wedge' courses (another scheme for the young unemployed to help them learn social and life skills). We mixed the singing with games and a technique of 'Will you show me how?' It happened that I had been watching rehearsals at Ottery St Mary where, in a laundry scene, some girls were using a posser and poss tub. I remembered such things in a back shed when I was a child up north, and I was sure they were being wrongly used in Ottery. Sure enough an elderly Dorchester lady came out into the middle of the circle and mimed how to use a posser. Other demonstrations followed. Thus, in a small way, we were beginning to encourage the old people to perform.

The MSC team also used video as a tool at the drop-in centre and at the youth club. They worked with young offenders on Community Service orders who thus became involved in making giant puppets and the like. It was the MSC team particularly who trained themselves in circus skills and passed them on, setting up street events as goals towards which everyone could train. Many people were involved in preparing, taking part and often videoing these events. As a result a significant number of people began to be involved in the play itself. It's worth saying, as with so much else of this work that, although there is tremendous potential for involving people, helping other people to achieve is far harder than doing it yourself and needs a special attitude of mind.

The results of such work can often be heartening. It's worth making the extra effort to reach every section of the community. It enriches the play and the community experience. It gives an opportunity for different classes within the community to really work together. One example: we managed to persuade a teenager to be in a play. He was an unemployed agricultural worker, hanging about on the edge of the drugs scene. To get to rehearsal he had to hitch a ride from an outlying village and, being a bit vague and laid back, was always late. He acted in a scene with a very upright, retired colonel, who became very irritated. Between them they sorted it out: the colonel and his wife used to pick up the boy from his house and take him to rehearsal. The colonel had time and a car, the boy had nothing. They became friends, each with a greater understanding of the other. The stereotypes were broken down.

FIRE OFFICER/THEATRE LICENCE

Theatre licences are required for all venues except possibly the open air. If the venue does not have a licence you will need to apply to your local district council. The amount of notice needed will vary, so make enquiries well ahead. The licence is virtually always issued on the sayso of the fire officer. Since community plays are very large and unconventional productions I always consult the fire officer, even if the venue is already licensed. The fire officer has the power to stop a show dead if he thinks something is wrong. Eight years ago promenade productions were unheard of in the south-west and the only way we could help the fire officer to understand the principle was to get him to think of it as a dance. Here he was on familiar ground.

This may perhaps illustrate how much care is needed in dealing with fire officers. They really do have great power. The fire officer will decide how many people will be allowed in the hall and the conditions under which they will be there: how many doors must be kept locked back or taken off their hinges, how many exit lights, fire extinguishers and stewards with torches will be required.

The requirements as regards exits are fairly clear: 100 people must be able to exit through a unit in $2\frac{1}{2}$ minutes (a unit measures 21 inches; if it is part of the same door 3 units would be measured 21 + 21 + 21, i.e. a 5ft door would equal three units). In any hall the fire officer will discount one door, i.e. with 700 people you need 7 units plus 1 door (Dorset Fire Brigade).

More in the realms of the fire officer's judgement is the placing of the doors, and beyond this there is obviously a certain area which is up to the officer's discretion and experience. You are never given direct guidelines. It is clear, however, that a stone church is less of a hazard than a wooden parish hall, children under the control of teachers are considered to be less at risk than a comparable number of adults. (So it may help to stress school involvement.) The fire officer will be weighing up all the considerations, including how careful and responsible your company is likely to be.

For this reason I preferred to talk to fire officers myself, preferably on a one to one basis, or with only a trustworthy and discreet assistant present (they are not needed but it's good to give them the training experience). That way I can concentrate solely on the fire officer. These meetings are amongst the most delicate and taxing of all negotiations. So much is at stake that I watch every eye movement, virtually every breath, sensing how much pressure to apply before the guy may get stroppy and dig his heels in. Every woman will know what I mean; but there's no use in messing about, it's too important.

Two meetings may be required: one very early on to get general approval of the venue and an unofficial idea of the numbers which would be allowed. Nearer production the fire officer will require a detailed plan of the arrangement of the hall and may as a result ask for a second meeting. He will, for example, want to know that there is space for wheelchairs and a ramp for access if necessary. Fire officers, although extremely busy, are very willing to help. They will provide you with copies of printed standard regulations as they apply in your county. They will also make available such things as recipes for cheap fireproofing, etc. I have often driven round two or three venues discussing with the fire officer what would be required in each case.

We are never sloppy or careless over fire regulations. They are there for a very good purpose and we observe them strictly, if only because the fire officer almost always used to drop into a show unannounced just to see that his instructions were being complied with. I have also know them come to a technical rehearsal and apply a lighted match to something to check that it had been properly fireproofed. Neither of these things has happened recently, so maybe our file now shows us as the co-operative people we strive to be.

PUBLICITY

Publicity is an area where the work is easily organised and shared, provided everyone is sure of their precise responsibility. You need to know your budget and when the booking will open, then apportion the budget and work backwards from the booking date.

Press

The Arts Council issues a very comprehensive press list, with names, contacts, addresses and phone numbers, etc., updated quarterly and obtainable direct from the ACGB.

Local press

It's a good idea to have one person as press contact who makes a friend of local reporters and feeds them weekly titbits. Try not to favour one paper more than another and take care with press dates. Paper A will get shirty if you appear to be advertising more in paper B. The local press may well be interested in sponsoring some sort of competition or event. In the past we have had painting competitions with the design supplied by us and prominently including the title, date venue and booking details of the play. Investigate the possibility of a full-page spread near production: local reporters prepare copy and photographs for the centre of the page which is surronded by local press ads of firms connected with the play or wishing it well. The newspaper will usually take responsibility for raising the ads. Look out for all the local 'special interest' papers: your Regional Arts Association bulletin should give strong support. Arts centre, church and community magazines are all possible outlets for a paragraph or two.

Display ads In the local press (you probably won't be able to afford the nationals). They are expensive: find out prices so you can budget. For reasons of prestige try not to have them too small. We have found that two ads are enough: one as the booking opens and another just before the start of the production. Display ads can eat up money if they get out of hand.

National press

It is too expensive to advertise directly in the national press but, since there is nationwide interest in this work and it gives people an extra kick if they can see their play is being noticed elsewhere we do try for some national coverage. The best hope is 'what's on' or 'diary' columns which like to include material from the provinces. Find out well ahead how much notice they require.

Critics

Send out invitations and a press release about three weeks before the show opens. Offer complimentary tickets, but don't send them with the invitation: you lose a lot of seats that way. The paper will telephone if they want to come. Obviously the local papers will cover the show. National papers may well send a local stringer; their national critics may come if it is a new play by a national writer and/or the work is of such standing that it should be judged by someone with an overall view of theatre, i.e. in national terms. Incidentally you don't usually need to 'nanny' national critics. They like to feel independent, booking their own hotel, etc., so that they are sure they are not being nobbled. Of course you can welcome them and give them a programme. I have my own private test which works nine times out of ten: if the critic loiters a little on leaving, perhaps asking the odd question or exchanging a word, then they have probably liked the show. If they avoid your eye and hurry out prepare for a bad notice. This is because critics are as mixed up as most of us and have a breath of honesty which inhibits the lie direct and a cowardly streak which means they prefer to be unpleasant at long range.

Television

Setting up a major programme is an extremely slow business and you have to be in touch with the relevant company at least a year ahead. Local TV news and arts programmes are best dealt with by press releases and personal calls. Send press releases to all the national programmes as well; they may pick something up. A good gimmick may be your best bet. In Dorchester we needed a live sheep in the play and had already found a charming hand-tame ewe at a local farm museum. However, this seemed an opportunity for publicity so we held a sheep audition (at the nearby village of Wool) which was attended by about thirty sheep, three TV stations and countless radio and press reporters and photographers. It even made a paragraph in the *Sun*, not a paper normally noted for its provincial arts coverage.

Radio

Certain national programmes such as *Kaleidoscope* are very conscientious about trying to cover important provincial openings. Send the press release to everyone you can think of. Local radio should give continuous support: encourage them to cover the play from the beginning and then have a composite programme, hopefully just before the play opens. This is the stuff of life to them.

Printed material

Play leaflet★ Enormously important: it will be working for you for months, from the public meeting virtually until production, and will be your chief means of spreading detailed information about the community play and inviting people to join in. As a guide: in Dorchester, pop. 15,000, we printed 10,000 leaflets.

The play leaflet explains what the play is and, in the limited space, the ideas behind it: the writer and the subject of the play, venue if known, patrons and sponsors, play officer and community play office and what they are there for, dates of play, etc. The play leaflet also gives notice of workshops, the fair, etc. Provide a tear-off section with space for name, address, phone number, school or organisation and so on, with boxes where people can tick off what they would like to do, with a few words to explain each. We list acting, music, technical stage management, electrics, costumes, publicity, scripts, tea-making refreshments, transport, stewarding, fair, fundraising, babysitting, accommodation and hospitality, secretarial help, manning play office/costume workshop. In future we will consider an open section for people to suggest their own ways in which they might like to help. Don't print information, which people may want to keep, on the back of this section. It's reassuring to say that by filling in the leaflet people aren't irrevocably committing themselves, simply showing interest and asking to be kept informed.

Play leaflets are first seen at the public meeting as part of the launch of the play. Leave them on the seats, hand them out. Encourage people to fill them in on the spot and give them to any member of the Organising Committee or drop them in a box at the door. They may also be taken away and handed in at the play office or some other convenient point; the Library is appropriate and has a good community image. Thereafter you distribute them constantly: leave them everywhere, get schoolchildren to take them home, always have a good supply available at any project or event. Simply by filling in the play leaflet people are beginning to associate themselves with the idea of the play. From now on you want to try and make them feel that they are part of something special.

Logo Favourite is to have a logo which can be used right through from start   finish (but see p. 58). It should appear in all supporting publicity, and at every event associated with the play. It's much harder to actually achieve this kind of detailed publicity than you might think – everyone is always so busy thinking of more immediate things. We managed it in Dorchester: chiefly because we had the help of an extremely talented professional designer, and a full-time play officer.

Posters Don't have them too big – they take up too much space in shop windows and so are not popular. Full colour is hideously expensive unless you can get preferential printing rates (a possible sponsorship) but you could compromise with coloured paper. As a rough guide we print 25 A4 posters and 50 A3 posters per 1,000 of population.

A possible difficulty: you can run into trouble with logo and poster design. In every venue there is someone who thinks of themselves as a designer and many people will tell you they are wonderful. You have to go very tactfully and try and assess if they can deliver. Apart from the play leaflet, the logo and poster are the most important general images the play will present to the world. The problem divides itself:

1 Is the artist good enough to produce a poster which will really reflect and sell the play?

2 Fine artists and graphic artists are very different people. Fine artists have strong ideas about the inviolability of their work, but they are seldom trained to produce a poster which is meant to reflect and sell something for someone else. They are used to creating a work of art which is significant and beautiful in its own right. Furthermore, fine artists seldom have much knowledge of print and printing or indeed of layout, and their highly developed sense of the integrity of their work sometimes makes it very difficult to discuss and alter what they have produced. Graphic artists, on the other hand, are trained to do just the opposite. They know all about print and will happily accept suggestions, discuss and alter.

Handbills Cheapest and simplest is to have a reduction of the poster: this gives coherence and saves money and effort. Have some gutsy copy about the production on the back. We normally print about 250 handbills per 1,000 of population, so you may be dealing with large numbers. Distribute through schools, shops, newspapers, libraries, etc., anywhere you can. Many local theatres, tourist offices, etc., have racks where the public can take handbills. Your local theatre and/or arts centre may be prepared to insert your handbills in their mailing (probably at a price); local newsagents may slip them into papers for delivery. Our most successful door-drop, from the point of view of image, was by the local milkman, but it's quite a lot of extra work for them. Boy Scouts have often helped and may expect a small donation.

Posters and handbills should be distributed only a few days before the booking-office opens. If they go out too soon shopkeepers won't put them up, and people will cease to notice them.

Car stickers We find that about 250 is enough whatever the size of the town. It doesn't seem very many: perhaps we are all so busy by the time the car stickers are ready – unlike posters we haven't thought ahead and don't distribute them effectively. The answer is probably to give the job to someone not involved in rehearsal.

Keeping in Touch

Card index With the information on the leaflets start a card index which serves two chief purposes:

1 If you should need a carpenter, typist, two beds for next weekend, someone who wants to help with publicity, you can first look in the card index.

2 All these people who have taken the trouble to say they are interested will constitute the core of the hundreds of people who will later be involved. They are enormously valuable to you. Take care of them; use them as much as you possibly can. You can start to keep in touch with them by means of the newsletter.

Mailing lists You will find you need several mailing lists:

1 People on the card index.

2 The cast (when you have one).

3 Postal bookings. This last should be subdivided into (a) groups, e.g. Women's Institutes, schools, amateur dramatic groups, other community plays, etc., who require plenty of notice to organise a party (b) 'attenders' – people who have come to previous shows (c) likely targets.

Newsletter* Once the public meeting is over it's a good idea to send out a newsletter to everyone on the mailing list and anyone else who might be interested (e.g. patrons). It makes a notice-board where you can ask for help on specific projects, increase publicity and generally keep in touch. The cheapest form of reproduction is obviously duplicating, but with preferential terms it may be photocopied. Computerisation is waiting for an opportunity here.

Other publicity

Direct mail (consult with the box-office manager). If you have a list of previous 'attenders' or, at the least, of people likely to be interested in the work, then direct mail, with a postal booking form, is by far the most effective and economical of all forms of advertising: the response is always extremely high. Possible group bookings, such as nearby amateur dramatics societies, Women's Institutes, etc., need to be contacted well in advance since secretaries will need two or three months to organise parties.

AA signs These are worth any number of posters. They only go up a couple of days before the show opens but they help raise the temperature and excitement enormously. The prestige and publicity are terrific. AA signs are also a very practical help as I know when trying to find my way by car to some other community-play venue. We contact the AA nearly five months ahead. (Ask for the Signs Administrator at your local AA Area Headquarters.) The AA will decide how many signs are needed and where they should go; they also erect them. In Dorchester twenty signs (the most we have ever had) cost £114 + VAT and it was money well spent.

Town banner There is often a banner you can borrow. If you decide to make one (we were charged about £30 for a banner with lettering by a professional signwriter in 1982), try and find out if there is any experience of trouble from wind: it can funnel up streets and wreak havoc with banners. You may need to mount letters on tennis net or some such to allow for turbulence.

T-shirts Have one person organise and get cash with order. Get key people to wear them and make them fashionable. They are worn for years after the play is over. People from one community will make up a coach party to visit another community play and all wear their T-shirts. I also hear stories of families wearing community play T-shirts being hailed as friends by total strangers who had also taken part in other community plays.

Badges and mugs If you can find a good local potter, mugs make a very special souvenir. Badges, besides having their obvious uses are sometimes great to give to numbers of schoolchildren who have taken part in a project or whatever. You can usually borrow a badgemaking machine.

Photographic record/book of the play There is usually an enthusiastic local photographer who will undertake to keep a complete record. It's important that they come regularly so that the cast comes to know them and they don't bring the vibrations of strangers into rehearsal. The photographer can recoup costs by selling prints to the cast, who much appreciate them. Incidentally, CTT does not allow flash photographs to be taken at dress rehearsals or performances. But anyone may take them at the technical rehearsal, when everyone is in costume but there is no risk of disturbance since we are stopping and starting all the time. The cast needs plenty of warning about this. Print an embargo on flash in the programme.

Have a member of the Publicity Committee keep a complete record of press cuttings, etc.

We always plan a book of the play, with variable results. More than a simple record, it is a collection of photos, reminiscences etc., all attractively put together and usually deposited in the local library. It's a rewarding job which can be undertaken by one person. These are distinct from the albums I made for early CTT productions (see p. 59) to show future possible communities.

Play sashes We have a few vivid sashes to be worn over one shoulder with 'COMMUNITY PLAY' written on them. These are worn by helpers at all sorts of events: the public meeting, street stalls, projects, etc. When people first notice that something is going on they will be less shy to approach if they have a little information. Play sashes provide instant identity.

Programmes CTT has always made a big feature of programmes, which we try and design in sympathy with the play, e.g. folded as an old-fashioned doctor's prescription for *The Poor Man's Friend* or as a despatch for *The Tide*. We often use sealing wax and ribbon, for there is an enormous amount of willing labour by the time we are preparing programmes. It's now a matter of pride with us to try and make the programmes special: a surprise, an extra treat. For this reason we never include advertisements even though revenue could be raised by this means. If your programmes are attractive and well produced they are souvenirs which people will treasure after the play. We have also found them useful when raising cash and enthusiasm for future productions, as a means of conveying some idea of our approach and standards.

You will probably need to print one third of your capacity audience. You may not sell them all but, as has been said, they make pleasant souvenirs. Make the cast responsible for checking the spelling of their own names. Put in as much interesting information as you can, including, of course, the 'thanks list' (make the copy larky if you can: this encourages people to wade through all the names). For late thanks we insert a duplicated extra sheet, or sometimes write up the names where the audience assembles before the play. The nightmare is leaving someone obvious off: encourage people to look it over and watch out for errors.

Outline publicity timetable for a production in mid November/early December (Table 2)

Approx. date	Main event	Action to be taken
	Big TV shows	If you want to set up a big TV show you need to start negotiating 14 months before the production
Jan–Feb.	Discuss general strategy	Check press dates of local papers/free throw-aways; establish contacts with local press and radio; radio may like to make a continuous record, describing the whole process of the play; consider possibilities of whole-page feature nearer production; handbill

Approx. date	Main event	Action to be taken
		insertions in other mail shots
	Mailing list	Start mailing list for groups, 'attenders', etc.; add to it as people make suggestions
	Street stall	Consider the possibility for later in the year, when the weather is warmer
	Logo design	
	Displays	Discuss possible displays and dates in library, museum, schools, shops, etc.; you need to book ahead
	Handbills to advertise public meeting	To be ordered
	Projects	Liaise with Projects Committee to organise publicity for projects
	Press cuttings	Have one person take responsibility for collecting all press cuttings
	Book of the play/ photographs/video	Do you want a book of the play? Consider keeping a continuous photographic record and possibly videoing key events
	Play leaflet	To be ready for public meeting
Mar.	Publicity for public meeting	Distribute handbills
		Place ads for public meeting
		Press release for local journalists, etc.
		Ring local papers and radio to remind them about the meeting and prompt them to send a photographer
Mar.–Apr.	Public meeting	This is very much a PR exercise. From now on, send regular press releases

Approx. date	Main event	Action to be taken
		to local press and radio giving news of progress of play and projects
		Offer speakers for meetings
	Start newsletter	Many people will fill in the play leaflet: use as base for mailing lists/card index
		Big publicity push for workshops
May	Start workshops	Check press dates of quarterlies, arts societies, Regional Arts Association bulletins, church newsletters, etc.
		Start making a list of the national press 'what's on' columns and note press dates
		Start talking to bus companies, etc., to see if they will display posters; special size/shape may be needed
		Consider town banner, badges, mugs, sweat-shirts
		Inserts in other mail shots, e.g. local theatres, community-service vans
	Play reading	Publicity push
June		Big publicity push for casting
Early July	Casting	
Aug.	Holiday	
Late Aug.	Order AA signs	
Sept.	Rehearsals start	Design posters, handbills
Early Oct.	Direct mail (to groups, WIs, etc.)	They require plenty of time to organise party bookings
	Programme	Check names of cast; programme to printers

Approx. date	Main event	Action to be taken
		Order town banner
Mid Oct.	Local TV	First calls to alert local TV for coverage in arts programmes, etc.
	Direct mailing	Handbills and postal booking form to 'attenders'; mailing list
		Big publicity push for box-office opening
		Distribute posters, handbills, car stickers, bus posters, etc.
Late Oct.	Box office opens	Shop, library, museum displays, etc.; town banner
		Second calls to TV, both national and local; get firm promises
		Press release to nationals and locals; invite press critics
		Display ads; TV commercials
Late Nov.	Production	Make sure that reviewers are well looked after, but not smothered

PUBLIC MEETING

This is an important point in the process of setting up a community play. A successful public meeting is an enormous source of strength, an unanswerable demonstration of support: '250 people came to the public meeting and voted unanimously for the play to go on.' A good public meeting will encourage the town council and others to help you and will give them the justification for doing so.

By far the most important message you have to get over at the public meeting is how much, and in what way the community will benefit.

1 Stress how tremendously exciting the project is, how idealistic, what a high standard it will be.

2 Tell them how it will refresh, stimulate and perhaps reinspire the

community: people will draw together and make new friends; there will be greater sympathy and understanding between young and old and, indeed, every section of the community.

3 The play will bring prestige and publicity to the town.

4 Its good effects will be felt long after the play itself is over.

5 Money will be attracted into the town.

It is important that the speakers stress their commitment to the community – their wish to work with it. They should be demonstrably warm, confident, sympathetic, modest, open.

We sometimes ask people from previous plays to come along and say what sort of a time they had. It means something when somebody who has been through the experience says they wouldn't have missed it for the world – and have bothered to come and say so.

Caution Don't run down the town in enthusing about the play. No one wants to hear that you think their town is awful. Try and infer that the play will provide an opportunity on which many good things in the community may focus; how rare it is to find a total community effort which can bring together hundreds of marvellous people from every section of the town, with all their tremendous potential for good and exciting work.

The particular purposes of the public meeting include:

1 To launch the project in the public eye; it's the start of a high-profile exercise in publicity and public relations.

2 To demonstrate support and enthusiasm.

3 To show that it is a community event and that the community itself is putting on the play.

4 To start large-scale involvement.

5 By the efficiency and general glamour of the meeting to project an image which people will trust and want to be associated with; a good public meeting is already demonstrating that the community play itself will be important, exciting and successful.

6 To take the play a stage further in formal terms, e.g. to have a show of hands demonstrating support for the play; to vote that the Steering Committee become the Organising Committee, etc.

We hold the public meeting eight to ten months before production. The process of putting on the play will in fact be well launched by this time. You have to start setting up the play long before the public meeting because a great deal of groundwork must be done and the writer commissioned. Indeed, in order to guarantee a successful public meeting you must already have a strong organisational structure. You can't hold the public meeting too soon because once you've held it you have to maintain momentum and this can be quite a strain. If the public meeting were such a disaster as to return a negative vote then, in theory, there is still time to turn back, or fight the decision. The writer's commission fee would still be payable (see page 143).

Setting up the meeting

The Organising Committee obtains a list of clubs and societies, etc., available at the public library, and works systematically through it, making contact with secretaries, etc. You can either telephone or send a duplicated letter and leaflet (or both), explaining the idea behind the community play and asking them to draw their committee's attention to the matter and to send a representative. This is all part of the basic job of getting people to join in and it's time, energy and money very well spent. If you don't do it, you may have a poor public meeting. It also ensures a broad base of contacts. The author will probably already have been talking to people in the town, gathering material, etc., and this also acts as publicity for the public meeting.

Publicity

Issue handbills advertising the public meeting, perhaps 5,000 in a town of 15,000. We use this opportunity to test out and develop channels of distribution for later play publicity. We issue a press release and press invitations, two or three weeks in advance, and we follow this up with a personal phone call to each of the more important papers, reminding them about the meeting on the day before, or the day of the meeting itself, stressing the importance of sending a representative and a photographer. Try and have a few gimmicks around to make the press photos a bit more original. We sometimes have people dressed up. In Ottery, a life-size horse's mask from a previous production which was part of the display was eagerly seized on by photographers as a centre piece for a photograph.

Testing people out

The public meeting is a very good opportunity to take note of who really does the work and organising – who gets on with it and how. Also, it's a good indication of how people relate to each other. It's an opportunity to try out local lighting and design people who have been recommended/volunteered. How talented are they? Do they react well to suggestion? Are they flexible? How do they relate to other people?

Status and glamour

The meeting should preferably take place in some recognised venue in the heart of the town, e.g. the town hall. It should be chaired by the mayor. Headteachers and other leaders should be present to demonstrate support. Enthusiastic and well-organised help should be much in evidence. The venue will probably be fairly dull and conventional. A little glamorising will help get the message across that the play will be out of the ordinary. We use a little stage lighting, an attractive and eye-catching display of photos of previous work, posters, etc., colourful costumes on stands. Sometimes we persuade helpers to dress up (this needs time and encouragement – don't spring it on them). Use flowers (a way to involve local flower-arranging groups).

Give a *free glass of wine* if you can (and announce it in the preliminary publicity). The wine may be homemade or the Organising Committee may know someone who can get it cheap. I have known shops give free wine as a form of sponsorship in kind. Wine makes a colossal difference: attracting people to the meeting and creating a party-like atmosphere. Have squash for teetotallers and children. Music helps lift the evening to a celebration. Try and get a local pop group. In Sherborne, the Yetties (who are locally based) sang and played afterwards and everyone joined in. In Lyme and Ottery St Mary, the musical directors of both plays made music; in Dorchester we had a local New Orleans jazz band.

Video

We make arangements to show videos of previous work after the main meeting. It's a good idea to have the video in a side-room, so that people who don't want to watch can go on talking and relating in the main hall. If it's a successful meeting/good community, and the atmosphere is right, they will want to linger a bit.

Arrangement of hall

I very much dislike having the speakers up on a raised stage and everyone else below them. It seems to demonstrate that you are bossing the whole thing about. I prefer the audience to be grouped in semi-circular fashion round the speakers. I slightly cheat by putting stage lighting on the speakers so that they are 'lifted up'. Never put out too many chairs: it's always much better psychologically if people pour in and you are seen having to carry in extra seating.

Costs of public meeting

You will have to pay for some or all of the following: printing of handbills (you may choose to take this out of the general publicity budget), hire of hall, possibly a small sum for display materials (i.e. Blu-tack, etc.) and wine. An informal raffle on the spot will raise £20–£30 – no great effort is needed: some chocolates, a homemade cake, a small basket of fruit, these can usually be donated. You will need a lottery licence from the local authority. This lasts a year and will cover any other raffle as well. Incidentally, don't just say: 'Would you like a raffle ticket?'; say: 'Will you help cover costs and support the community play by buying a raffle ticket?' We also ask people for a donation for their second glass of wine; don't sell it: that's illegal unless you have a licence. By such modest means you can recover the costs of the public meeting.

Order of meeting

Although you make it as much fun as possible, the meeting has a serious purpose. Here is the agenda of the Ottery meeting:

Meeting commences 7.0 p.m. Allow time for people to drink their wine and look at the displays.

1 Introduction from the Chairman of the Town Council, Mr George Hansford.
2 Chair introduces Crosby Chacksfield, Head of Drama at King's School, to talk on the value of a community play to the community itself and to the school.
3 Chair introduces Ann Jellicoe, Director of the Colway Theatre Trust, to talk in general about community plays, relating to past experience and the proposed work in Ottery.
4 Chair introduces Sheila Yeger, the commissioned writer of the community play, to talk about her own background; how she works and how she hopes to relate to the town.
5 Chair invites questions from the floor.
6 Summing up by the Chair. Show of hands to demonstrate that the town wants to do the play. Request to meeting to accept the Steering Committee as an Organising Committee.

Difficult questions

These will come up at any time but almost certainly at the public meeting.

Q   *What will the play cost and where is the money coming from?*

A Warminster town councillor, speaking against the motion that the town should contribute to their community play said, 'It's a complete waste of £17,000 which would be better spent on a kidney dialysis machine.'

This may appear a hard question but in fact it's beside the point: how does he propose to raise £17,000 for kidney dialysis? Who is going to raise it? If the councillor will take it on himself, good luck to him! We are talking about community plays and the benefits they bring.

If you specify early on exactly what the play is going to cost then you must be prepared for the information to be used as a weapon against the play. People have to come gently to the idea that art costs money and that professionals require to be paid. Amateur theatricals are associated with voluntary, free help and it is quite a jolt to find that artists must earn their living by their work. In the early stages of community plays there are plenty of doubters and antis. By the time people have been through the whole process and seen the complex operation, how hard and effectively professionals work and how they hold the huge productions together, as well as the immensely high results that are achieved, few people will question the cost of the undertaking.

Bear in mind that if you announce the budget before the community is psychologically prepared there is a real risk that certain people will be angry and offended. The local Arts Centre may be struggling on a pittance of £500 a year, the Music Society likewise. When you sweep along asking for, and getting, quite large sums it will be hard to avoid jealousy. (The best way round the difficulty may be to gain their friendship and advise them on how to raise more money, suggest sources and improve their approach.)

In the early stages, CTT produces budget proposals, but they are not budgets on which we would be happy to make a stand. All the figures in the early budgets will be flexible and negotiable. Even within the rehearsal process, the budget remains flexible within the overall figure.

For these reasons, I personally prefer not to publicise budgets to begin with, although of course they are shown to the chair of the Organising and Fundraising Committees, headteachers, where directly involved, and sponsors.

What you are trying to avoid is:

1 The town rejecting the play too soon because they are frightened of the money involved.

2 Being constrained in moving around within the budget, so that you don't have to waste time and energy justifying having an extra stage manager and the cost of travel, etc.

3 A situation of 'greediness', where people think that there is so much money, they start wanting to sell you their old piece of carpet, instead of giving or lending it.

The following points may be made:

1 A normal, commercial project of this type might cost over a quarter of a million pounds and while the cost of a community play may seem large to people who are used to the scale of amateur productions, the costs are in fact very low indeed. (The production absolutely depends upon the maximum of giving and sharing by everyone concerned.)

2 The play will bring money into the town (see Bridport analysis* in the Appendix), as well as many other benefits.

3 CTT would also stress that it is substantially subsidising the play through the work of its officers and the use of its facilities. The Trust also raises considerable amounts of money itself towards the play, e.g. through the Arts Council. Colway Theatre Trust itself makes no profit out of the plays.

4 Audited accounts will be presented at the end of the exercise.

Q *What happens if there is a loss?*

This is a grey area indeed and one where the person who takes the question should be as clear as possible in their own mind. I have heard of disastrous deficits due to over-optimistic, amateur budgeting and insufficient control. The safest course is to be able to reassure the questioner that the play has raised guarantees against loss. This is what we do at CTT, although we only once called in a guarantee (for bookkeeping reasons when the funding body concerned, although calling it a guarantee, let us know that it was in fact to be regarded as a grant).

Q *What happens to any profit?*
It's almost certain that any grant aid will be given on condition that if
there is a profit it must be used to pay off the grant. This is reasonable
enough: why should public money go to fund the charity of your
choice? In fact you are aiming for a very slight loss.

Q *Can people from other communities be in the play?*
You can get a kind of chauvinism. There is a wartime Home Guard
story from the village of Musbury in the Axe Valley, one and a half
miles from Axmouth, saying: 'I'm damned if I'll go and defend they
buggers at Axmouth.' We work in rural areas and roughly take in the
catchments of the school. You have to decide whether you want
'outsiders' in or not. I like them in, since I don't like exclusiveness.
Also, outsiders have to be very enthusiastic to travel 10 or more miles,
and enthusiasm is probably your most valuable commodity. Also, it
may mean you'll be able to use people who have been in previous
shows and they provide a very solid influence as regards work
attitude, promptness at rehearsals, etc.

Alternatives to a public meeting
In setting up *The Tide*, our second play, we didn't have a proper
public meeting, partly because I hadn't worked out the need for it,
and also because the area was so huge that although it cohered
artistically after the play, it certainly did not before. But when the play
had been cast and before we went into rehearsal, I happened to be in
contact with a friend, the actor Edward Fox, and asked if he would
help us launch the play. We had an enormous tea party, to which
everybody brought food, and at which a local group sang. Edward
spoke, signed autographs and was photographed with his arm round
everyone. It wasn't strictly a public meeting in the sense which I have
described, but it was good publicity, fun, glamorous and gave
rehearsals a great start.

In Bridport, we had a second public meeting for the benefit of BBC
TV's *Arena* programme. They wanted to film the whole process and
had missed the public meeting proper. I wanted to make sure that
everyone in the town would have a chance of seeing themselves on
television. Our excuse was that we were wanting to tell yet more
people about the play and ask them to book for auditions and
rehearsals.

Working with Writers. ▲ Sheila Yeger (*right*) and other members of the production team talk to Otteregians at a stall in the centre of town.
▼ David Edgar and Ann Jellicoe discuss the script of *Entertaining Strangers*.

David Edgar gives the first reading of his play *Entertaining Strangers* in Dorchester.

Towards Performance. ▲ First read through of _The Tide_; a section of the cast shows the mix of age and social background.   ▼ A group of people clean and prepare a space which has been loaned for set and costume making.

First rehearsal of *The Poor Man's Friend*. Dividing the cast into their families and social groups (*see p.220*). *Seated centre:* Howard Barker (author) Andrew Dickson (composer) Rex Trevitt (conductor).

◀ One of the advantages of a specially commissioned play is that parts can be written in for everyone.

▶ The cast has divided into 'family' groups for discussion: listening to a young actor.

◀ Local history: at Beer, a group of actors from *The Tide* research smuggling.

▶ Wardrobe and costume making. Note the many bundles of material, much of it donated.

▲ Group improvisation during a big rehearsal; this is a direct follow up to workshop experience.

▼ A sewing party. Over a hundred people may be involved in helping with costumes.

PROJECTS

Over the three most recent productions in Lyme, Ottery and Dorchester, projects have become much more structured. This was partly due to the character and personality of my assistants. Also, we received financial help from the Carnegie Trust and the MSC which made it possible to be much more adventurous. With each show we grew in confidence, experience and boldness. Almost all the projects in Ottery helped with fundraising, but at the same time these projects raised consciousness and involved a high standard of artistic self-help which prepared the ground for what would happen when the play was over. There was a masque performed by torchlight in an inner courtyard at Cadhay, an exquisite, small Elizabethan house; this was organised by Nick Brace, the musical director, who was a native of Ottery. A local string quartet gave a concert in the library of Chanters House. This room, designed by Butterfield, must be one of the most beautiful and least known in the South West, since the house is not open to the public. Both these evenings gave a sense of occasion and uniqueness and raised a lot of money. At the same time, there were buffet parties, coffee mornings and a bring-and-buy sale, a children's circus display, a sponsored ladies' cricket match, a concert of New Orleans jazz, an evening of poetry reading, a medieval banquet, a huge Christmas dance, a float in the town carnival, a painting competition and a raffle where the prizes were locally made arts and crafts. All this activity spread over nine months is bound to have an important effect in a town of 3,500 people. Even while Ottery was in rehearsal, we were setting up the Dorchester Play and building on our Ottery experience.

Dorchester was a very different community to Ottery, with a different Projects Committee and an utterly different approach. There were many more open air street events. Dorchester's main shopping street is largely closed to traffic and so the town has created a lively arena for itself. If you set up a street event in Dorchester on a Saturday morning, you have a ready audience and can create a great deal of interest. We used masks, giant puppets, stilt-walkers, jugglers and street music. The Projects Committee also set up a huge 'Fun Day', a non-stop event of dancing, theatre and improvisation, involving every possible group in the town, with food, sideshows, decorations, etc. This was a terrific success, except that in this case too much work fell on the play officer; we should perhaps have enlarged the Projects Committee or set up a special committee for this one event.

In Beaminster Jon Oram, the new Director of CTT, with his strong
visual sense and experience of working with the Welfare State Theatre
company, set up a series of events and projects of a more free and
fantastical nature. One such was 'Garland King Day' held in late May.
The charming little market cross was decorated with flowers, and
shopkeepers around the square were asked to garland their shops –
about a quarter did so (following the success of the event, more will
join in in future; encouraging people to take part next time is partly
what projects are about). Early on Saturday morning local people
brought flowers and greenery to the school and everyone made
garlands to be hung from poles, and decorated horses, carts and hats.
Escorted by a band (very important to bring people out) the Garland
King and Queen rode at the head of a procession through the town.
(They were led by a police car: why didn't they garland that?) There
was a maypole and morris dancing in the square, and a parade through
town. Garlands were hoisted up by the church and, after the singing,
everyone retired to the pub.

Garland King Day confirmed two observations I've previously
noticed with carnival parades and the like:

1 If you are are wearing a flower-bedecked bowler hat and walk
down the street people will smile and say 'hello' to you, and you
yourself will feel liberated.

2 People watching a parade or procession love to be drawn in,
perhaps by simply being waved at and waving back. Or you can use
'tickling sticks' (a long light pole with feathers on the end), very light
balls on elastic, and the like. You're not aiming to assault the
onlookers, rather to mildly tease so that they feel part of what's going
on. Have people handing out play leaflets along the route so as to
follow up this sense of involvement.

Don't plan to have big projects during rehearsal

Once the production team are embarked on rehearsal there will be
little time or energy left for projects, except for an appearance at the
odd coffee morning, etc. Nor will you want the cast to dissipate the
energy needed for rehearsal. With *The Western Women* we had
innocently planned ahead for a big spoof hockey match to take place
on a Saturday afternoon about a month after the start of rehearsals. It
was an attractive idea: 'Parliamentary Fellers' (i.e. girls in boys'
costumes) versus 'Royalist Ladies' (boys in drag), with the Lyme
Regis town band; kick-off by the Mayor and running commentary
from the Town Crier or some such extrovert. This would have

entailed an enormous amount of organisation: use of wardrobe facilities, etc. etc. We had to abandon the idea.

Weekend workshops

We use weekend workshops to increase skills and raise consciousness in a slightly different way to projects. In 1984, having read how children could quickly attain proficiency and a sense of achievement in circus skills and how they improved co-ordination, balance and reading skills, we set up a weekend workshop, taken by Reg Bolton, chiefly to teach ourselves, but open to everyone. Similarly, we had a mask-making workshop, given by Jenny Carey, an artist of great sensitivity, where she taught a simple and effective way of making masks directly on to the face. We also learned skills of giant puppet-making from various friends who had attended Welfare State training sessions and then passed their skills on. Jon Oram in Gainsborough set up workshops in how to make your own musical instruments: horns which cannibalised car manifolds and bits of old vacuum cleaners, cellos made out of tea-chests, etc. The aim was to take the mystique out of music-making and make it cheaply available to all kinds of people who would never for one moment consider themselves musical. The opportunities are endless and delightful and it is a way of feeling oneself refreshed.

Once we ourselves have learned the basic skills, we pass them on to children and others and set up a series of events to provide opportunities for people to work towards demonstrating these new techniques. However, we have begun more and more to incorporate these particular skills in the actual productions, at first in the fair preceding the play, although in Dorchester we also used stilt-walkers, jugglers, masks and giant puppets in the production itself. People often tend to become interested in these skills at a more personal level: one boy became a really dedicated monocyclist and it was a charming sight to see him weaving round the town with people looking on in amazement and pleasure. It's important to stress that there is enormous potential for involving people; projects are hard work because helping other people to achieve something is much harder than doing it yourself, and it needs a special attitude of mind.

Raising contributions in kind

You will often need relatively small amounts of goods and materials in connection with projects: anything from tea-bags to newsprint. This is an opportunity to involve a whole area of small shops and businesses which may not want to give cash but will be prepared to donate goods in kind. Remember these requests are very common (some shop-keepers say they get 40 per week), but this request is different as it's for the community, and maybe you are hoping to draw the shopkeeper in to play a wider and different role.

Since this is a job which is likely to be taken on by assistants, or local people who may be new to it, a word of help may be useful: asking for things requires a certain amount of nerve until you've done it once or twice, but you learn a technique and get tougher. Remember you are asking for the play not yourself. Work in pairs if you can. It's more fun and you give each other confidence. It's always more effective to ask for things face to face, but there is an equation to be drawn between the amount of material required divided by time and energy.

Suppose you have a fairly long list of your requirements and decide to do the job by phone: sit down with the Yellow Pages and an exact list of what you need.

1 Ask to speak to the manager. If you can't reach him or her don't leave a message: only the boss will have the authority to let you have what you want; you are going to present a careful spiel and all the message will say is, 'They want such-and-such.' Ask when the manager will be back and say you'll ring again.

2 When you get the manager say, 'I'm Katkin Mayne from the Beaminster community play.' Then explain briefly about the play, including the fact that hundreds of local people will be involved and that it is a charity (you'll get very good at doing this succinctly).

3 Explain that you are holding a fundraising event on 25 July which will again involve many local people; explain what it is.

4 Let them know that you are looking for contributions:

K.M.: Is it possible you could give us some sugar?

Prospect: Mm.

K.M.: We are aiming for twenty pounds.

At this point the Prospect will say either 'Yes' or 'What!' or 'No, I'm sorry'. If they say 'What!', try lowering your amount. If they say 'No' ask if you can have it at cost or discount price (then go on and try and find it free elsewhere).

Assure them that any help will be credited in the programme. Small shops sometimes don't sufficiently appreciate the value of a credit, particularly if production is a long way off; but it will actually be very worthwhile for them to be associated with such an event.

In all requests for sponsorship in cash or kind, and many other situations when you are trying to persuade people to do something, I have had two very worthwhile tips from commercial travellers; they apply particularly in face-to-face situations:

1 Give the Prospect a few moments, friendly chat before you start on the main topic. This puts you on the level of an acquaintance rather than a petitioner: it's the old foot-in-the-door technique.

2 'When you hear your own voice coming back at you, you've lost them.' This last is curious but true and you can learn to recognise it.

4
The play and the writer

A good community play must be theatrical, well written and appropriate to the needs of a particular community.

It is easy for amateurs to understand the importance of the director of the play: directors are very visible and amateurs are used to them. It is much harder for them to appreciate the value of a writer. Amateurs usually never see an author and work from a printed text where the writer's name is printed small. But the play is the basis of all and the playwright's role is fundamental. Nor do people usually appreciate that real writing talent is rare.

THE NATURE OF THEATRE

Theatre is based upon imaginative identification and the actual conflict with reality which this presents. Thus I am me, sitting here in my seat, but I am also Hamlet, Prince of Denmark, discovering that my father has been murdered. In this dichotomy lies the essential theatrical experience. Confident dramatists will sometimes intensify this experience by challenging it. Thus Oberon says, 'I am invisible' but remains foursquare upon the stage; all the actors treat him as invisible; we accept that he is invisible – but he isn't. This is a common, indeed ancient device, often used in pantomime, and it intensifies the theatre experience.

This direct physical challenge to belief, and the acceptance, indeed, connivance of the audience is what makes theatre quite different from TV and radio. These are forms whose very natures are so flexible and magical that they can do anything and make it appear real: change a pile of stones into a bag of gold, make a man age in five seconds. They are so magical that magic has no meaning. The very limitations of theatre, the way it must rely upon the audience's acceptance and imagination, are its unique strength.

The other characteristic of theatre is, of course, its live audience. The audience is exerting an immediate influence, changing the performance, not only making it easier for the actors one night and harder the next, but actually seeing the play in a different way. So that what is in most respects the same play is quite differently perceived in Edinburgh on Friday to London on Monday.

How this process works is perhaps less commonly recognised. The audience exert an irresistible and unconscious influence not only upon the actors but also on each other. You think you are making an objective judgement about a play but, without your being aware of it, your response is coloured by those around you. I first noticed this with my play *The Knack* while it was on tour before coming to London. At that time we still had stage censorship and I had had several conversations with the Lord Chamberlain's office, in typical British fashion an apparently quaint body but powerful enough, staffed by ex-Guards officers who might be trusted to know what was best for us ('Ah, Miss Jellicoe! I'm afraid this is going to be a rather embarrassing conversation. Haw! Haw!'). The censor had wanted to cut some really quite inoffensive jokes and I had managed to persuade him to let me keep them in. The play opened in Cambridge where it played to packed and delighted houses of undergraduates and I knew I had been right. It then went to Bath where there were half-empty houses of elderly people. I began to be worried: the play really did seem to be obscene – had the censor been right? When the play came to London I was sitting one night in the Royal Court Theatre and suddenly felt, 'But it's so innocent. So childlike!' When the lights went up I saw that in front of me was a row of extremely sophisticated film people. In every case, without my knowing it, my reaction had become the same as those around me. This is one reason why promenade performances are profoundly theatrical: they encourage the audience to mingle with each other and the actors and so intensify their influence upon each other.

Good and bad writing

Good plays, like all good art, are coherent. From the smallest detail to the overall form they are artistically integral. The ideas are clear, strong and original, the lines written so that the placing of stresses and the arrangement of sounds reveals and reinforces the meaning. The characters are consistent with the demands of the action and interact so as to put pressure on each other and bowl the action along. Every character, thought, action, every syllable, word, line, pause, scene, is part of an infinitely subtle structure. However complicated, the form will be economical in its own terms: everything not needed, anything which might blur, confuse or slow down the play will have been pared away. The play will capture the audience's imagination and then lead it through a series of experiences, building and releasing tension to the play's final climax and resolution. Paradoxically, a really fine play, which controls the actors, does not make the actors the play's slaves; it frees the actors, allowing them to put their energy where it truly belongs, into the interface with the audience. With a good play you fly. It's like jumping off a springboard.

Bad plays are bad in endless ways but fundamentally because the writer's thinking is not sufficiently energetic and clear, and their theatrical sense or experience not great enough. The ideas are dull and conventionally expressed. The characters are flat, their actions imposed and not justified. Instead of interacting they 'gossip', i.e. they witter on in flabby, superficial dialogue that does not engage, so that nothing has advanced by the end of the scene. There will be dialogue and indeed whole scenes, lying around with no purpose, simply for the sake of passing time. Thus when an actor speaks the line, s/he has to work against the blur and try to force some meaning through. In a bad play the actor has to do the playwright's job: testing every single moment in the play against artistic truth or the discipline of a single, energetic idea. Even if this is possible, it drains the actor's energy from where it should properly be used.

Note This differs from actors improvising and devising plays. With *improvised* plays the action is either extremely short or, as with *commedia dell'arte*, based upon an agreed simple, standard plot. With *devised* plays the work is done in two stages: (1) the actor as playwright creates the play (2) the completed play is rehearsed by the actors.

Monkeying around with the text used to be, and sometimes still is, a popular pastime with vain and arrogant actors because they do indeed have a single idea and one which often conflicts with the text: how to make themselves look most attractive to the audience.

Plays, pageants and carnival

It is sometimes mistakenly thought that a play of this size must by definition be a pageant, but they might more correctly be termed 'epic plays'. A pageant is a series of loosely connected scenes which usually have no formal link with each other beyond being a sequence of events from the history of the town. Frequently, different sections and scenes are rehearsed by different groups of the community, e.g. the Women's Institute takes the Signing of Magna Carta, the Boy Scouts

take the Burning of the Cakes, etc. What this means is that a pageant is
a very cool form: the emotional temperature cannot rise because there
is no build-up.

A play, on the other hand, has character and plot which are related
in an organic whole. We identify with the heroes and heroines and are
swept along by the story through the switchback of the play and the
building and release of tension to the climax.

David Edgar makes a further interesting distinction in an article he
wrote for the *Guardian* (but of which this section was cut on
publication):

> Quite early on in our work together, Ann Jellicoe made an
> important distinction, between a play (organic, with breadth
> and bulk) and a pageant (a linear form, its sum merely the
> arithmetic chronology of its parts). But although *Entertaining
> Strangers* is, I hope, absolutely a play in the sense of that
> distinction, it has (and must have) some of the elements of
> pageant, of huge, almost self-contained units of action or
> sequences of event, passing the fixed point of the audience's
> perception. What is wrong with a pageant is that it is *merely*
> processional, lacking the dynamic of purpose, a medium of
> heritage rather than history. Carnival, on the other hand, is full
> of life and aim, even if those aims can be contradictory, and its
> vivacity crackling with danger. And increasingly I think that
> what Ann Jellicoe has created over the years are not plays or
> pageants, but kinds of carnival, and it is that reality which
> provides the sense of an event not just of commitment and
> energy but of moral force and artistic scale. And of course the
> point of a carnival is that it is an event of sufficient size and space
> to encompass both the most high aesthetic endeavour and the
> most untutored communal enthusiasms; not community or art
> but the two together. Which is, I'm sure, why playwrights, who
> find it so difficult to find houseroom in the professional theatre
> for statements of scale, may follow the people who attended the
> Lyme conference into the realms of the community theatre.

In conversation, David Edgar further describes carnival as 'like the
medieval mystery plays having a beginning, middle and end'. He also
defines carnival as: 'those really thrilling scenes where lots of things
are going on at once *and it doesn't matter*'. And again: 'not just plays
which celebrate, but events which are themselves celebrations'. I
think I glimpse what David Edgar means by carnival: something of

scale and form, encompassing risk and celebration. Perhaps indeed something between a play and a pageant.

THE PROBLEM OF COMMISSIONING ONE WRITER

Until recently we assumed that a specially commissioned community play would have 11 performances and that would be that. A play being specially written for a unique community would never be performed again. But recently Nick Darke's community play for Restormel, *The Earth Turned Upside Down*, and David Edgar's play for Dorchester, *Entertaining Strangers*, have both been bought by the National Theatre. The authors are rewriting them in order to reduce the cast to manageable size. These are very significant developments for it means that there is now a possibility of a far greater return for the writer financially and artistically and it makes community plays an even more attractive proposition.

Even if there is a reasonable chance of further life for the play, it is very unlikely that you can afford to commission more than one writer and all your fortunes are in that frail vessel. Professional theatres will commission several writers. They don't usually need a play for a particular occasion and they always have more than one production in the pipeline. If the commissioned play does not come up to scratch they need not produce it. But you have to make a choice of writer and stick with it and you won't really know that everything is all right until it's almost too late to do anything about it. This is one of the most precarious aspects of the work. If the writer's talent, personality or attitude is wrong, you can be left with the shreds of a script and rehearsals which start in two months' time.

To be especially written

The play should be especially written for the town. It won't do to simply revive *Oliver* or to adapt *Bleak House* and I don't think revivals of mystery plays are enough unless you write your own mystery play. An original play will not only be written to the precise needs of the community but it will provide an enormous sense of occasion, something unique. It will also mean that you have a contemporary statement written for our times. This will be so whether the subject is historical or not. It is impossible to write a play, even one set in the remote past, which is not actually about the present.

In theory, there is no reason why you shouldn't have a contemporary play set in the community today. But if your aim is to reconcile the community, to bring it closer together in harmony and to celebrate it, then you may be in for trouble with a play which discusses problems which divide the town today.

Politics

In West Dorset, we live amidst a very right-wing, even feudal community. If we set out to challenge the basic political feelings of the communities we serve, we will alienate large sections of them and lose their support. We might even provoke them into active opposition, but far more likely they will simply melt away and not join in, or drop out. The Colway Theatre Trust comes to a town to help reconcile a community, hopefully to enrich it. Politics are divisive. We strongly feel that the humanising effect of our work is far more productive than stirring up political confrontation. In a sense, our task must be made easier by the fact that in the rural south-west we don't have to face the enormous problems of the great industrial cities – we live more or less in one-class communities. Even though unemployment is high (20 per cent in some areas), so far as I can tell there is little or no sense of 'them and us' in class terms. While the extreme left would doubtless say there is no possible ground where everyone in a given community can meet without dishonesty, we strongly feel that these plays do provide just such a ground.

After the opening of *The Poor Man's Friend* Howard Barker spoke on the BBC programme *Kaleidoscope*:

> I didn't realise I had learned anything particularly, even till perhaps the first night, and then I realised that it is in fact a completely different form of theatre. I didn't quite realise that when I started. The kind of theatre I normally write is more or less the theatre of the battlefield: it's about division and it's about hostility. Seeing that production, I realised that theatre is also a civilizing influence. I don't mean civilizing in the sense that a writer and a producer are coming to a town, offering education to the people, but of the civility of a community which is drawn together and develops its strength from sharing in an artistic experience. That's very novel to me. And by that I am also saying that it's an experience of celebration in a way that no professional production I have ever worked on before is a celebration. I have tried to make sure it's a celebration of the right things from my point of view: I think they celebrate

solidarity in times of oppression and they celebrate things like survival and coming through, which I think the whole community is able to tangibly feel.

The interesting thing here is that Howard Barker is a Socialist playwright and there emerged the consideration not only of what he might do to Bridport but what the experience of writing a community play might do to him. In this connection, Sheila Yeger, who wrote the Ottery St Mary play, is very articulate. Speaking at a writer's conference held by Colway Theatre Trust in 1985, she said:

> This question about to what degree one would be compromising one's principles taxed my brain a lot to begin with. I felt I'm going to write this very strong statement, this very strong socialist statement. I knew that I was going to say the things that I always say and I was going to say them in the way I always say them and no one was going to stop me, not even Ann Jellicoe. I wouldn't think Ann Jellicoe would even try to stop me. When I presented my first draft I knew that I had aimed a kick at the groin. And that a kick at the groin was not what was called for in this play.
>
> It took some subtle and gentle persuasion and a certain amount of ego-stripping for me to relinquish some of the things in my first draft. When I read the play at the second draft I was very glad I had relinquished them.
>
> What had happened was that a very, kind of, coarse play, one in which I made my usual statements in my usual way, had somehow been transmuted into a much more subtle and, I think, a much more human play. I was somehow persuaded off my customary soapbox and it had been a good thing that I had been persuaded. What happened and continued to happen during the process of rehearsal was that I started looking at how these ideas, these responsibilities if you like, could be addressed in different ways. I know now that it's not always necessary to spell out things in words of one syllable. I learnt that it's not necessary to offend an audience, that there is such a thing as actually persuading the audience in a way that doesn't turn out to be offensive.

It has certainly been my experience that amongst eminent or accomplished writers, the most generous in time and energy and relating to 'ordinary' people are generally socialist. They take their obligations to a community with great seriousness and sensitivity. They have by and large recognised that here is an opportunity to relate to people. They find it a great problem when they are asked not to write a 'political' play and a great deal of my time and energy has been spent in talking them through this problem.

Sensitivity regarding image

This is perhaps surprisingly an even more explosive issue than politics. It has taken me a long time to realise (at first with incredulity) how deeply and sensitively people feel about their own image: their family, their business. I am afraid if everyone had their way, their background in the widest sense would be pristine, pure, unsullied, not necessarily interesting, but absolutely and certainly spotless.

You cannot be rude about local people or their forebears by name, unless you wish to antagonise them, even if the facts are true. If we carefully analyse a great many devised plays, it's likely we shall discover three things: (1) nothing really rude or unpleasant is ever said about the member of any working-class family connected with the play; (2) the villains are all people against whom the community can comfortably unite, e.g. the wicked capitalist landlord or entrepreneur; (3) the devisers, being socialist, will be tempted to see the working-class through rose-coloured spectacles (oh yes they will).

Peter Terson tells a story (at the same writers' conference) of a situation when he found himself destroying a local myth:

> I was drummed out of Whitby. I went to live in Whitby to write a play, sort of looking into the area and the history and all that. Whitby had the St Mary Church on the hill with a monument to the 1861 lifeboat disaster: a great marble monument up there. I looked in the records and found that on February 11th, 1861 a great storm blew up and wrecked a ship. The gallant lifeboat crew pushed out and saved them and they've got this monument and I thought, 'That's wonderful!' and I started getting all the newspapers out. It made fantastic reading.
>
> I found that when it came to the gallant lifeboatmen, they had refused to try out a new Sub-Viking lifeboat and wouldn't practice in it. They were wearing the old-fashioned cork life-jackets around the waist that turned them upside down like ducks in the water and wouldn't try the new jackets that had been issued, and this attitude just went on and on. On the day of the storm, everyone rushed down to the harbour because you

got an extra sixpence for every time the lifeboat was launched. They were fighting each other to get in. They were all half-starved because it was February: they'd pawned all their gear at the beginning of winter. They kept on going out to the ship and going out again for the money and some silly bugger was feeding them with rum every time they came back, so that by the end, apart from the cox, they were all blind drunk. They were all drowned, except a bricklayer who had gone in wearing the correct life-jacket. And I wrote the play and the press got hold of it and I was driven out of town within a fortnight. Whitby hasn't ever seen my play. It didn't go on there.

Of course you cannot write a play that is pap. But organise your villains so that if possible they come from out of town: people whom the community can comfortably unite against.

CHOOSING A SUBJECT

Must it always be historical?
For such political and personal reasons, CTT tends to use historical subjects. If the story is placed reasonably far back in time, there are few actual descendants of the characters portrayed who will worry about them. If you show somebody's ancestor in a bad light, you must be prepared to make an enemy, even if the story is accurate and well researched. No one likes their neighbours to know that their great-great-grandfather embezzled the corporation funds, or that their aunt was the town whore.

At the same time, history lends distance to what may be bitter political arguments. In *Entertaining Strangers*, the Reverend Henry Moule gives a very strong speech in a formal situation: a presentation in the town hall. His speech, naming the Prince Consort and Duchy of Cornwall, Landlords in Dorchester, is essentially a Marxist call: 'I will not rest until this wrong is righted. For it is a species of oppression and it will and should provoke resistance'. Were those words put into the mouth of a contemporary vicar of Dorchester, it would place him and the town in an untenable position. But nonetheless, the dramatist has made the statement and drawn the moral.

Who chooses the subject?
Sometimes the subject thrusts itself forward, as with *The Western Women*, for example. The story had exploded in our minds and we

were quite clear that we wanted this and no other. On that basis, we commissioned the writer. In Ottery, the town, by a series of meetings, virtually chose the story, or at least its main incident, the Great Fire of Ottery. Such is my respect for writers that, all things being equal, I rather prefer that they themselves should find the subject in consultation with the townspeople, for the writer must have a subject to which s/he will respond. However, it is fundamentally important that a subject is chosen which favours women. Ideally, the story must actually depend upon women, so that it is possible for women to have leading roles.

Selecting a good writer

Good may be relative in social terms. You will wish to balance quality with the need for the writer to relate closely to the community and to be seen to be relating. It is a consideration which may make you pause before commissioning a writer of national standing. Your luckiest solution might be if you had a writer of national standing who lives locally, e.g. Nick Darke, the writer of the Restormel community play, who is a Cornishman. Before you commission a local writer because they will be obviously part of the community, take a moment to consider that local writers may be local for very good reasons. If you are going to release people's talent, they must be free and confident. A good play, by its technical, artistic and emotional power, will thrust the actor into that extraordinary space where actors and audience confront each other and lift off.

Alternatives
A national writer

If you wish to commission a well-known writer of experience who will deliver you a very fine, well-made play on which you will be able to rely, there are certain difficulties: not everyone will be able to approach a well-known writer and not every writer will accept such a commission without knowing the person who is approaching them. However, you have something unique to offer: no play in the commercial theatre, including the national companies, can now have a cast of more than 30 people; community plays offer casts of 100 or more. This is a commission that writers will find nowhere else. If you can somehow demonstrate the excitement of the work and your skill, the invitation is almost irresistible. David Edgar: 'If Ann Jellicoe said, "Come down and do a community play with a cast like you get at the

Royal Court," I'd have stayed up in London riding about in taxi-cabs. I'm down here because there's nowhere else I'd get 150 people.'

You do need to be familiar with the writer's work and sometimes their personality. Will they think they are slumming and not bother? Do they deliver on time? Do they like to be prodded or left alone? You are depending a great deal on the integrity of the writer.

A 'fringe' writer

If you cannot persuade a writer of national standing, or have not had a great deal of experience in coping with writers and think that a heavyweight might walk all over you, your best bet might be to choose a writer of emerging talent: someone who has demonstrated their potential around the fringe or the regions, but who hasn't yet made it on the national scene. The chances are they will see the play as an enormous opportunity and put their heart and soul into the work. However, at this level it begins to be a toss-up to whether a local writer might not be a better idea.

Local writer

An attractive option for obvious reasons, but remember there may well be other local writers and their friends whom you have not asked to write the play and who will resent your choice.

Devised plays

A dramatist works to reveal and discover the integrity of a single idea or attitude. S/he is working to find and give body to artistic truth. This process will be partly intellectual, partly intuitive, at the best an experience of possession, of being 'breathed through'. In theory it is possible for a group of people to create a play in the same way, but they need many hours of discussion to clarify their goals, which may continually change and emerge as they pursue the nature of the idea. It is probably a great deal easier if such a group shares a common, strong idea, e.g. all are left wing, or perhaps come from a common background. In theory it should be possible for the community to devise its own play, but I have never tried it because the numbers are so vast. It's hard enough to organise rehearsals, but to organise rehearsals without a real play seems insuperable. We did a great deal of improvising in Sherborne but that is quite different to the diffi-culties of devising a whole play from scratch. With Lyme Regis and *The Western Women* the atmosphere at rehearsal was so very good that we improvised from strength: we weren't trying to make a dodgy script better, rather the good and confident atmosphere allowed us to take risks and make discoveries which enormously strengthened the play itself.

If you have a poor play it is still possible to end up with a success in community terms, but not in artistic terms. A great deal of self-congratulation will tell you that you have done well, but this is to descend to the lowest level of amateur dramatics – it is a form of self-indulgence and self-display. You may well think it worthwhile to use a local writer and you may be right, but do not underestimate what you are giving up. The play is the structure which allows everything else to happen.

THE WRITER'S CHIEF PROBLEM AND OPPORTUNITY: SIZE

Organising the writing to cope with 100–180 parts is chiefly a technical problem. Numbers of names are always confusing and hard to remember. Most roles don't really need to be identified by name (though it's vital that the actors know exactly who they are). What is important to the audience is that people can instantly be recognised and remembered by role, attitude, social relationships and import-ance in the story.

My own technique is to take individuals and set them into relation-ships. I spend most of Act I identifying people and groups in terms of action and story; this frees me to let rip in Act 2. In practice the characters fall into three groups:

Leads Have as few big leads as possible. I much prefer 12 secondary leads to two starring parts. The leads are probably identifiable by name but it's not always necessary.

Medium-sized parts By far the largest group. I aim to give these people a good entry in at least two small scenes with their own speeches together with appearances in all the big scenes where they will improvise, etc. It is surprising how even a small part can be worked up with entrances in 'baskets' (see below) and care that they are brought forward in rehearsal. In this way even the smallest part can begin to grow, particularly if the actor has their own secure social identification.

Very small parts Obviously you keep these to the minimum. In *The Western Women* there was only one almost invisible part played by a French girl with a heavy accent who couldn't come to rehearsal very much. She only appeared in crowd scenes but even so had 'family relationships'.

Baskets

The writer should make provision for small groups which can be varied in size without too much trouble. Thus you can put people into the group or take them out merely by adding or redistributing a few lines. 'Baskets' are almost essential because you are bound to find that you have more people than you bargained for, especially women and children. Thus we have had 'baskets' of women gutting fish, preparing cricket teas, ladies' friendly societies, girls washing clothes, boys playing chicken games, etc. etc.

A basket is always made up of individuals who have their own separate identity and relationships. One person may be in several different baskets.

Building parts

Using *The Western Women* as an example: the Gaitch family consists of Gaitch, a baker, his wife, daughter, son and two shop assistants. We first meet Gaitch (a secondary lead) as a town councillor in Sc. 5. We see him in his shop in Sc. 10; he then becomes a trusted assistant of Colonel Blake (lead), Commander of the Lyme Parliamentary Garrison.

Gaitch's wife and daughter are seen (just) in the town council, and have a clinching appearance in the shop. Mrs Gaitch has a good scene in Act 2 when women, fearful of the approaching siege, are making bandages (this scene was also a basket). Gaitch's daughter has an important moment when she becomes spokesperson for a group of women (a basket) begging Blake to let them help the men.

Tom Gaitch also belongs to a boy's basket (as does a shop assistant) which brings important news of the approaching Royalist army. Young Gaitch also has his individual moment when he runs through the audience excitedly yelling that Colonel Blake wants to see his father. The girl shop assistant also belongs to a basket of girls washing clothes in the River Lym with a paired scene (see below) in Act 2. (Both these groups, consisting entirely of children and Blake, a school teacher, could rehearse in the valuable 4.0 p.m. time just after school.) The shop assistants also had their own families.

Identifying people in terms of action/story/form, etc.

The whole background and basis of the story of *The Western Women* was set up in four very short scenes and one very large scene at the beginning of the play. The first scene (starting in the middle of the hall and moving to a side stage) crashed into the fair with a violent argument on religious matters: Mr Seeley (a secondary lead) is tortured by a question of fundamental puritan philosophy which led directly to the siege. All the time the men are shouting at each other the women dandle a charming (real) baby. The laws of theatre (the eye always takes precedence over the ear) and babies being irresistible, we watch the women, and the men have to fight like mad for our attention. Thus background and identification are provided in terms of theatre and story.

The second scene is also basically a statement of the religious position and shows an extreme protestant belief of that curious and passionate time (it was important that the audience thoroughly understood quite a lot of non-conformist thinking). A town councillor in bed, as he thinks, with a tart is desperately searching for his socks so as to be in time for the mayor-making; he is constantly distracted by the girl who turns out to be a member of an extreme sect: 'Before thee can be redeemed thee must passionately embrace all things, all sins one after another.'

The third and fourth scenes each scarcely last two minutes and are basically building Seeley's dilemma. We have now met 12 characters, including two secondary leads, 3 Councillors and the Town Clerk and their women. It is time to 'set' these characters as well as going forward.

The fifth scene, the mayor-making, involves the whole cast. We recognise our friends sitting with the other town councillors up on the platform. The scene is set very much in terms of men equated with power and women shown as trivial-minded and ineffective in public life. Each town councillor, identified by name, makes a formal statement of support for Seeley, stating why he too would not take the oath (more background information). At the same time their wives/sisters etc. on the floor sketchily identify themselves (but it helps set them in the audience's mind when they appear in later scenes).

There are 29 scenes in Act I and by the time it is over almost all the characters have been introduced. The Act ends with an intensely quiet scene of men guarding the defence perimeter waiting for the Royalists to come. It's an echo of a previous scene when the same men and a few others (including Gaitch's shop assistant) have been digging the same defences. These paired scenes are a very useful device: reminding the audience of who people are and giving a sense of cohesion in sprawling plays. We now know all these men. Not necessarily by name but we remember the happy-go-lucky town councillor who went to bed with the girl, etc. Here they all are under new stress. The final new characters, introduced in this scene, are two young secondary leads whose story promises to take the action, and so our expectations, forward. And that is virtually the last of new characters. Act 2 is concerned with the chaos and excitement of the siege itself, and how people change and develop.

It really is a question of technique. You build individuals into relationships. You show them reacting to a given situation trying to introduce each character as economically and clearly as possible, in terms of action and background information. You control how much, and what, the audience needs to remember. You don't particularly ask them to remember the name of Mrs Hassard but present them with the image of a woman, married to the ex-Mayor, with a sharp tongue, who bullies her servants. With her characteristics established she later becomes a useful development of the story when her bossiness enables her to organise the hospital. A drudge scrubs the town hall floor in Scene 3, speaks up in Scene 5, receives charity in Scene 9, is seen taking part in baskets and large scenes; she later shows the shake-up the siege has given to status when she comforts a woman, her social superior by far. It's totally unimportant to the audience, though vital to the actress, that her name is Bess Podger.

PRACTICAL DEMANDS OF THE SCRIPT

The play should have lots of action. It should aim to be popular. It may be serious – people love serious things as much as they love comedy. People like to see work scenes, especially when they concern the local craft, e.g. carpet-weaving in Axminster, rope-making in Bridport. This draws on local pride and you will be able to involve local craftsmen, sometimes teaching children the old skills. Local allusions are much appreciated: one gets an amazing amount of simple pleasure from hearing a familiar street or building named.

Duration
The play should last 2–2½ hours with an interval. Any longer is really too long for a promenade performance and it also means that there is more material to be rehearsed, which can be an unforeseen but very practical difficulty.

Cast: size and constitution
120 is a good size. 150 is beginning to be rather large. Above this figure, all the logistic problems seem to grow at a compound rate.

Women

There are always three times more women than men wanting to join in. The play should deliberately cater for this and should have plenty of good, strong parts for women and girls. This really cannot be emphasised strongly enough. It is no good delivering a play with 4 big male leads, 70 good parts for men, 1 female lead and 30 to 40 walk-ons for women. But this is what will happen if playwrights are not given the strongest guidance. We have been taught to perceive history in terms of men: men as initiators, women as passive. Theatre was one of the strongest image-makers in our society for over three hundred years until around 1920, when radio began. Theatre as we know it was virtually created by men, who see society and history in male terms. Men, even the most humanist, will not accept this, but it's true. Ask a man to write a play and it will be virtually all about men. Women writers are more aware but even they have problems in delivering a play with the necessary ratio of women to men. In historical plays in particular a writer has to make an enormous conscious effort to write women's parts, and in this connection it's wise and very helpful to start with a story which is about women so that they will naturally be pushed to the front (e.g. *The Western Women*). You must then, at every moment in the writing, remind yourself of the problem: could this part be played by a woman? Are the men taking over, looming too large? Stop! Go back! Think again and develop the women more.

Why more women should want to act than men, I do not know. It's maybe that they are freer in their outlook, less inhibited, less worried about possibly looking odd or strange. It may also be their willingness to adventure in the imagination. I hesitate to use the word 'fantasise', which has a derogatory sound. I think it's enviable to have a rich, imaginative mind, so long as you don't lose your grip on real life and practicality, and few women are tempted to do that. Whatever the reasons, there are always more women than men and it is neither fair nor right that while the men are doubling two or three parts, women may only have two or three lines each.

Named parts
There do need to be named parts, not just crowd scenes, though these can be made up by people who have small parts elsewhere. Getting

people to join in is not easy to begin with; their egos seem to need the promise of a part, however small. This is the reality of the situation. Beyond this, named parts, where each person has a family and an individual background, leads to extraordinary richness and depth of characterisation. People are locked into the play all the way through and this is very important in a promenade production, where actors are in the hall all the time.

How many big parts?
The best amateur actors are very good indeed – quite as good as most of the professional actors I have worked with. It is a temptation to use the very best actors in big parts and, of course, the form of a play this size often demands one or two huge parts to hold the thing together. Even so, it is better to have, say 8/12 strong, medium-size parts than 1 very large, starring part.

Children
Remember there may be technical acting problems with children: poor projection, often astonishingly poor articulation. If children have little to do, their concentration will sag. It's unwise to plan for large numbers of children to be kept quiet for a long time in dressing-rooms.

Bear in mind the problems of calling children to rehearsal. It's sometimes almost impossible to get groups of children from different schools together for rehearsal at the same time. (It's usually easy to get an individual child for rehearsal.)

Incidentally, remember that while a girl of fifteen can look like a grown woman, a boy of fourteen years old may pass for ten.

Technical
It's likely that financial resources will be very constricted, both in terms of the professionals who can be employed and the amount of materials bought. The community joins in to an extraordinary degree but will not have the skill, teamwork or resources of say, the National Theatre. The writer should probably think in terms of the simplest possible staging, including using existing stages, and building as little extra as possible. The play should be performable in an interesting way in what may be a dull environment.

RESEARCH

How the writer may relate directly to the community

All the Colway plays have demanded a degree of research, some more than others. Since I have always been interested in social history, and have been a co-curator of our local museum, when I was author the job was half done before I started to write. As it became clear how closely 'visiting' writers must relate to the community, it was obvious that we must begin to structure the relationship more carefully. The opportunity was first properly grasped in Ottery where we had extra resources and so some time to think. We learned a great deal from Sheila Yeger who went about her task with sensitivity and method born of her previous experience as a community worker.

First of all the play officer set up a very wide range of encounters and meetings between Sheila, individuals and groups. She met and talked with all the obvious people: local historians, teachers, gate-openers, etc., but she also sought out peer groups and the disadvantaged, e.g. unemployed youths near the fish-and-chip shop, mothers waiting outside the infant school, etc. We arranged that Sheila should have a table in the library where she would work when in Ottery, being available if anyone wanted to talk to her. When she was out of town she left a notice saying when she would be returning, and also a suggestion box.

The consensus seemed to be that they wanted a play about the Great Fire of Ottery of 1866. Having established this, Sheila made an appeal for help,* listing about twenty historical events of the period and asking for any memories or stories of the time which might have been handed down. She also set up a series of meetings* to explore local history. They were well attended: we had made sure that at least 4 people would be there but over 30 turned up each evening. They included boys and girls of 14 as well as older people, e.g. the Chairman of Ottery Town Council whose family have lived in the district for hundreds of years, and people who had recently moved into the town.

From the start it was clear that Sheila had done her homework and already knew a good deal about the background history of the town. She made it clear she wasn't only looking for basic facts but 'faction', a kind of imaginative feeling of what it must have been like because, she said, 'That's what a play is: it is not historical fact.' Amongst other things this attitude made it possible for relative newcomers to the town to play a useful role.

On a typical occasion Sheila started by reading a contemporary newspaper account of the Great Fire which contained many names of places and people. This sparked off discussion and reminiscence. People contributed, enjoyed themselves and much material came to light. On another evening, people were requested to bring their music and recitations to the party, and had an evening of the kind of family entertainment which might have been typical of the period. These meetings not only stimulated ideas and threw up research but were also valuable in another way. Sheila's evident grasp of the subject, the work she had already clearly done in background reading, talking to local historians and the older generation, the mixture of the audience and their really valuable contributions, made it a piece of high-profile imagemaking. Those meetings must have gone a long way towards establishing trust in the town and the feeling that the play was seriously attempting to involve people.

As a further means of reaching people we set up a stall, with lots of information about the play, in the main square on one or two warm Saturday mornings. We all wore sashes with 'COMMUNITY PLAY' written across them, and gave out handbills. The handbills gave us an excuse to go up to people and talk to them. The sashes warned who we were and so removed some of the stress – or we could be avoided. Sheila described one of these occasions and vividly tells of the moment when inspiration may come to a writer:

Once, when we were doing the stall, a women, maybe in her fifties, maybe older, was sort of flirting with the idea: she was looking at the stall and walking on, pretending not to be interested and hanging about a bit. So I began to talk to her. She spoke with a very broad local accent and she started off by saying: 'Well, I'm just an ordinary woman, you don't want to talk to me, I can't tell you anything.' And I very quickly thought I did want to talk to her but it was a lot of trouble persuading her that she might have something to tell me. So I made an arrangement to go and see her the following week. I went to her house, which is on one of the poorer estates.

Now everywhere I went I was wined and dined. I had cream teas and homemade Victoria sponges, and sandwiches, and what have you. I ate myself silly. On this occasion I went to the front door and her husband was watching the television and didn't leave it the whole time I was there. She had prepared nothing. I never had a glass of water. She didn't take off her pinny nor did she apologise for not taking off her pinny. What ensued was the most amazing monologue in which she told me her life story and the life story of her mother and grandmother.

This was fairly near the end of my period of research and, as she spoke I – it was actually like a light on the road to Damascus – I'd been researching, and I'd been looking for a story, and there was a very obvious event in the history of the town which people were pointing out: 'If you're going to write a play about Ottery it's got to be about the Great Fire: that's really the only thing that's happened here.' It's difficult to make a fire dramatic and so forth and it hadn't – let's put it like this – it hadn't actually caught my imagination. I recognised this as a potential subject but I was waiting to find a flash point that would set my mind going. As Mrs Luxton (which is not her real name) was talking about her life in service, and her family's life in service, she said to me: 'What really gets me is that we are always at the back of the queue. Times have changed. Conditions have improved OK. This town is not what it was in Victorian times: housing conditions are better, people have more money, we have free education. But me, my family, we are still, relatively speaking, at the back of the queue.'

And I began to see a potential, within the subject which I had already decided upon, for showing an historical event from the point of view of people who are at the back of the crowd. Not those who were attending the church restoration in their summer bonnets alongside the architect and the vicar, but those who couldn't quite see because of the crowd. Who were standing right at the back on tiptoe, lifting their children up, trying to work out what the hell was going on. They were starving, the people had spent a lot of money restoring the church. How do you make sense of that? I began to define two of my areas: I wanted to look at the situation of women and I wanted to look at historic events as seen by those who are not protagonists, those to whom they are being done, if you like, who are watching from the sidelines and trying to make some sort of sense of events in relation to their everyday lives.

In Dorchester we built on what Sheila had taught us, but necessarily in terms of David Edgar's personality. We arranged numbers of meetings for him, and he was a great hit as a public speaker. He appeared to have moments of discomfort when parading about the market place wearing a community play sash; nevertheless he did it.

Rather quickly a number of people who were interested in research began to gather round him. The Research Group found terrific energy and began to burrow in the museum, library and Public Record Office, finally putting in well over a thousand hours of work on background research and uncovering much new material about the town.

> They produced a great deal of information and the play's too long partially because of it. They went through the *County Chronicle* – not noted for its economy, indeed truly bulging – and of course they got very enthusiastic and recognised even more names . . . and you do sort of think to yourself halfway through . . . My God! Have I got something that so-and-so researched . . . I mean have I actually got a bit from everybody? You have to start getting ruthless and say, 'The Fat Baby Competition of 1853 will have to go.'

Once he saw the potential of the Research Group David began to have a vision in which every single person would actually have lived in Dorchester at the time of the play, been of the age and filled the social role in which they would appear.

> The play covers 40 years and 173 characters. I very much wanted that people would be able to go to the Public Record Office for 1841 and say, 'Here I am. Here's my address. Here's what I do.'

He began to be absolutely meticulous about accuracy and would ring a member of the Research Group and say, 'Can you find me ten women aged between sixteen and forty in 1830 and still alive in 1854? I need six of them to have lived in Fordington, four can be middle or upper class.' When he ran out of people who lived long enough to span the whole era of the play he combined them and their daughters into one part, e.g. Martha Tilley (mother) having inconveniently died sometime in (say) 1860, the same actress went on to appear as her daughter, Mary Tilley, for the rest of the play. The audience weren't lumbered with this (although it appeared in the programme), but the actress and David knew.

It sounds complicated and it was. David also still had to deal with the basic challenges of a community play:

> Your major problem is the number of characters. You have to start from characters and count them out. The way I write plays

is that I have a series of scenes with more than three people in them. So you have the main characters and then you get other people to appear as sort of additional characters and you think, 'Oh great! We could bring him in earlier', and your minor characters build up as you write. And you realise that in Scene 8, this character who delivers the post would actually be very interesting if you wrote him in Scene 2. You combine. In a play with 173 people that way madness lies.

You have to start from a chart. My crucial mistake was thinking that, in theory, I wanted almost everyone who died in this cholera outbreak in history. We know who they were . . . I wanted the fact that they died to be ironical, or to have been prophesied, or all the things that do happen to people. I thought, 'Well, I'll get to the cholera and then work backwards; get to that point in the plot and then I'll have to do a bit of rechecking; I've got to remember where they all are . . .' It was just incredibly hard work . . . You know with most plays there comes a moment when the dust has suddenly seemed to clear and all the research material has gone, when you can sort of just run on because you know it's all there; you don't have to keep looking it up. That never happened because you are always looking up. You think, 'God! I've got to bring back the guy who was married in 1833!' And you go back to the ringfile and look it up and check what age he'd be now, because you can't remember 173 people's lives.

David was meticulous about accuracy and nearly drove me crazy, but there is no doubt that it did a great deal for the cast. They really did go and look themselves up, visit their characters' graves and discuss lives and background with members of the Research Group. It must have added greatly to the actors' sense of their own significance as individuals, to the reality of their characters and to a vivid sense of the living past in their town. They were walking the streets these people walked. David's approach, based on the work of the Research Group, was one of the things which gave the play a particular authority. In Beaminster, having learned from Dorchester, David Cregan is also working alongside a Research Group albeit less obsessively. Another town, another writer, another style.

RELATING TO THE WRITER WHILE S/HE IS PREPARING THE PLAY

This is always a very sensitive time. You and the writer have to learn to trust each other and this is a process which is being built up from your first meeting. You cannot force this trust. It is a most difficult and delicate relationship and has been the source of the greatest satisfaction and considerable misery to me. Due to my training at the Royal Court, I probably tend to leave writers alone and to respect them too much. Some writers are obsessed with the inner process of creation. Some like to have check-points along the way; discussions, outlines, scenarios, etc. You have to discover how best to support and encourage each different writer, so that they do their best work. But you have to respect a writer and their talent. You cannot write a play for another writer. If you want to write your own play, get on with it. Writers must not be mucked around. On the other hand, they have to be helped and you have to keep an eye on them, because if the play is bad, the town, and you, are going to suffer.

WHEN THE SCRIPT ARRIVES

The playwright will be waiting with extreme anxiety (repressed or otherwise) to know what you think of the play. S/he has had to digest all the information from research and has been working virtually alone for the last three months or more, spinning the play from his or her own gut. The writer knows as well as anyone how much depends on the script, so they may well be very tense. I am as anxious to read the script as the writer is to hear my opinion and so I read the play fast, without stopping, to get a first reaction. I am always positive with the writer. Even if my heart sinks, I'll find something I can praise without lying and without having to eat my words later. The worse the play, the more closely you are going to have to work with the author, helping to make it better. You must keep up the author's courage and confidence.

It's far more likely that the play will be good. In any case, your next step is to work through to try and understand it almost as closely as the author does. At this stage I generally make a careful written analysis of what is actually happening moment by moment. This is rather different from a scenario which merely gives a résumé of the story. I may also lay out the form of the play diagrammatically on large sheets of paper, showing an essentially horizontal progression with big blocks for big scenes, linked diagrammatically by smaller blocks which may be different in shape (the feeling of the smaller scenes is different). Colour may be used for different scenes, large arrows linking up different parts of the plot, crescendos mark the building of tension, an exploding star for climax, etc. etc.

These devices help me to get into the play, to see whether the action is really going forward, where there appears to be confusion. I am also checking all the points previously mentioned. I look for underwriting: this is when the playwright has given insufficient explanation, time, dialogue, or stage directions to make an action or character clear to an audience. I also look for overwriting: does the play need cutting here? Is the playwright giving too much explanation? (This often happens when writers don't trust directors and actors to do exactly what they want.) Could such and such an image/piece of action be more powerfully conveyed by the actors with fewer words? Is the dialogue too 'literary', i.e. launching into an inflated, bookish, poetic tone during which time the action simply stops until the author has had their little say. Every word that can be cut without damaging the play will make it stronger and more powerful.

Try not to write the author's play for them. Every writer has their creative attitude and voice and will solve problems in their own way. Everyone pays lip-service to 'positive criticism', i.e. making positive suggestions, but I'm not sure that negative criticism isn't more valuable. In the end, the play and writer will be stronger if the writer finds the answer him/herself. It may actually be more helpful to say, 'Why is this scene set in the dark?' rather than, 'I think you should set this scene in the light.' 'Why does Mavis enter so late in Act 2?' will encourage the author to explain and clarify the ideas, whereas 'I think Mavis should enter sooner' may put the author on the defensive. Alternatively, your suggestions may be accepted all too eagerly because it's great to relax and let someone else do the ghastly work of writing for you. A good writer knows that a work of art is a totality, vertically and horizontally, a process of discovery as well as creation. Alterations may well be needed, but the writer must weigh every suggestion (his/her own and other people's), against complex, intellectual and intuitive considerations. The writer may well be unable to give a coherent answer to all your questions at first. S/he may indeed have to search through the text like anyone else. Authors often forget why they did something, but at some earlier point they may well have had a perfectly valid reason for doing it; the process of creation is often layered. If you impose your own creative pattern by saying, 'Wouldn't it be great if they were all Hussars?' you may be tearing a great hole in a series of patterns which are not yet clear to you and which the author has virtually forgotten, but which are an extremely important part of the play. Of course, finally, a good deal of positive suggestions may be made, but watch out: it's a great temptation to meddle in someone else's creation.

This period of working together with the author to refine the play is even more important than with a normal professional production. It can be very hard to alter a community play once it is in production because so many people may be affected and disappointed. Try to cut and rewrite before casting and rehearsal. As a final check, we have sometimes found it helpful to have a quiet, private play-reading with a small group of experienced actors doubling up the parts – their reactions are often very revealing.

Allow time for consultation and rewriting. Resist the temptation to produce interim scripts before the final complete version is ready. If you are having people read the script themselves rather than a play-reading, time may well be short and there will be pressure on you to get out some form of script. We have made this mistake on two occasions and it cost extra effort and money. In one case the earlier version was not liked and led to tensions in the town. Had we waited, people might have been more positive towards the play and been saved anxiety.

THE WRITER IN REHEARSAL

Many directors don't like writers in rehearsal. This is because the director lacks confidence: s/he knows that the writer knows more than anyone else about the play, which gives him or her enormous authority with actors, so the director may lose 'authority'. There is a danger that an irresponsible or stupid writer may make the director's job difficult by arguing with the director in front of the actors (though this is perfectly acceptable and possible if the atmosphere at rehearsal is good and the director confident), or by allowing him/herself to be used by a difficult actor so that the director is made to look incompetent and foolish.

I welcome writers in rehearsal. They have an absolute right to be present at rehearsals of their own plays. I would be happy to have them at every rehearsal except that I find it more valuable to have them coming just from time to time and keeping an objective eye on things. I welcome them precisely because they do know more about the play than I. The director's skills are in discovering moves, controlling pace, handling actors so that they give of their best, etc. These are not the skills of the writer, though s/he may have suggestions to make. The director has to interpret the text theatrically, and to do this you have to understand it. Time and again a writer has clarified a point for me and everything has fallen into place. At the same time the writer can be shown in rehearsal that something is not working, and be persuaded to alter it.

In working with a writer on a community play the problems are similar to those with any other production. You must find out how skilled and flexible the writer is in talking to other people. S/he has to find out how much s/he can trust you as regards not monkeying about with the play. It's probably best to have an agreement with the writer that to begin with they only speak to the cast through you, until you discover how well you work together. The writer has a secondary job of encouraging and supporting. S/he must encourage people in general terms and should exude satisfaction and *bonhomie* in relating to the actors. In private the writer may protest vigorously to the director, who should listen carefully. This is the price the director pays for asking the writer to be quiet in rehearsal. Once trust is established between them and if the atmosphere is confident and good, then it will very likely be easy to allow the writer to speak fairly freely if s/he disagrees with an actor or the director, but the writer must always be ready to react to 'stop' signals from the director. Maybe the actor has a problem the writer doesn't know about. The writer must remember that it's now the director's responsibility to bring the play to a successful production and while paying close attention to everything the writer says, the director must decide on the allocation of time and energy.

It's enormously refreshing to have writers come to rehearsal and put in new ideas. All the best writers I have worked with have been both tactful and experienced in their relationship with me as a director, and it's very encouraging to have a chirpy but critical writer at your side. Howard Barker, particularly, is an expert at judging the correct moment to drop in a fresh, key idea.

CONTRACTS

The company which commissions a play and mounts the first production will have certain financial rights if the play transfers or is produced elsewhere within a specific time. There are also various other rights and obligations which should be set down in black and white. This is extremely important, as quite large sums of money could be involved. Any writer of standing will have an agent and all agents are on the side of the writer and holding their corner firmly. This is quite as it should be, but it means that you must have professional advice in drawing up the contract.

Payment

The Arts Council supports new writing on certain conditions. You should obtain their booklet, *New Writing*, from the ACGB Drama Department. Your local regional arts association may also support professional writing. These two funding sources have enabled us to raise our commissioning fees to writers, in our time, quite dramatically. We now pay £1,000 on commission and £1,000 on delivery (plus VAT), together with around £500 for subsistence and travel during the whole period. The latter should not necessarily be automatic. You may like to ask the writer to submit an expense claim. These figures are independent of royalties. We pay a standard royalty of $7\frac{1}{2}$ per cent. Bear in mind that the writer may be eligible for more money if you apply for a Royalty Supplement Guarantee from the Arts Council (details also in *New Writing*). There is a temptation to forget VAT, but it may sometimes amount to a quite substantial sum – and it won't be covered by the ACGB grant. There is now pressure to raise fees to a level comparable with those paid by provincial repertory theatres.

Delivery dates

You need to allow 3 weeks for rewrites and 3 weeks for reproduction and binding, and have the scripts ready for distribution at the public reading, which will take place about a week before casting begins. Thus you need the final draft of the master script at least 7 weeks before casting. Writers are *always* late in delivery so allow extra time. If you have to start casting on 1 June ask for the script by 1 March and have this written into the contract. If you really do get the script by that date it will allow you to introduce some preparatory work on the text into the pre-rehearsal workshops.

Talk through the dates with the playwright at the earliest stage. The writer may have other commitments which will make delivery difficult, they may be nervous and want to make extra time for themselves, or an agent may try and make time for a writer. If the writer can't promise to deliver in time you may be prepared to take a risk on delivery or you may prefer to commission another writer. Either way, look at the problem clearly. You really cannot cast without a script (some authors will try and make you do it with a list of names and descriptions).

HISTORY AS ART

You may need to warn people that a play is not a historical thesis. It is history shaped by art to tell a story, make a point, reveal a truth. People tend to expect when they share a memory or a piece of research that it will appear on the stage exactly as they tell you. Quite apart from the impossibility of two people seeing the story in the same way there will actually be a great number of gaps. No one can know everything about someone else's life, even about the key points in it, and if we did know everything we couldn't put it all in. A selection would have to be made and this is where the difficulty arises. History may be all the facts as we know them; art is a selection and organisation of facts so as to present a sequence of images, having a relationship with each other which leads to a climax or resolution. The playwright must present the facts as s/he sees them in a certain relationship and must imagine what happens in the empty spaces. People may have to be educated that there cannot be total historical accuracy, that it doesn't exist, and if it did exist it would still have to be reshaped to make a play. We have sometimes made this point in general newspaper articles and have used the following as a paragraph in a newsletter:

> Commissioning a play is not like asking an architect to build a house. The writer is creating a work of art which begins in a sense to have an inner spirit or life of its own which may very well affect the final shape of the play. We need to be careful not to build up a picture in our minds of what the play will be like. Sheila's play is bound to be different and it is bound to surprise us.

David Edgar, well aware of the dangers, covered himself in the two opening speeches of *Entertaining Strangers*:

FIRST PERSON.   Good evening. My name is — and I'm a
                        real person. These are photocopies of
                        various documents concerned with the
                        characters in the play you are about to

see. In fact, we know a great deal about them from newspaper reports and certificates and censuses and wills, and even old family notebooks full of legend and rumour. But of course none of these pieces of paper tells us how they spoke or what made them laugh or, for that matter, cry. So we don't know if everything that happens in our story actually happened but we know it could have done.

SECOND PERSON.   Hallo. My name is — and I too am a real person. And these are copies of a lot of sermons, pamphlets, monographs and tracts by or about another central character, who was also as real as they come and of whose output this is but a fraction. Which gives us a great deal of information about him, but even so in everything he wrote or was written of him, there is hardly anything about the most desperate and tragic happening in his life, which we portray towards the end. So how we treat *that* too can't be how we know it happened, just how it could have done.

THEATRICAL JUSTIFICATION FOR CROWDS

It is not difficult, and very effective, to set up crowd scenes involving large numbers as when audience and actors become a church congregation or take part in a courtroom scene or a cricket match. But large numbers of actors and the promenade form present an even subtler opportunity which has been identified by Howard Barker: how to create scenes for large numbers of people in uniquely *theatrical* terms. I would quote as successful examples: the scene in *The Poor Man's Friend* when the ghosts of those who have been hanged with Bridport rope come back through the audience trying to justify themselves, whingeing, blathering, blustering; Moule's nightmare in *Entertaining Strangers* when he is supported and carried, tormented, writhing and trembling, all over the church. The scene in *The Western Women* when the women gradually find confidence and a voice finally demanding, with almost ecstatic vehemence, the right to share danger with the men.

5
The professional core

Once, when giving a pep talk during a 'mid-rehearsal sag' (see p. 230), I defined the difference between amateurs and professionals. Amateurs are lovers of art: they do it for love. Professionals are those who have professed, have taken a religious vow. This is high-flown, but it has grains of truth.

There are several advantages in using professionals:

1 They are trained and have learnt the discipline of their art.
2 They have (or should have) measured themselves against the highest standards.
3 Their training and talent give them the freedom to be bold and innovatory if they wish. Equally, it allows them to be extremely economical and to eliminate. It is usually the mark of an amateur designer that they try and put/leave too much in.
4 They have a full-time commitment and responsibility to the work. The play is their main job, not something they do in their spare time. This is an enormous relief when you have to consider and work round the private lives and work commitments of so many other people.

Professionals must be as good as possible at their job. Inexperienced 'professional' directors should not be encouraged to have a go. I have known an instance where a Regional Arts Association, asked to recommend a suitable director, totally misjudged its opportunity and responsibility and suggested a lighting person who thought he would like to try his hand. The result was ludicrous and in a way tragic for it betrayed the amateurs and shamed professionals. Those who made the recommendation were wholly to blame. Directing a community play demands and deserves greater experience, not less. (Small-scale amateur productions, like small-scale professional productions, may legitimately be used by those seeking experience.)

The ability to relate well to people is not reckoned a necessary quality in most practising artists but is naturally very important in a community play. We find that, given the right attitude, a professional who has lived in the town for several months, working intensively and warmly alongside hundreds of people becomes just as much part of the community as someone who may have lived there many years without bothering to relate very much to other people or help the town.

THE ROLE OF PRODUCER/MANAGER

In the professional theatre the producer, or manager as they are sometimes called, is finally responsible for all the financial and administrative organisation of the production. Since the producer also commissions the writer, director and professional staff, s/he is also indirectly responsible for the artistic side of the production as well. It's a job demanding strong nerves, steadiness and tact, and since the producer has to know when to intervene, a little experience does not come amiss.

The producer's chief day-to-day responsibilities are: enabling the artists to function so that they give of their best, and administering the show to production. To a very limited extent, insofar as s/he has knowledge and experience, the producer may give the director the benefit of their views on artistic matters, but the director is not bound to accept them. The understanding is that particular artists have been retained because that they know their job and must be allowed to get on with it. More than that, they must be supported in getting on with it.

In CTT productions I, in effect, always filled this role, with the support of the Organising Committee, even when I myself was directing. It may well, however, fall to the Organising Committee and perhaps particularly its Chair.

The producer's most important relationship is with the director. The producer must remember that the director has an enormous responsibility for presenting the show on time and to the highest possible standard. Directors must be able to be confident that their base is steady. This will free them to put all their energy where it is vital to the production. So the producer, while tactfully and carefully keeping an eye on the director (e.g. controlling him or her if s/he wants to go over budget), must be extremely reassuring and supportive.

While relating warmly to everyone in the show the producer must remain objective and above all never seek to encourage any division in the production team, or any disloyalty to the director. It may well be that, given artistic temperament, strain and dissension may appear and the producer will be appealed to as arbitrator. In such a case the producer must behave with great tact, supportiveness and caution, certainly helping to sort things out, but trying not to appear to be taking sides or stirring things up.

In judging which course of action to take in any situation it helps to bear the ultimate aim in mind: you want the production to be ready on time, to be an enormous success and everyone to have a great time. Make your decisions taking into account all the personalities involved and the great pressure which they are under. Take action according to the simple yardstick: what will most help the play?

The producer certainly has final authority, but it should be so confident as to be worn lightly and not provoke people. If authority has to be exercised it should be done in terms of guidance, discussion and suggestion rather than outright orders. As a producer handling directors I have frequently given way on minor matters to gain a greater point, or carried the can because I knew my shoulders were broad enough and I was not under the same immediate strain as the director.

TERMS OF EMPLOYMENT

Fees and wages

CTT has paid its professional employees in three of the following ways:

Paid by fee (no National Insurance) director; designer; musical director; lighting person (if paid); stage manager.

Salaried play officer (if paid); assistants of all kinds (if paid); MSC personnel

Unpaid voluntary (usually on DHSS, which means they must be available to take up paid employment elsewhere should it be offered) play officer; some assistants and/or trainees.

The figures given under individual job descriptions (see below) indicate the level of salary that Colway Theatre Trust community plays were paying in the last quarter of 1985. They represent reasonably good salaries in fringe and provincial terms, but low salaries in national terms. They are of course negotiable up or down. But CTT is trying to employ the best possible people and these salaries may represent some sacrifice on the part of those individuals, indeed, a kind of exploitation. People should be paid what they are worth.

Contracts
Writer See p. 142.

Letter contracts All paid employees are entitled to a written note of the terms of their engagements.† This is much less complicated than it sounds. CTT issues simple letter contracts with job descriptions, length of engagement, including particularly when the employee is expected to start, whether they must stay for the production and cleaning up, etc., how and when they are paid. Letter contracts may include terms under which the employee may be dismissed or given notice, if appropriate, together with certain general terms (e.g. all keys must be returned at the end of the engagement). The best course might well be to have a solicitor prepare a general letter contract which you then alter and amend according to specific needs. CTT has sometimes been lax about contracts, but they are a wise precaution: however good the feeling between you, it's best to have the chief points covered in writing. This may save much vagueness and bad feeling.
Verbal contracts In legal terms these are not worth the paper they are written on, as Sam Goldwyn might have said. They are simply so that any unpaid assistants know where they stand. Since professional assistants are probably on the DHSS anyway, it's important to remember that they must be available for paid work if something suitable turns up.

† See Cotterell, Leslie E., *Performance* (Eastbourne, John Offord Ltd, 1984), for advice on the legal aspects of employment.

JOB DESCRIPTIONS
Director
As Director of Colway Theatre and, in effect, at the same time, manager and producer of the plays, I also took on a large administrative role, virtually organising the whole structure as laid out in this book, as well as attending 90 per cent of all committee meetings. However, we have occasionally employed outside directors, who were responsible only for getting on a play in the normal way, while I have filled the role of producer/manager.

If you are using an independent director, then it is wise to engage him or her early and possibly involve them in commissioning a writer. The better the writer, the more interested they will be in who will direct. An experienced, professional director with a known track record is a guarantee of quality, and vice versa.

You will want the director to liaise with and advise the Organising Committee on every aspect of setting up the play, including choice of venue. The director will talk with the writer regarding the play. If there is to be a large musical input, there will probably be early discussions with the director, musical director and writer about how much music there will be, etc. and indeed the whole nature of the work. The director will continue to talk to the writer at such intervals as both may think appropriate, and will read interim drafts as required. When the writer delivers the final draft, the writer and director will work together for the improvement of the text as necessary.

The director will advise on the choice of designer, musical director, stage manager and the whole structure of the professional team. Throughout the work, the director will be responsible for these people, discussing their contribution and guiding them in their work.

You will want the director to advise on the structure of the acting workshops, perhaps also suggest names of tutors, etc., and to be prepared to take some workshops him/herself.

The director is responsible with the author for casting the play, but will need help from the play officer and possibly the musical director. The director is responsible for preparing rehearsal schedules and organising rehearsals, and has overall responsibility for every aspect of rehearsal, and for bringing the play to performance by an agreed date.

The director should be prepared to advise and discuss publicity, programmes, poster design, etc., and to help with publicity (giving interviews, etc.) as required. S/he should also be prepared to serve on committees connected with the play as mutually agreed with the Organising Committee.

The director will have overall responsibility for the running of the professional team and for every other aspect of the production, technical and artistic, except financial responsibility. However, the director will be expected to encourage all departments to keep within agreed budgets.

If the director is to be paid a total of £3,500, Colway Theatre Trust would normally pay £875 at the following times: on signature of the letter contract; on casting; on the day of the first rehearsal; at a point

midway through rehearsal; and on the opening night of the production. (See also rehearsals, page 211.)

Co-director

This may well be the drama teacher of the school, but this could mean
less commitment in terms of time and energy than with a professional.
CTT has also used very experienced directors who wanted to learn
specifically about community plays (e.g. Joan Mills, Jon Oram). This
is an area where there is great scope for development and learning.
They must obviously have some experience as a director, capable of
taking rehearsals on their own and generally standing in for the
director of the play. The co-director is frequently in charge of the fair
which may include organising side-shows, small performances and
scenarios. The co-director attends all committees, except possibly
fundraising. S/he is needed for the period of rehearsal and probably
performance (14 weeks). If paid: £980–£1,400.

Play officer

A full-time commitment. A comparatively recent role, but of great
value in large productions. If there is no play officer, then the job must
be shared amongst a number of volunteers. Ideally, the play officer
starts work as soon as the play office is opened. It's the kind of job
which develops and alters according to the energy and talent of the
person involved. It is an extremely complicated and arduous organising and executive position and it would be hard to say what are its
limits beyond the fact that the play officer is not concerned with the
artistic side of the play. Essentially, the play officer runs the play
office, including handling mail, answering the phone, coping with
queries, etc., keeping card indexes and lists, co-ordinating information regarding people and resources, helping to organise and service
committees, getting the newsletter together and organising its distribution, initiating discussion regarding play packs for schools and
helping to prepare them, helping to set up street events and projects
and clearing up after them. The play officer may oversee the work of
the MSC team. S/he is responsible for an enormous amount of contact
and development work before the play begins and thereafter helps
organise rehearsals and the hundreds and thousands of problems that
crop up during production. The play officer could also be the actual
administrator of the play.

The play officer should have authority to spend small sums of
money for petty cash up to an agreed amount but must be prepared to

produce receipts for all purchases. S/he may be voluntary, paid by the play management, or by the DHSS: we have had all three, and mixtures of them.

Designer

Prior to the start of rehearsal, you will ask the designer to relate to organisations in the town with a view to involving them in projects connected with the play. This may or may not be possible, according to how much time the designer can give you. S/he may not be able to start until just before the production goes into rehearsal. In any case, it is the designer's job to design the costumes, sets and properties for the play and to organise, supervise and help in the making of them: to be responsible for procuring materials, either buying (with the authority of the Organising Committee), borrowing, hiring or receiving as gifts; to collect, store safely and return promptly and in good condition any items borrowed or hired; to organise and supervise the dyeing and treatment of any materials as may be necessary; to organise and run the costume workshop and to supervise any assistants, helpers or dressers; to organise, supervise and help with wardrobe care, storage and setting out costumes for performances; to organise a dress parade, as far as possible in good time for the technical rehearsal and in consultation with the director; to organise the cleaning, washing and repair of costumes and their return in good condition to wherever is appropriate; to help and advise the director of the play and the Organising Committee in any other way which may be connected with design. You may wish to state precisely at which dates the designer will join the production and when they will leave, and if they are to have any breaks in the middle of the process.

The designer should have a float and be able to spend up to an agreed sum without first obtaining prior authority. They should of course produce receipts for any expenditure.

If you are paying the designer a fee of £1,750, you may prefer to divide it into four or five instalments, according to whether you wish the designer to stay for the production or not. Bear in mind that there is a great responsibility for seeing that costumes, sets, properties, etc. are returned clean and in good condition to wherever they should go, within a few days of the end of the performance. If this is not the designer's responsibility, then it must be covered by someone else. (See also pp. 160–165.)

Musical Director

You will want the musical director to be prepared to discuss any aspect of the music with the writer and designer at any stage while the play is in preparation, and to compose such music as the play may require, bearing in mind that it is a community play and may need a special approach both in rehearsal and composing. You will probably ask the musical director to take one or more music workshops prior to rehearsals and you may want him/her to help with casting if there are special musical requirements. The musical director must rehearse the music and attend for rehearsals as the director requires, by mutual arrangement (the musical director, being part-time, may have other commitments which s/he has to work around). The musical director, with the help of the play officer, may be responsible for finding the people to play in the orchestra and is responsible for rehearsing the orchestra. You will probably require the musical director to conduct all the performances unless other arrangements are made. The musical director should agree that certain excerpts from the music can be used for publicity purposes (e.g. short extracts on television, etc.). If the musical director is to be paid a total fee of £1,000, then it may be appropriate to divide it into four instalments: £250 payable on signature; £250 at first rehearsal; £250 at the first and last performance. (See also p. 165.)

A stage manager

There is nothing to touch a really good, professional stage manager but they are as hard to find as good designers. The job is so important, and carries such responsibility that you need someone whom you trust and you know works hard and efficiently. I have used intelligent assistants in the role. They don't have the touch of a professional but I'd far rather work with an amateur whom I trusted than stage manager whose work I didn't know and who turned out badly. Sometimes you may get help from the local amateur dramatic society team but I have the impression that some amateur stage managers are very exclusive – a touch of the old siege mentality. On the other hand, *ad hoc* technical teams who come together for the play – and may indeed stay together after it – have given amazing help.

SM Responsibilities
General
The stage manager has overall responsibility to the director for setting up all the practical and technical aspects of the show, for running the performance. When the show is over the stage manager is responsible for clearing up and returning any items which may have been borrowed (apart from costumes), and for locking up and unlocking all venues.

The stage manager is responsible for the *book of the play* in which every change of text, character, scene order, etc., is written at the time it is made. This means that by the end of rehearsal there will be a complete master-text. This is important in working on a new play. The book of the play may, or may not, also be the *prompt copy* in which the stage manager lists every technical, lighting and sound cue, etc., and any other information which s/he needs to run the show; also prop lists, etc. Some directors will require all moves to be noted in the prompt copy. The Stage Manager or deputy attends all rehearsals.

During rehearsal period
The stage manager is responsible for:
1 Distribution of rehearsal schedules, seeing that copies go to other interested parties (e.g. designer, school caretaker).
2 Liaising with whoever is responsible for the building where rehearsals take place; if given a key the stage manager is responsible for its safekeeping and for locking up the building.
3 Calling all rehearsals and checking on those who have not turned up; checking rehearsal diaries after each rehearsal.
4 Organisation of rehearsal room including marking up the ground plan with masking tape, and for reinstatement of the room after rehearsal.
5 Safekeeping of sweets, Mars bars, etc., and their sale to cast. Provision of refreshments, tea, etc., is a stage management responsibility during conventional productions but is too large a task in community plays. However, the stage manager or assistants should check that refreshments will be provided in big rehearsals.
6 Keeping the designer informed of any changes in characters, etc., which may affect design.
7 Prompting: reading in for cast not present at rehearsal.
8 Properties: their finding, collecting, borrowing, making,

buying and safe storage. Substitute props and sound effects.

9 Building and/or getting together the set (in consultation with
the designer), including transport, and if necessary painting,
stripping, dressing, etc.; liaising with/helping carpenters,
etc., who may be building the set (again an area shared with
the designer).

Production week

1 Preparing the hall – i.e. clearing it; sometimes overemphatic
curtains need to be turned so that their quieter linings show
(you still need the curtains for blackout); removing and
safely storing any stage curtains; remembering whether any
doors need to be removed from their hinges, etc.

2 Borrowing a scaffolding tower, ladder, lorry (a driver with a
heavy goods vehicle licence may be needed).

3 Organising erection of scaffolding, remembering that lights
probably cannot be hung until scaffolding is in position.
Covering scaffolding seating surface with carpet, laying
strips of gaffer/heavy coloured adhesive tape or other to
mark out seats, checking that any dangerous ends, etc. of
scaffolding are protected.

4 Arranging light masks over doorways.

5 Organising storage and safety of props and any set when not
in use during the performance.

6 Seeing that the demands of the fire officer are met.

7 Rehearsing set changes with the director.

8 Arranging for any notices to be made and hung (e.g. 'NO
SMOKING'); we also have a large notice prominently
displayed near the entrance: 'THIS IS A PROMENADE
PERFORMANCE, IT HAS BEEN DESIGNED TO BE
SEEN FROM THE CENTRE OF THE FLOOR WHERE
YOU WILL ENJOY IT MOST.'

9 Security of hall and any other rooms in use.

Fair
Organising sellers in and out.

Performance

1 Checking all the cast have signed in and taking appropriate
steps to cope with absentees.

2 Calling: half and hour, quarter, five minutes, beginners.
3 Running the show.
4 Sweeping and tidying up after the performance – with help from the cast.

After the Production

SM is responsible for reinstating the venue including dismantling scaffolding, cleaning etc., and for the safe return of any borrowed items. This is a heavy task but there will be much willing help from the cast and others. The stage manager generally has a small float which s/he may spend without further authority; receipts must, as in every other case, be provided for all purchases.

Salary

Current Equity rates for stage managers are £171 per week so it's unlikely you will be able to afford one for the whole rehearsal period. You can compromise by having a copper-bottomed, diamond-plated professional for $6\frac{1}{2}$ weeks, i.e. for 4 weeks before production and 3 days clearing up afterwards, or you can get someone less experienced, and therefore cheaper, for a longer period.

Lighting person

We have generally used professional lighting people. The advantages of using professionals are: skill, flexibility and full-time commitment. They are usually very co-operative and good about involving amateurs and will frequently train them in how to light the show, etc. In practice, the lighting person generally seems to acquire two unpaid assistants, probably enthusiastic sixth formers, as volunteers who will help during the show. The lighting person usually needs a good deal of help in setting up and dismantling the lights, and for standing in during plotting of cues; help which is easily found since it is for a limited period and people like to learn technical skills.

There is an unexpected disadvantage in using professional lighting people: since they are accustomed to having a great deal of equipment at their disposal professionals recognise only too well the difficulties of the situation and may oversimplify the lighting, using too few, too strong lamps, etc. On the other hand, amateur lighting people, who are used to lighting shows under considerable difficulty and who know their job, will very often rise to the challenge and attempt the impossible. If they are attached to a school or amateur dramatics society they may also have quite large resources at their disposal.

Lighting is not merely a technical matter of hanging the lights and switching them off and on. The play needs to be lit sympathetically; lights can be operated dead on cue and yet be intrusive and out of key with the performances. A gifted lighting person can feel the play so precisely and truly that the lights seem to breathe with the production. One of the best lighting people we ever had was the physics master at the local school who usually lit local amateur and school productions. It may be that people who spend their lives amidst the technical and scientific feel a yearning to express themselves creatively. Certainly, the man in question not only took great trouble, but was an artist with his lights, totally unselfish in the service of the play.

The lighting person will be required to: work through the script with the director discussing cues, style, etc.; attend some rehearsals, usually the large general rehearsals and/or run-throughs so as to get the feel of the production, begin to sense out problems, etc.; produce a lighting plot and talk it through with the director; find the necessary lamps and other equipment by hiring or borrowing, within an agreed budget; collect and safely store any such equipment; lay any cables and hang the lights as soon as possible after the play gets into its venue; light the play and perfect the plot, cues, effects, etc. through the technical and dress rehearsals and at other times; operate the lighting-board during performances; dismantle all the lighting, etc., and be responsible for its safe and speedy return. The lighting person will probably also be responsible for recorded sound effects.

If paid: total fee £500. Half fee on an agreed date; half at last performance or when goods have been returned.

Assistants to the director

Must be full time. This is an excellent training area for young, enthusiastic professionals, who want to learn about the work. If they are bright and intelligent there are enormous opportunities in such large productions. They attend almost all rehearsals and are responsible for a great deal of liaison work and organisation, e.g. keeping the designer and others informed of any cast changes, checking the spelling of names for programmes, seeing that tea is available, organising children's transport. They will be responsible too for following up non-attenders at rehearsals. A great deal of their work is shared with the co-director, play officer and stage manager. Assistants will be required to read in for people who are not there and very often take small acting and singing rehearsals. They may help with the fair. If they are skilful at PR they may well help the harassed director cope with the media. They may attend all committee meetings and share minute-taking with the play officer. They will probably be attached to stage management or design for the period of production and, since they are generally very enthusiastic, may also have a small part in the play. They are needed for rehearsals, production and the clearing-up period.

They may receive a small salary of about £70 per week or be paid by the DHSS.

Assistant designers

We have found that we must have at least one full-time, paid assistant, usually a maker. This is preferably a professional, or semi-professional seamstress. S/he not only fills gaps in the making, but will also help organise the work, being responsible for helping to organise all the voluntary aid, checking work in and out, talking to people who come to the workshop, etc. Required through the period of rehearsal and probably as wardrobe person during performances. The designer's job is so heavy, s/he may need a second assistant.

Probably paid, since it would be suicidal to lose them. £70 per week.

Assistant stage managers

At least one full-time ASM is needed, paid by the play management or DHSS, or a volunteer. This is an area where one is grateful that professional friends will often turn up to lend a hand just before production.

Paid or unpaid. If paid: £70 per week.

MSC SCHEMES

CTT makes increasing use of the MSC schemes to help with secretarial work in relating to the community and in working on the plays themselves. The greater proportion of our funding now comes from the MSC – more than from any other organisation. The MSC, while applying strict conditions of employment, pays basic salaries (at present £69 per week) with a support figure per person of £440. Within the salary structure you can move about, i.e. you can employ someone part time and pay them say, £35, and add the other £34 on to another full-time worker, who will thus receive £103 per week. You can also top up the salaries out of your own funds if you wish. There is a considerable amount of book-keeping involved, but the larger schemes may also have their own administrator/supervisor. Ask at your local MSC Community Programmes Office for details. Schemes are constantly being developed and new ones introduced.

Although MSC schemes are a godsend to many community organisations, there are difficulties. The conditions of unemployment for entering an MSC scheme are very strict and, in a rural area, even one where unemployment is high, we sometimes have difficulty in finding people of the right calibre. Having found them, they receive a year's excellent training but then under the conditions of the scheme are forced to move on and we have to start again from scratch.

DESIGN AND DESIGNERS

Three things give a production its essential quality: script, director and designer. Weakness in any one of these will fundamentally affect the production. It may perhaps be a temptation to underestimate the work of designers, to think that any reasonably talented artist can do it. But theatre design is a very special skill. Even in the relatively wide field of professional theatre it is not easy to find a really fine theatre designer. In a sense, their work is a conflict in terms: they have to have the vision and drive of fine artists but be ready to find their satisfaction in sublimating their own ego to the interests of the play. They also need experience and knowledge of the demands of theatre and the technicalities and resources of set and costume making. In addition, community plays need makers who will think in terms of the community, who have sufficient modesty and tact, and an outgoing personality, so that they don't try and do all the work themselves but share it out; who can organise and enthuse local helpers, as well as demonstrating and explaining.

The work of designing a community play is so arduous and demanding that you must have full-time professional help, but the task is so huge that it would be impossible for a designer and one or two assistants, however dedicated, to do all the design and making. By its size and nature the work must be shared, but the designer needs the temperament to cope. In Newbury, they commissioned a professional designer who delivered the sketches and then left the amateurs to get on with it. In my opinion, admirable though the designs may have been, this is professional involvement which is nearly meaningless. The professional must work alongside local people and be prepared to discuss colours and dyes, cut and construction: to relate to local skills and maintain a good relationship with the community.

CTT has tended to use fairly young designers who have had some experience on the fringe but who are looking for a chance to get up the next rung of the ladder, and to widen their experience. Many art colleges have schools of design and all have end-of-year showings of their students' work; you can often find young designers who have talent and some experience. There are also those who are assistants to older, more experienced designers and obviously keen to do their own production. We give these young people every possible support, but finally the responsibility is theirs. What generally happens is that they suddenly perceive the scale of the undertaking and realise that they must use dozens of people to get the job done. Guts and personality get them through. It's a capacity-building experience.

We have sometimes used older and more experienced designers, and the sheer terror that grips every designer at some point on such a project has occasionally turned them outwards to seek help from their professional friends; borrowing costumes, etc. from theatres all over the country. This is not what the work is about: not only are the amateurs short-changed, but it's surprisingly expensive, involving transport, insurance, cleaning.

Design meetings

Dozens of people will have filled in the play leaflets, saying they want to help make costumes, do technical work, etc. With the help of the play officer and assistants, everyone on this list should be contacted and invited to a special meeting immediately rehearsals have started. At this meeting the designer explains the nature of the work and how it will be organised. Those attending should also be asked to find more help(there really cannot be too much). In Dorchester, we had a public 'open evening', where the whole complex of workshops was on show, with plenty of people available, ready to explain/take names/suggestions, etc.

Costume workshop

You need a minimum of about 250 square feet (and this is very small) with heating, tables and chairs, mirror, running water, toilet, changing space, electrical points, etc.

The costume workshop should be as near the centre of town as possible. You want somewhere where people will drop in readily to collect and deliver materials, work, etc., and you want to make them welcome and give them coffee, so that they will stay and chat and be drawn in. However, this can be extraordinarily distracting for the designer who may be in the middle of a piece of work. There need to be other people around, assistants, or people from the community, who can take on the important work of giving callers time: talking, explaining the work, thanking them for bringing materials, etc.

The costume workshop also needs to be central to prevent the design team becoming isolated. This can easily happen, partly because of the personality of many designers themselves, but also because the production team will be very busy and, unless they have reason to go to the costume workshop, contacts may falter and this can allow strains to develop.

Wet workshop

Space for dyeing and drying of wet materials, somewhere where you can make a mess. Beg or buy an old second-hand washing machine.

Over the years we have been through varied experiences with design and costume workshops and are now convinced that it's best to try and find sufficient space for everyone (i.e. play office, stage manager and design) to be under the same roof. In Ottery St Mary, we were fortunate enough to get several rooms in the town council offices, in the heart of the town. Here we had the play office, costume workshop, and a third room doubled as storage space and for meetings. In Dorchester, we had half an old school, within yards of the church where we were to perform, with plenty of space for wet and dry costume workshops, storage, play office, stage manager's office, etc. If you can manage this sort of confluence, then the whole problem becomes simpler: the place is always full of people who are ready to welcome callers and explain the work; the designer is only round the corner from the director and so on. Since there is always lots of activity, someone who comes to be fitted for a costume may find themselves painting a bench, typing some rewrites or making tea.

Sets

It's an enormous task getting out 150 or more costumes and organising other people to make them. Sometimes the set gets neglected unless the designer is very set-minded. There is never much money. If the set is behind, you are going to have to get somebody else in at the last moment and juggle the budget. For this reason, and because I prefer economy ('maximum of effect with minimum of means'), I prefer to keep shows technically simple: there is not enough money, skill or resources to match the glossy, close-up perfection of TV design or the elaboration of West End spectaculars; but then that is not what the work is about. We are always prepared to build but, where we can, we use the portable butterfly stages which can be borrowed from most schools. The attraction of these stages is that, having dimensions of 8 × 4 × 1 or 2 feet high, you can build them up into any size stage you want, and when folded, then can be wheeled through a doorway. However, to transport them you need a drop-tail van which allows you to wheel the stage on board. It takes four strong people to lift one.

You'll never have much difficulty in finding technical and carpentering help, though you may have to drum up more from time to time. People can become amazingly enthusiastic and attached to what they are doing. In Dorchester, the technical team made a movable stage 12 × 8 × 4 feet high. With minor cunning alterations it became in turn a coach, a great cauldron for boiling infected clothing, a cart and a haywain. It could also be dismantled and stored. The team took tremendous pride in their masterpiece and used to come to rehearsal to pat their stage and see how it was getting on, revelling in the appreciation and admiration it aroused in us all.

The economy of this stage – the way it could be used in many ways, was very much to my taste. I much prefer simple sets, with perhaps a few three-dimensional objects (chairs, tables) which are as exactly chosen as possible. The banks of alert faces on the scaffolding then become part of the setting. I don't even mind the school hall, hardly glimpsed because of the bright lights, but still there and reminding us of the layers of commitment behind the play.

However, in Restormel (set design by Jim Still) the School Hall was elegantly transformed and the walls and ceiling entirely covered in rough, dark slats made from orange boxes. In Ottery (design by Sue Dart) there was an ambitious environmental design, which hid all the boring bits of the hall, mostly achieved with dyed cloth. In Worcester (design by Chris Croswell) the subject of the play was 'Woodbine Willy', the Reverend Studdert-Kennedy, and the play was performed in his own church, a faintly ugly red and black brick building, with the same energy that Woodbine Willy must himself once have had. It had a fairly elaborate set in black and white, backing into a series of niches. The Dorchester community play was also performed in a church which was relevant to the subject, but here we used hardly any setting. The audience was banked at each end, cutting off the chancel, but above, catching reflected glints of light, was the richly carved screen, and over the whole soared the pillars and vaulting of the roof. It was not a particularly beautiful church but perhaps more interesting than a school hall and the setting became charged with significance as the play developed.

I find that the more experienced the designer, the more enthusiastically he or she reduces the setting to its essence. In Dorchester, Di Seymour, with her great experience, wit and sensitivity, produced a very few, exceptionally strong three-dimensional images which gave the play an extraordinary style. The hardest thing a designer has to learn is what to throw away and what to keep. The danger of using an inexperienced designer, albeit even a professional, is that they may neglect set design and so find themselves in trouble at the end, or attempt too much.

Appeal for materials*

Certain materials you will have to buy and the designer or the town will know where is cheapest, but you not only want to keep costs down, you want to involve the community. Make an appeal for materials. You will get some of your best stuff this way. It will call for a good deal of cutting and dyeing, but it's a very effective way of involving people: when they give things they are committing themselves.

Shoes and Hats These cost money and are hard to fake. Try and build up a collection.

Measurement chart

We used to take measurements right through the first read-through, when we could be sure that virtually all the cast was there, but it's exhausting, can be distracting, and you don't always finish in time. We now issue a measurement chart at auditions and provide tape measures. People can either be measured then and there, or take the form away. The form is printed on two sides, male one side, female the other, so we don't have to worry about picking up the right one.

Keeping the designer in touch

The designer must of course have a full and accurate cast list with descriptions of characters, but there are inevitably changes, partly because the cast is so large: people drop in and out, we improvise in rehearsal, get fresh ideas for costumes from movement sessions, new interpretations, etc. This is always the case in any production, but with 150 characters or more, the designer's problem becomes enormously magnified. The designer must immediately be told when changes are made, and s/he has to have the temperament and be sufficiently organised to cope.

It's extremely important that the designer comes frequently to rehearsals to sense how things are going and to keep in touch with the actual process. It's the designer's responsibility and one that cannot be delegated.

Trip list

It is not a bad idea for the producer, director and designer to discuss a timetable or 'trip list' (e.g. 'All the men's costumes will be out for sewing by 8 February and then we shall start to cut the women's costumes', etc.). Such a list requires real thinking out and if the designer is inexperienced in working with such large numbers, it focuses the mind and will reassure both designer and director.

Costume parade

Should take place on 2 or 3 evenings – this avoids too much hanging about for the cast – and should be well in advance of the technical dress rehearsal. Thus it provides a time target for the designer and allows a little space for alterations or catching up, etc.

Dressers

Not many actors will need much help in dressing, but there should be people to keep order, set out and put away costumes, find lost items, repair damage, supply pins, hairgrips, inspect actors as they leave the dressing-room, etc. Actors must be taught to respect the costumes, hanging them up properly, checking them, etc.

Identification

Everything should be labelled and every hanger should have a label with all the articles of the costume listed on it, name of character/actor, etc.

MUSIC: COMPOSER/MUSICAL DIRECTOR

Music can provide both comment and emotional surge and release. To me a community play without music would be like eating on a diet. It also brings in a whole new section of the community.

The musical director, like all professionals working on a community play, must be especially aware of his/her opportunities and responsibilities. S/he should be extremely positive and encouraging, prepared to share skills, and have a very positive belief in the potential of everyone.

CTT has always used professional composers and musical directors except in the first play where we hadn't realised the immense possibilities of music. We use professionals because writing music for the theatre is a special skill, and we have hitherto managed to commission men (alas no women yet) who were experienced in the demands of music theatre. In Bridport we experimented with asking the school music teacher to work alongside the composer and to conduct the band. Although both parties were extremely generous, the partnership was a little uneasy since Rex Trevett, who has his own terrific big band, likes things to be written down and Andy Dickson, a hugely talented, professional musician who has done three shows for us, preferred to improvise and teach parts by ear. There were also slight problems with the amount of time Rex could give us. Quite justifiably he felt that there were limits. In the circumstances in which we have to work few professionals consider limits.

Like all artists, directors and designers included, composers can be blinkered. In dark moments it sometimes seems as if the professional team are behaving like race horses asked to pull a coal cart. Musicians sometimes appear to regard the play as an irritating and largely irrelevant interruption in the music. If not experienced in music theatre, the musical director may think that the music is not being sufficiently respected unless the play stops dead and we all stand and listen. For the same reason background, or 'incidental' music is not popular.

Everyone pulls for their corner and some of the most exciting moments in our productions have been musical: the 'traditional local tunes played with ravishing poignancy' as the Times Educational Supplement described Steve McNeff's music for The Tide; the huge chorus, celebratory yet ironical, 'It was well done! It was bloody well done!' at the end of The Poor Man's Friend; the rollicking 'Welcome to the Digby Tap!' by Nick Bye (a marvellous composer of good tunes); Gordon Jones's great rolling 'And this is England!' for Crediton; Nicholas Brace's music for The Western Women; and the dazed, whispered chorale as the people of Lyme realised that the long siege might be over.

6

Finance

WHAT THE PLAYS COST AND
HOW TO RAISE IT

The Reckoning (1978)

The Reckoning started from a minus base: there was no money. I managed to raise £1,350 from South-West Arts, Marks & Spencer, the school PTA and various other sources. The play cost £2,233.67. We gave 4 performances and took £878.22 from ticket sales and programmes, so emerging with a loss of £5. Costs were low because people were paid little or nothing. The designer, Carmel Collins, lived in my house. We both finally received fees of £250. This was hardly adequate pay for 14 weeks work on her part and 18 months on mine; it was simply a token acknowledgement that we were professionals. At this time, in my innocence, regarding Arts Council grants as a form of charity, I did not apply for a Writer's Award and so received nothing for the script. Costs were also low because Exeter University gave us a great deal of help with the lighting design, free loan of equipment and a stage management team. Medium Fair Theatre Company allowed us to duplicate scripts on their electric machine and their actors took part in the play at no charge to us. They also, via their charitable status, accepted money on our behalf.

As has been described, I now set up the Colway Theatre Trust as a charity. It is better to do this through a lawyer who understands the Charities Commission, otherwise it may take some time. We also began to receive funding from the Gulbenkian Foundation and the Carnegie Trust and, after two years, SWA began to give us annual funding. In budgeting these plays this background funding should be borne in mind. In 1984/5, our funding from SWA, which included their contribution to each play and help with paying the writer, was £20,000. This covered office and administrative expenditure, some travel, salaries for permanent staff and virtually all 'forward' work in setting up community plays. This was a low figure for the work which we undertook, but it is nevertheless a hidden cost of the plays themselves which must be remembered when budgeting from scratch.

The Tide (1980)

I raised much greater sums for *The Tide*, although I still had much to learn. Devon County Council gave £1,000; Seaton Town Council gave £50; the three schools involved gave £450 between them. I began to ask the town itself for money: £295 was raised in small sums by an appeal to local businesses, but I still did not know how or what to ask. *The Tide* was concerned with carpet-making; Axminster Carpets is a small and relatively prosperous firm. I went to see the managing director. 'How much do you want?' he asked. Very timidly, I said, '£25?' and he nearly fell off his chair in his delight to write out the cheque. *The Tide* was a much bigger undertaking and with this production we had a larger professional team including co-director, designer, composer, stage manager and deputy stage manager, and they were paid more. The wages bill came to £3,550. These salaries were still very much on the low side. Giving 10 performances we were able to apply for a Contract Writer's Award from the Arts Council, which meant that the writer (myself) was beginning to be paid something, on this occasion £720.

The Poor Man's Friend (1981)

The shows continued to grow in size, as did the production teams and general costs. Our wages bill for the Bridport play was £5,198. This was slightly larger than anticipated because there was an emergency over design – a not uncommon happening – and we had to bring in extra help which cost over £400. Production costs too seemed to go out of control and we had to pay twice as much for scaffolding as I had anticipated. Indeed, almost everything went over budget. This was never to happen again in the same way and I am not clear quite why it should have been so with the Bridport play. I can only suppose that it was our largest show to date, involving more people and more expense, and I had not perhaps fully learned the need for iron control. It is neither an easy nor pleasant task saying no to people who are quite rightly fighting for their interest, or who think they should stand out for higher wages as a moral duty and who, at the same time, do not appreciate the realities of fundraising. It has been a source of satisfaction to me that I am still in touch with some of the people involved and, over the years, they have realised, perhaps through personal experience, what the problems were. One person who was grossly underpaid, considering his worth and the time and energy he gave us, was the author Howard Barker, who nobly and idealistically gave us his play and his attention for a total of £1,118, including commission fee, royalties, VAT, travel and expenses. The show had been budgeted at £8,193 but finally cost £9,975. Fortunately, I had been extremely conservative about how much we could make on ticket receipts and we actually made £1,700 more than I had anticipated.

I was also becoming more successful in raising money in the town itself. We were in Dorset and so could expect no help from the county council or West Dorset District Council, but Bridport Town Council did give us a guarantee of £100, the only time this has ever happened in the county. However, I was able to engage the interest of a businessman, who runs an international trucking company and lives near Bridport, but I didn't yet know how to present a request for sponsorship. 'What's in it for my firm?' he asked, and I had no ready reply. But he was friendly and helpful and set up a meeting of local businessmen and worthies, whom he persuaded to pledge £150 each and so raised £1,500 in one evening. £150 was a perfectly reasonable sum for these people or their firms to give, but it was done very economically in terms of energy and, at that stage, I certainly wouldn't have been able to raise it myself from those sources. The school gave £500, trusts and individuals brought a further £950, South-West Arts and the Arts Council between them gave just over £1,600.

This was a fairly complicated fundraising exercise for which I was taking complete personal responsibility and it was no light burden. I was extremely worried near the end of the production in case we should make a loss. Tom Sharpe, the novelist, who lived in Bridport and is a patron of Colway Theatre Trust, as well as being a member of our Council of Management, and who had already helped with a donation of £250, came early one evening and, seeing me looking (I suppose) depressed, asked me what was the matter. I told him my worry. Twenty minutes later he reappeared with a further cheque for £250, saying he had talked it over with his wife and they wanted to help. I went away to a dark corner and cried, the relief simply overflowed. There is a rider to this story that in the end, we didn't need Tom's cheque, since our ticket sales were so unexpectedly high. Instead of returning it to him, I put it towards the Sherborne play. I think he slightly resented this high-handedness and never gave us money again. It was my inexperience. Raising money always seems such a huge burden and I should have not passed the money on to

Sherborne; but I shall never forget my feeling when he gave me the cheque.

Bridport analysis* of money coming into the town
No one really has any idea of the effect of arts funding in commercial terms. We were now well into the Thatcher era and so much thought was directed towards money. It seemed a good idea to try and produce an analysis of the money a play might be bringing into the town. We therefore prepared a form which we asked everyone who came to the play to fill in, showing what they had spent (apart from ticket money) on coffee, at the fair, etc. during the play. There was also a section for people coming from out of town in which they were asked to say how important the play was in their decision to come to Bridport, and how much money they had spent in the town on meals, petrol, hotels, shopping and the like. To encourage people to enter, we offered a small draw prize of a book token. This analysis revealed that £10,979 came into Bridport from outside and was spent there. This was apart from ticket money and was a conservative estimate.

Ssh! (1982)
This was our first village play. The Director, who was also musical director and author, was paid by Colway Theatre Trust. Otherwise, there were nominal fees and costs. It was really done with small scrapings of money that we were left with at the end of the year and a contribution from the Queen's Silver Jubilee Trust.

The Garden (1982)
With the experience of going over budget on the Bridport play, I was very careful indeed in Sherborne. There was a large cast (perhaps too large) of 180 and costs were rising all the time. Nevertheless, the play cost only £970 more than Bridport and we managed to stay around this plateau for the next two or three productions. In Sherborne, for the first time I passed funding responsibility to the town and they agreed to raise £3,000 themselves in support of the play: they were to find the money, not me. In addition to contributions from schools and small sums from local individuals and businessmen, the town itself raised money from community activities (a sponsored walk, a raffle). This fundraising by the local community marked a significant development. It was the beginning of structured community projects leading up to the play which have become a very important part of our work. The town showed in the most positive way that the play was needed

and it totally changed the relationship between me and the town. Up to then, I had been almost apologetic in my approach. I was now much more confident and, because the town helped financially, it was demonstrating that it really wanted us. There was no help from the local authorities because we were in Dorset, although there was a great deal of moral support and encouragement.

Colyford Matters (1983)

This was another village play. Colway Theatre Trust made considerable financial input, for example, paying the director. Nonetheless, the village itself gave £250, which was recouped by selling amazing amounts of delicious food during the play. Small amounts were raised by a raffle, badge-selling, sale of programmes, etc: East Devon District Council gave £233. The author was a local writer and so not paid. Ticket sales were £1,220. There were only 6 performances and, as usual, the play made a very small loss.

Today of All Days (1983)

As already described, Crediton was the triumph of mind over money. We received no funding from SWA, but mercifully CCT was helped and heartened by a grant of £3,000 from Television South-West, half of which we passed over to Crediton. TSW has continued to fund Colway Theatre Trust ever since and their money has sometimes made a crucial difference (as indeed in this case) between being able to go ahead with a project or having to abandon it. In our need, we also began to turn to the MSC for the first time and this aspect of funding was to grow until in 1986 the MSC became CTT's biggest source of revenue.

Crediton took responsibility for raising its own money, with the difference that up to this date, although CTT productions had more or less broken even, I had had a nasty scare over Bridport, and it was a great, unresolved and continuing anxiety as to who should pay if any play made a loss. With Crediton, where I was so far away and so had little control, I had to say firmly and openly that Colway Theatre Trust could not guarantee to underwrite the production. In the event, Crediton did make a slight loss which was in fact borne by the CTT to save argument.

The Western Women (1984)

The second time round in Lyme, the town raised over £2,000 through a Fundraising Committee – a significant change of attitude to *The*

Reckoning. Just as interesting was the way we began consciously to use fundraising events so that they would also have a publicity and consciousness-raising purpose and indeed become community events. As part of the MSC scheme, I now had a very lively assistant, Sally-Anne Lomas, and, working closely with the Fundraising Committee, we structured a number projects linked to the play, which drew in more people.

The Ballad of Tilly Hake (1985)

With this play costs rose dramatically. This was due to 3 factors:

1 For the first time we began to budget for certain CTT background expenses and charged the town for part of the salary of the play officer. (We were able to appoint this officer and undertake further experimental work as a result of a grant for development work from the Carnegie Trust.)

2 We were under very great pressure from the ACGB to begin to pay the writer a reasonable fee, and so Sheila Yeger received a total of £3,056. Of this, the Arts Council gave £1,250 from its new Writing Scheme and South-West Arts gave £1,000, so we were covered to some degree and the increased budget costs were more apparent than real. (In future we were to find that whilst both the Arts Council and South-West Arts insisted that we meet this increased obligation, they themselves grew less generous.)

3 We had to employ an outside director, since I was engaged in putting on the Dorchester play.

Entertaining Strangers (1985)

The cost curve continued to rise. This was by far the most ambitious production to date and it was reflected in all aspects of the budget. We were forced into a difficult position because of the drastic reduction in funding from South-West Arts during the year. The Dorchester play cost £25,654 and begins to reflect the true cost of these plays, although it still falls a good deal short of the actual cost because it did not take into account CTT costs, including my salary and travel over the very long period leading up to rehearsal. Dorchester itself raised £4,238 (in a town of 15,000).

Sponsorship

There were significant financial developments in Dorchester. The first was that we had our first major sponsorship for a particular play. Our funding from Television South West was certainly sponsorship, but it was for the central administration of Colway Theatre Trust and the plays in general. Up to now, most business sponsorship for the plays had really been in the form of charitable donations – a relatively low level of small sums from small businesses – but it was becoming easier to make successful approaches. One of the great problems of the rural south-west is that we have very few big industrial concerns. However, money exists in pockets and it should be borne in mind that the larger centres of population probably have greater resources.

Eldridge, Pope plc is a family brewery, one of the largest employers in Dorchester. With my eye on 1985, I had invited Christopher Pope, its Chairman, to come and see *The Western Women* in 1984. In his own words, he was 'electrified', and wrote a kind letter: 'One's only fear is whether Dorchester can possibly rise to anything so good; but I much look forward to hearing the plans.' Such a letter is not going to have to wait long for an answer. I carefully prepared a sponsorship proposal:* we now had an electronic typewriter (bought with our original capital grant from the Carnegie Trust) and the proposal looked very attractive. I presented this proposal to Mr Pope and he read it with the greatest care. Our deficit was budgeted at £8,200. A few days later we met again and, having consulted his board, he offered sponsorship of £2.50 for every £1.00 raised by Dorchester itself, up to a limit of £5,000. This was an imaginative gesture for it recognised that fund-raising is in itself a community activity. The town rose handsomely to the challenge.

MSC
The second important financial development in Dorchester was the setting up of an MSC scheme to work in the community, building on our experience in Ottery St Mary.

Summary
The costs of *The Reckoning* and the village plays were kept artificially low. The work was either very poorly paid, volunteers were unpaid, and/or certain people were paid by Colway Theatre Trust. The production (costume, lights, etc.) was simplified.

The costs of the plays rose from £7,128 for *The Tide* in 1980 to £25,654 for *Entertaining Strangers* in 1985. Production costs rose from £2,885 in *The Tide* to £12,715 in Dorchester. Wages rose from £3,550 in *The Tide* to £12,939 in Dorchester.

We have brought all the plays in more or less on budget and have done so by raising more money to finance the plays from every possible source. Ticket receipts have consistently rested at just under 50 per cent of costs; these receipts have been raised by slightly increasing the number of performances and by having paid previews instead of extra dress rehearsals; we have also varied the cost of seats. The lowest priced ticket for *The Reckoning* in 1978 and *Entertaining Strangers* in 1985 was 50p for both shows; the most expensive ticket was £1 for *The Reckoning* and £5 for *Entertaining Strangers*. Thus we have been able to keep faith with our poorer patrons, while at the same time charging higher prices for certain especially popular nights.

BUDGET

It is vital to draw up a budget which is clear, detailed and, as far as possible, accurate. Amateurs and many professionals sometimes don't appreciate the importance of carefully working out a budget and then keeping within the overall pattern when changes must be made to it. Some people are likely to say: 'The door receipts will cover it' and blithely order another newspaper advertisement without properly thinking out the comparative costs.

Budget for a large community play 1986/7 (Table 3)

This budget is based on a rehearsal period of 11 weeks, 2 weeks performance and half a week clearing up.

Expenditure

Writer	On commission	£1,000	
	On delivery	£1,000	
	Travel & subsistence	£ 500	
	Royalty (7½% of box office receipts)	£ 915	
	VAT (15% of commission and royalty if writer is registered)	£ 435	£3,850
Fees	Director	£3,500	
	Designer (14 weeks)	£1,750	
	Composer/Musical Director	£1,000	
	Co-director (if paid – 14 weeks)	£1,260	
	Stage Manager (see note)	£1,080	
	Lighting Person	£ 500	£9,090

Making a giant puppet.

Puppets and stilt-walkers in performance; part of the Grand Parade in *Entertaining Strangers*.

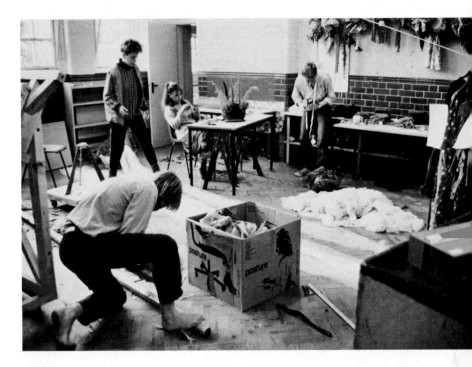

▲ Making sets and costumes. Note the row of bonnets on the wall.

▼ This exquisite 'sixteenth-century' door was specially made by a student of the School for Craftsmen in Wood at nearby Parnham House. It was so well designed for its theatrical purpose that, in spite of its great weight, it was easily shifted by two people.

A costume parade should take place in as calm, methodical and relaxed a manner as possible.

▲ Erecting scaffolding.
◀ The designer checking costumes before the dress rehearsal.

In Performance. ▲ The fair before *The Garden* including the 'Yetties' folk group who are locally based in Sherborne.

▼ *Ssh!*. Burton Bradstock village play. The actor on stilts (who was unemployed) made his own helmet and so discovered a whole new area of skills. He later went on to work in theatre design.

Workscenes. ▲ *The Poor Man's Friend*. Real rope is being made as part of the action. Note the arrangement of extra seats on the stage itself (*see p.249*).
▼ *The Tide*. Actors mime carpet weaving.

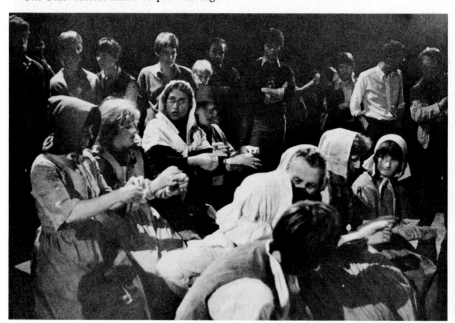

Wages	Play Officer (paid/unpaid or MSC)		
	Notional figure of 34 weeks @ £90 per week	£3,060	
	National Insurance	£ 215	
	Assistant Stage Manager (paid/unpaid or MSC)		
	13½ weeks @ £70 p.w.	£ 945	
	National Insurance	£ 66	
	Assistant to Designer (ditto)	£ 945	
	National Insurance	£ 66	
	Assistant to Director (unpaid or MSC)	–	£5,297
	Carried forward		£18,237
Production & Administration	Costumes	£1,200	
	Staging & properties	£ 450	
	Electrical hire	£ 700	
	Scaffolding (notional)	£ 500	
	Publicity	£1,200	
	Transport	£ 90	
	Sheet music, tapes, records	£ 40	
	Scripts	£ 150	
	Insurance	£ 350	
	Accommodation & entertaining	£ 200	
	Travel	£2,000	
	Administration, postage, stationery, telephone, secretarial	£2,000	
	Town fundraising expenses	£ 700	
	Programme & merchandise	£ 500	
	Hire of hall (notional)	£ 500	
	Audit	£ 300	
	Contingencies	£ 566	£11,446
	Total cost of play		£29,683

Income

	Ticket sales (85% of total)	£11,730
	Programmes & merchandise	£ 1,200
		£12,930
	Deficit	£16,753

How deficit may be met

	Regional Arts Association (project subsidy)	£ 2,500
	(writer)	£ 1,250

Arts Council (writer)	£ 1,250	
Local authorities, trusts, donations	£ 2,000	
Major business sponsorship	£ 5,500	
Town fundraising (including minor business sponsorship)	£ 4,255	
	£16,755	
Add ticket sales, programmes, merchandise (as above)	£12,930	
Grand Total	£29,685	£29,685

Ticket sales (Table 4)

Based on an audience of 400 (20% children) over 11 performances, i.e. 320 adults, 80 children

First week		(£)	(£)
Mon. (preview)	320 @ 1.00		320.00
	80 @ 0.50		40.00
Tues. (preview)	320 @ 1.50		480.00
	80 @ 0.75		60.00
Wed. (Civic Night)	320 @ 2.50		800.00
	80 @ 1.25		100.00
Thurs.	320 @ 3.00		960.00
	80 @ 1.50		120.00
Fri.	320 @ 3.50		1,120.00
	80 @ 1.75		140.00
Sat.	320 @ 4.00		1,280.00
	80 @ 2.00		160.00
	Total first week		5,580.00
Second week			
Tues.	320 @ 3.00		960.00
	80 @ 1.50		120.00
Wed.	320 @ 3.50		1,120.00
	80 @ 1.75		140.00
Thurs.	320 @ 4.00		1,280.00
	80 @ 2.00		160.00

Fri.	320 @ 4.50	1,440.00
	80 @ 2.25	180.00
Sat.	320 @ 6.00	1,920.00
	80 @ 3.00	240.00
	Total second week	7,560.00
	Total for two weeks	13,140.00

Seating

80 seats × 11 performances × 75p	660.00
Grand total 100%	13,800.00
85% (including allowance for discounts etc.) of Grand total	11,730.00

Notes on budget

Writer There is now pressure from the ACGB to raise the commissioning fee because the small number of performances does not adequately reward a good writer.

Fees and National Insurance People designated as self-employed receive fees and pay no National Insurance.

Stage management You have a choice between a first-rate professional stage manager, who is not cheap, for a shorter period, or someone less experienced for a longer period.

Transport You may be able to borrow a lorry, but have to pay for the driver who must have a heavy goods licence. Allow 2 days for collecting and 1 for returning. It makes a very long last day, but people usually prefer to get it done.

Insurance Go into this carefully. Anyone in your employment, the cast and audience should be insured, as should lights, borrowed properties, costumes, etc. Insure against damage to the venue and watch out that you are covered for unexpected items, such as damage to vehicles while on loan to you.

Accommodation and entertaining Dozens, if not hundreds of times, someone, probably the director, is going to have to take people out for a drink to sort things out, quiet them down, butter them up. It's a very important way of relating to people. It may be necessary also to take certain key people out for a meal.

Travel Do not underestimate. Professionals should have return rail fares from London. (CTT actually allows 2 return fares, since the work is stretched over such a very long period and it's good for people to have a break.) The professionals and the play officer will probably cover quite a large mileage by car. CTT pays professionals 18p per mile while on strict business travel. (As a comparison: in 1985 BBC Radio paid 23.3p per mile and ITV paid 28.2p per mile.) Sometimes the musical director comes and goes according to his own timetable and receives some petrol money. It is possible to estimate fairly accurately the likely cost of transport by simply working out the probable number of journeys and the distances involved.

Administration costs Telephone is a heavy item. It's possible to get voluntary secretarial help, but this is an area where you want fast, accurate work with a high standard of presentation. You need to be able to rely on somebody being there at definite times.

Hire of hall You may get this free or at low cost. Careful explanation regarding community involvement and using a large proportion of schoolchildren may mean that you can get a school free.

Contingencies CTT allows 2 per cent of the total.

Repaying expenses Insist that receipts are always produced for expenses. It helps to have a standard claim form. Amateurs sometimes don't understand the system and have a feeling that it doesn't matter. You may say, 'You can spend up to £10 on materials for the display' only to find that they blithely tell you they have spent £18 with no receipts to show for it.

Amateur expenses This is a grey area. Of course amateurs must be reimbursed for any items they buy with authority, on behalf of the play, and for which they produce receipts. Very few people make a claim for small journeys, a few phone calls, a little postage, but if these items are going to mount up, the community play should pay for them. There is a variation, according to the circumstances of the person involved.

Ticket sales

Tickets do not automatically sell out, even with such a large production. What people are really waiting for is to hear what their friends say. If it is a good production there will be a scramble for tickets. A good reputation is a guarantee. With *The Western Women*, our second production in Lyme Regis, the play sold out 3,300 tickets in a town of 3,500. In Ottery St Mary, we failed to sell out 3,500 in a town of 7,069 (but sold enough to cover the projected budget figure). In Dorchester, population 15,000, we sold out 4,000 tickets before the play opened. It's an equation between size of town, reputation, quality of product and publicity.

In arriving at the price for tickets, you have to balance out what you need against what experience will tell you the market will stand. When you first price tickets people will always say they are too high.

Sliding scale of prices With our first play, in 1978, we charged a flat rate of £1 per ticket, half-price for children. With subsequent productions, we found that there was usually some slowness in selling out the first few nights. Once word-of-mouth had spread, we would have to turn people away. We therefore developed a price structure which encouraged people to book ahead for less popular nights, while making the final performance, for which there was an enormous demand for seats, relatively high in price. We sweetened the pill on the last Saturday by calling it a 'Gala Final Performance' and considered issuing a special souvenir ticket, but in the end didn't bother. It sold out anyway. The excitement of the final performance, the speeches, bouquets, make it sufficiently 'gala'. Since Dorchester sold out before it opened, perhaps we did not need that elaborate price structure, but it meant that poorer people could still see the play and were in fact subsidised by the more wealthy.

Half-price children's tickets/school parties We are now questioning the value and wisdom of encouraging schools from out of town to bring large coachloads of children, which they can do relatively cheaply, given the discount and half-price children's tickets. In future CTT may only issue half-price tickets to local children; all the rest will have to pay the full price. The problem is that teachers sense a great opportunity to teach history or English. To 14-year-olds the play may seem an extension of school and they sometimes behave as if they don't particularly want to be there and are extremely cool, laid back and uninvolved. Twenty teenagers at a promenade performance, bunching up, giggling and making snide remarks can be extremely irritating, though I may be being oversensitive. Incidentally, if I do discover a group of difficult teenagers during a performance, my technique is simply to go and stand amongst them and quietly focus on the performance and I find they generally quieten down.

Discounts We allow a discount of 25p per ticket for parties of 25 and over, except on the first two cheap preview nights. This offers a real inducement for people to bring coach parties and it's very encouraging early in the booking period to be able to say, 'We have a coachload of 60 coming from Manchester on the first Thursday.'

Seating We have always seated about one third of the audience on scaffolding at no extra charge. In the past this has led to people rushing in and grabbing seats which they hung on to grimly. Previously I never had the time or peace of mind to organise paying for seats, chiefly because scaffolding is a dodgy area anyway and I didn't want to add to my anxiety by committing myself to a precise number of seats. But in Ottery St Mary, where I was not directing, we tried charging £1 per seat and 50p for OAPs (for whom the seats were really intended). We met some resistance to the £1 charge and as a result, the seats were not all filled. In Dorchester, where space was extremely limited, it was important that we should have every possible body off the floor and so we charged a flat rate of 50p, though in future we may charge 75p. Since 80 or more people a night will be seated, this may bring in around £600, but you must remember that you will give away quite a number of seats free to local dignitaries on Civic Night, and to the Press, sponsors, invitees, etc. It's best to calculate the number of available seats very conservatively: you will be selling tickets long before the scaffolding is up and you may find certain places cannot be used. In any case, it's convenient to have a few free seats to be filled on the night.

Budgeting for the percentage of ticket sales If you sell all your tickets, you will have a figure representing 100 per cent of capacity, but it is very unwise to budget on this figure: you may not sell out; you will have to give away a few complimentaries; the proportion of seats sold at half price or at discount may vary. As a guide, the Northcott Theatre, Exeter, budgets at 55 per cent of capacity and this is general for most professional reps. CTT budgets at 85 per cent. This is actually a conservative estimate since we almost always take 95 per cent at the box office, but it would be foolish to budget at this figure because there are so many variables.

Deficit

If you subtract income from ticket sales, merchandising, etc., you will almost certainly find you have a deficit. The following suggestions given for covering the deficit are only intended as a guide (the local authority, for example, may be much more generous). It is surprising how much a town will raise once an energetic committee gets going and providing they have sufficient time.

Control of cash/responsibility

Credit and deposit accounts should be opened in local banks and as much money as possible kept on deposit. Signatories are usually the Chair of the Fundraising Committee, possibly the Chair of the Organising Committee and the Administrator/Treasurer of Colway Theatre Trust, any two of whom may sign (you must decide who actually disburses money and holds the cheque book). I myself, as Director of CTT, had no authority to sign cheques, although I authorised payments and controlled the budget. It is the job of the Fundraising Committee to raise money, not to control the budget but, naturally, the Chairs of the Organising and Fundraising Committees must be given the fullest facts.

COVERING THE DEFICIT

Local fundraising

Schools In the past, we have raised £150–£900 from this source, but we no longer ask state schools, since education budgets are so tight. Private schools are another matter.

Projects and events

These will be organised by the relevant committee. Each town will raise money in its own way, according to its nature. Since you are putting the responsibility on the townspeople, you will, of course, be guided by them. Don't try and force them to work in a way which is against their nature. Ottery St Mary, for example, preferred to raise its money in relatively large parcels of £500, while Dorchester liked small events, raising only £100 to £200. Both towns found substantial amounts each in their own way.

We have raised money in the following ways:

Sponsorship All kinds, including 24-hour improvisation (use competing teams), walks, cricket matches, stilt-walking etc.

Diminishing tea parties If these take off you can, in theory, make a fortune. Some towns like the idea, some don't. One person holds a tea party for 10 people (have leaflets and literature available about the play), each of whom gives 50p. They go away and give a party for 9; these nine give a party for 8; and so on. It's a good way of fundraising because it spreads the word and forces people to search the community for invitees. People are encouraged to make new contacts, because they run out of friends. What is dispiriting is if somebody breaks the link in the chain and pays money instead and so the compound multiplying process is lost.

Street events You need police and local authority permission for street events and collections. Incidentally, people can be astonishingly generous during street events, even if the rain is pouring down, provided you look cheerful. If you ask them for 5p they will frequently give you £1.

We make street events as lively as possible with stilt walkers, people in rough costumes, lots of visual interest, etc.

Paper-chain race 5p a link; 2 competing teams, which team can make the longest chain? Names of teams associated with the play.

Collapsing Roman wall We had this in Dorchester (a Roman town): 2 teams (Romans and Saxons); loads of polystyrene bricks; 5p to the Romans puts a brick on the wall; 5p to the Saxons takes it off.

Stately homes, etc. Food and drink adds to the pleasure; concerts using local musicians; in Ottery we held an Elizabethan masque; dances and balls; a medieval banquet.

'Great Dorchester Crossword' Shops sell the form (20p). This is popular and good for £100 or so.

Treasure hunt Again the shops sell forms: too complicated and it took a long time to explain that the answers to the clues had to be found round the town and that the answer to where the treasure was hidden could be found amongst the clues, etc.

Jumble sales and coffee mornings Don't despise these humble ways of raising money; it's all part of the community relating to each other and you can raise £40 from the humblest coffee morning – more from a jumble sale.

Raffles You need a lottery licence (from your local council) which lasts a year and will cover any other raffles, such as that at the public meeting. A good raffle will make £700 with donated prizes of goods or services. You can make quite a feature of this and it's a useful way of involving businesses which don't want to give cash. Have a care. Don't be tempted to make the prizes too big and pay for them yourself. A large raffle in one town had prizes of £500 cash and only made £200 because so much money had to be raised before it was in profit. On the other hand, a tiny village raffle with a bottle of whisky and a bit of fruit (both donated) raised £175 with no effort.

Miscellaneous

Hotels list In a suitable town (e.g. Lyme Regis) with a big seaside complement of hotels and guesthouses lying idle in winter, we charged £10 for appearance on an accommodation list which was sent out with every postal booking.

Vice-presidents Popular with amateur dramatic societies and such. Invite lists of people in the town to become vice-presidents (or whatever) at a cost of £5. Their names appear on the programme and maybe they get priority booking.

Salisbury Fields Fun Day We had this in Dorchester. It was an open-air event which took an enormous amount of organising, but raised £500 and got a great deal of publicity. There was non-stop music, improvised theatre, dancing displays, etc. surrounded by stalls selling food, drinks, ice-creams, crafts.

First-day covers This is very exciting and has tremendous possibilities for publicity and image projection. CTT has not yet used first day covers, but other organisations have successfully raised up to £1,000 or more. There is quite a heavy initial outlay. Ask the Post Office for details.

Business sponsorship

An excellent sponsorship manual has been published jointly by the Association for Business Sponsorship of the Arts, 2 Chester Street, London, SW1X 7BB and by W. H. Smith. Colway Theatre Trust uses this manual constantly. Incidentally, ABSA is a very lively organisation and might well be able to help you in finding a sponsor.

Major business sponsorship

This may take time to set up. Sponsors are looking for promotion and publicity. They want to be associated with an event which is prestigious, successful and relevant to their product. It's vital to have a personal meeting with the key person. Try and get him/her to come and see your work; find out all you can about the firm and get hold of a company report. Image is important: look at yourself from their point of view and decide what you would like to see; don't distort your image, but you must reassure them that you are what you say. Have your proposals well prepared and clearly typed, giving succinct details of the production and the possible benefits to sponsors; a budget and a timetable. Be prepared to go through the documents carefully, so that the sponsor clearly understands the principles of the work and what is offered.

It's never easy to persuade a business person to sponsor an event: they have to be utterly convinced that it will be good for their image and that they will not be called to account for foolish misuse of money by colleagues or stockholders.

Bear the following in mind: a firm will usually budget to spend $1\frac{1}{2}$–2 per cent of its expected turnover on publicity. The turnover of a medium-sized firm may be upwards of £2 million. Of course this money will not be lying around it will be earmarked to finance advertising and perhaps salaries. £5,000 will buy half a page in a national newspaper or five full-page advertisements in trade papers. However PR, i.e. mention in editorial pages, TV coverage, has far greater credibility and is infinitely more valuable than mere advertising.

If a firm orders fewer trade advertisements but gains editorial mention, TV and radio coverage, its name printed on all material relating to the play, an exhibition of the product in the foyer and fifty free seats for clients and staff, it will have made a very good bargain – provided the play is a success.

This is an expanding field and one where there is an opportunity for the sponsor to have some fun. If you are successful in raising sponsorship, look after your sponsors. Keep them informed and involved. You are offering much more than an opportunity to do business. An association with the arts will be something new and intriguing for the Chairman and others. If your sponsors have a good time and you deliver what you promised then it's likely they will want to sponsor further events.

Business sponsorship of a particular night's performance
A useful, medium sized sponsorship. The business gives £150–£500 to sponsor a particular performance. For this they receive 10 free seats, hospitality (i.e. coffee and/or wine), their own advertising in the foyer on the night of the sponsorship and mention in the programme.

Sponsorship and charitable donations
There is a clear distinction to be drawn between business sponsorship and charitable donations. With sponsorship the sums involved may be relatively large and you offer something very positive in return. It's a business deal and the company can set the sponsorship against their Corporation Tax. Charitable donations generally range from £10–£200 and for this you would offer an acknowledgement in the programme and probably display the company's logo in a relatively minor position, the company might also ask for a few seats, but watch this or it may become too expensive.

Local Authorities
There is an extraordinary variation between local authorities in funding community plays. Monmouth Town Council (population 7,509) voted the product of a 1p rate over 2 years to finance a community play in 1987. This will raise £16,000. Ottery St Mary in Devon (population 7,069) gave £250 and much help in kind. Apart from Bridport, which gave a guarantee against loss, no town, district council or local authority in Dorset has given any money to any community play. Colway Theatre Trust has an operating base in Dorset, 300 yards from the Devon border; it's registered address is in Devon; I tried endlessly to raise money in Dorset, personally lobbying district and town councils. Colway Theatre Trust has given enormous value to Dorset ratepayers, but the county will not give a penny in cash, although it has given help in kind, usually accommodation for the play office and rehearsal space. It is not lack of appreciation: I made it my business to invite the Chairman and Chief Executives of Dorset County Council and West Dorset District Council, the Chair-

man of the Dorset Education Authority and the Chief Education Officer. They all love our shows: they write letters to tell us so; they give personal donations of £10 or £25 but, as local authority officials, they maintain they have done sufficient by paying their contribution to South-West Arts. In 1985/86 Dorset County Council gave South-West Arts £8,222 and West Dorset District Council gave £1,015. In the same period, Devon County Council gave South-West Arts £25,000 and East Devon District Council £1,410.

Devon do not only generously contribute to South-West Arts. You can lift up a telephone and talk to a representative of the EDDC or DCC and receive cash and guarantees with very little trouble and a great deal of understanding. Is it any wonder that Devon has a far livelier artistic life than Dorset? As a glance at South-West Arts' Review Calendar of Events will show, I am convinced that this has led to a far richer intellectual life in Devon and indeed a more prosperous business life, though which came first and is a symptom of which, it is hard to say. Dorset is notoriously feudal and rather proudly behind the times. Its philistine attitude to the arts is both a reason for and a result of this attitude. We *should* get help from our local authorities: communities are transformed and jobs created as a result of what we do; new life and new money are brought into the area. Support from local authorities is vital: it visibly demonstrates local support and so is extremely important in raising support from elsewhere.

Grants from Regional Arts Associations and the Arts Council of Great Britain

The policy varies from region to region and the emphasis is always changing. This is probably your most hopeful source of money since, although their funds are committeed from year to year, there is still a relatively large pool of cash. RAAs are very approachable and you will easily be able to go and see the relevant officer and talk the whole thing through. They will give you guidelines as to what policy is current.

ACGB If you are in the provinces, you are unlikely to get direct funding from the ACGB, except for the writer.

Trusts

Get hold of the *Directory of Grant Making Trusts* published by the Charities Aid Fund of the National Council of Social Service, 48 Pembury Road, Tonbridge, Kent, and put in some homework. You have to be very clear and businesslike. It's no use sending out a blanket application. You must write an individual letter and keep it short. Enclose if you can a full budget and try and tailor your application to what you gather is the relevant field from the *Directory of Grant Making Trusts*. For example, if it's an educational trust, stress the educational aspect of what you are doing. We have raised a considerable amount over a period of time from this source. It sometimes pays to argue, if you think you have a case. At first I received a negative answer from the Carnegie Trust, saying that we did not meet the requirements of their Trust's aims. I felt this was wrong and wrote a long, strong, rational reply, whereupon Geoffrey Lord, the benign and wise Secretary of the Carnegie Trust agreed to meet me, and as a result they gave us £5,000 for capital expenses, and later funded development work. Things get easier as you become known: we raised £1,000 from a particular trust because the son of my correspondent had seen our work. Another trust sent us £50 totally unsolicited.

Gifts, donations and covenants

We sometimes have a form in the programme of the current play, explaining the principles of our work and inviting covenants and donations, occasionally with touching results: old ladies have pressed £1 in my hand from time to time; generous friends have sent cheques of £25 or so. For larger sums, you need to approach possible targets directly. I find that rich artists, or connoisseurs of art give the most ready response. They understand the process and the difficulties and may wish to compost their money back.

Covenants In approaching individuals, covenants are most desirable, because not only can you claim from the Government the difference in tax between what your covenanter pays and what you yourself pay, but the money rolls in for at least 4 years (you may have to gently remind your benefactor each year), thus giving you stability ahead. We have raised about £1,000 a year from covenants.

Follow up leads Strike quickly. Someone told me of a generous donation an elderly lady had given to another organisation: 'but she's moving'. I quickly wrote off a letter and received by return my own letter with a scribbled message, 'Will this do?' and a cheque for £1,000.

The rules for raising money

1 Offer careful proposals and not too much indigestible information. Write a letter which excites you and which, if possible, you enjoy writing; not more than two A4 pages in length.

2 Try and make personal contact. Very few people can refuse you face to face. Retain the initiative. Say, 'May I phone you?'

3 Dress the part.

4 Keep your funder informed. Draw them in: keep them interested and feeling they are appreciated and valued. Try and give them some fun/interest for their money.

7

Working with the actors

ACTING

Since we were born all of us have had to employ communication skills
using speech and body language to try and reveal what is in our minds.
We all have this curious problem of presenting ourselves, of trying
either to hide or reveal what is inside. Even when we are trying to be as
simple, clear, sincere, truthful as possible we still somehow have to
externalise an interior idea or image by means of what we say and how
we say it. It's simply unavoidable – it's part of life. We have to present
an image, we have to communicate, otherwise we are mad or dead.

We must present an image even when we are asking for 3 lb of flour
in a shop: we are also maintaining a higher, equal or lower status to the
shopkeeper; we are being friendly or indifferent. There is nothing
that we do, in relating to other people, which does not present an outer
image of something which is going on inside us. Thus a child begging
its mother for 20p for an ice-cream, a doctor reassuring a patient by his
calm and sympathetic manner, a schoolboy boasting to his mates: all
of us, all the time, are employing communication skills which when
developed become acting.

Why do people want to act?
Since you are hoping to persuade people to join in these plays, many of
whom will never have acted before, it's perhaps important to try and
understand why people should want to act and what they may get out
of it.

1 Acting is an experience of possession. When we are on stage,
every single part of us focuses towards a single aim, the world
narrows. We feel that our whole being is concentrated and projected
and nothing blurs this focus. It is comparatively rare and extremely
exciting to feel totally committed, concentrated towards a single aim.
There are really few situations where we can be so completely focused
at so little cost to ourselves, as it were, each night on demand. I have
many times had the experience, watching actor friends in promenade

performances when they simply did not relate to me as an individual or indeed recognise me; their eyes were glazed, they were in character, they did not know me as a person; they were possessed.

Here is a comment from someone who took part in a community play, never having acted before:

> I could never understand why so many show-biz people – particularly the young – took drugs. However, now having experienced the tremendous high it is possible to reach when performing in front of an audience I can see the desire to prolong the 'high' might be very great.

The experience of possession is not merely common it is at the heart of acting and is described in many biographies. It is akin to what is loosely described as 'inspiration' (the person is taken over by breathing in something from elsewhere). An inspired artist feels the picture paint itself or the piece of writing write itself. With acting the experience is peculiarly intense and much more common, because the presence of the audience provides a stimulus, a challenge, a support, and a creative element of risk.

2 There is an element of pleasurable fantasy and compensation in acting. Your own life may be a mess; you may feel yourself unattractive and unsuccessful. By acting you can give yourself a holiday from your boring self. It is pleasant even for people who may be shy and introverted, although of course that introversion may actually mask a desire for display or power.

3 Most of us like to feel that we are commanding attention, we are being looked at. Through the course of rehearsal, many people discover this in themselves and it makes them more confident and assertive.

4 It's really enjoyable to work closely with other people towards a demanding and exciting climax. In such a situation, you get to know other people really well.

The best actors are probably intuitive and naturally talented; it just comes to them. Fine actors are not necessarily intellectual or even clever, their gift is in acting, as a sculptor's gift is in his hands. They have a natural sense of timing, and without appearing to be particularly imaginative in everyday life they seem able to shuffle on another character as someone else will put on an overcoat. Their voices and bodies are both free and controlled. They focus and project truthfully, powerfully and economically. In working with perhaps fifteen hundred amateur actors over ten community plays I have come across two such outstanding natural talents and possibly eight who were nearly as good. I consider this a high proportion.

Beyond these special talents there is a very large body of useful and acceptable talent. The skills then shade through all degrees of excellence down to people who appear to be virtually non-actors. But non-actors, above all, want to gain something: they have volunteered to take part, so there is clearly a high degree of self-motivation. It may confidently be promised that everyone can increase their acting skills and so their self-confidence; perhaps they will also become vocally more effective and more assertive. They may also gain insight into themselves and others.

WORKSHOPS

Reassuring people The mere word 'workshop' may scare some people because they don't know what it means or what to expect. Explaining the nature of workshops★ makes a useful feature in the newsletter and for general publicity.

Uses of workshops

Workshops are designed to develop trust, sensitivity and supportive-ness amongst the group, to increase acting skills, to begin work upon the play and the ideas behind it, to introduce people to the practices of rehearsal, to draw in and reassure people who may never have acted before.

They are a vital and very effective part of the process towards performance. Not everyone who will be in the play will come to the workshops but there will be a core of about 60–100 people who will have attended all, or at least most of the workshops, who have worked together over three months and who have developed attitudes towards each other and the work, which will colour the whole approach to rehearsal. By the end of the workshops there will be very strong group-feeling and sensitivity and, allied to this, an approach to the work which is based on not blocking, willingness to experiment, hopefully a new attitude towards 'success' and 'failure', considerably increased acting skills and a sense that a very important preliminary stage in creating the play has been successfully achieved.

Names We keep a record of all the people who come to workshops collecting names at the door. This way you not only find out who is most committed (and who may have missed a certain important workshop), you signal to them that you care and are taking notice. From the very first workshops the principle is established that everybody is called by their first name be they headmaster, 14-year-old, town mayor, or nonagenerian. I clear this beforehand with people who are likely to be sensitive, but have never had any resistance. Being named is important because it means you are being respected as a valued individual and perceived to be as important as anyone else. This helps give you confidence, assert yourself, and show what you can do. Since we are all called by our first names, the play becomes neutral ground and, hopefully, we can begin to leave certain factors which inhibit us outside, make a fresh start and have a new relationship with the world. In the first few workshops, to help learn the names of 60 or 70 people, everyone wears a sticky label with their name written on it and we have a number of name-learning and introducing games. (See Appendix p. 298 for workshop booklist.*)

Workshop practice

Almost all workshops start with a circle, because this is an image of equality and supportiveness. I am not too keen on people sitting around outside the circle and not joining in, unless there is a real physical reason, such as a bad back. As they become ready for it people are going to be asked to do some fairly silly and unusual things. If we are all in it together, it's easier; if someone is watching it may make us self-conscious. It's very rare indeed that people don't join in. The pre-publicity often says, 'No one will pressurise you to take part' and on those terms, at the first few workshops, I would accept people watching, provided they were sympathetic and tactful: no one would be allowed to stay who giggled, talked, whispered, or made remarks while not joining in. Likewise, I am asking for a true circle. If people hide behind others – 2 or even 3 deep – it means they are not committing themselves.

I then try and sense the feeling of the people there and may start in any of a number of ways. If the people seem apathetic and slow, I'll start injecting bounce and energy. If they are over-excited and talkative, I'll wait in a perfectly relaxed way, simply withdrawing all judgement and movement and letting my glance flow gently round. There is no sense in demanding attention or 'punishing' people for talking. I don't talk to anyone, or let anyone talk to me. I simply wait quietly until I have their attention and then speak in a gentle tone. This is an almost foolproof way of gaining the attention of even the rowdiest and most excitable group, but it may take a few minutes. Then, according to the nature of the group, I have warm-up games of a fairly basic nature.

Physical and vocal warm-ups Start from the basic circle so that you are not messing people around. *Orange, Lemon, Grapefruit* is useful (set up for musical chairs with one person standing in the middle; everyone names off alternately 'Orange!' or 'Lemon!'; or use names appropriate to the play). Encourage the players to speak up or yell; it's a good start. If the person in the middle calls 'Orange!' all oranges must change seats; lemons, likewise. If 'Grapefruits' is called, all change. The person in the middle finds a seat and the one left out is the next caller). This is a reassuring game because people feel that a chair is their base and it gives them security but, in all the noise and fun, they discover that it's possible to relinquish their base without feeling too insecure.

We may then go on to games involving physical contact, such as *Hug Tag* (you can't be caught if you are hugging someone: this encourages people to touch each other and the excitement loosens inhibition). A *Human Chain* (all hold hands, the leader leads the group into the most complicated knot possible and then unravels) is another acceptable way of encouraging touching. After a few work-shops, if I feel they can take it, I might do *Log Rolling*: (remove shoes, watches, anything which may catch or injure. Everyone lies face down on the floor in a tight row, shoulder to shoulder, hip to hip; encourage people to squash up; you want as little space as possible between bodies. The person at the end of the row begins to roll over the others, followed by the second and so on. On reaching the end rollers join on the line of bodies until all have rolled over – make sure there is sufficient space before you start). This is a really demanding, unavoidable physical contact and also encourages lots of groaning, screaming, laughing and protesting.

In time, these physical warm-ups develop into much more sensitive and controlled contact. They are also the beginning of understanding the use of our bodies in space and how to make them more free and expressive. This will be followed by vocal warm-ups, often linked with the physical warm-ups, for we produce our voices physically, and if we can free our bodies, then our voices will be more expressive also. The vocal warm-ups will be followed by games which encourage the use of words in a free situation (e.g. *Customs Officers* (divide into pairs; customs officer dives into imaginary suitcase and demands to

know why traveller is carrying fifty kilos of bird seed/ a broken grand
piano/ five plastic bags ful of gin, etc. Traveller must volubly justify),
which is the beginning of improvisation.

Trust games Leading on from the warm-ups, we play a number of
trust games, which make increasing demands, remembering that
learning to trust is also learning to be responsible; from the very
simplest, where two people rock a third between them, to groups of
about 15–18 people, all of whom are responsible for carrying one
person around the room, making accompanying verbal sounds if that
seems appropriate. This is an exercise which encourages great
sensitivity.

Group sensitivity Sometimes, combining the physical, verbal and
group work, we'll begin to *play the room*, when the whole group begins
to move as they will, to find a rhythm amongst themselves, developing, intensifying, making verbal noises, tapping their bodies, the
room, the furniture, each other and, as a group, they allow the
movement to start, develop, reach a climax, subside and cease when
the group senses the moment.

A variation is to divide the group into As and Bs. Start the whole
room from stillness. The As are to move off, sensing as a group when
to start. They may develop a group rhythm as above if they sense they
want to. The As cease moving when, as a group, they sense the
moment. At the moment the As stop, the Bs start moving. The group
can go on working together like this for some time. This is also a useful
and refreshing exercise in rehearsal if people are becoming a little
insensitive to each other.

A development of this is for groups of people, standing very closely
together and lightly touching, to be asked to cross a space and to sense
(not push or guide) when the group wants to move and at what speed.

In all these exercises you can begin to encourage a feeling for sound,
perhaps first finding rhythms through tapping or hitting, moving on
to humming or other verbal sounds. The linking of voice with
movement helps people become less inhibited about making sounds.
It also prevents them from tightening up and producing their voices
with strain. It's fun and a further development of group feeling if you
set up an exercise where the group, holding each other closely (the
physical proximity is important) speaks with one voice (the group says
'I' not 'we'). The tutor asks simple questions ('Have you had a nice
day?') and gets more complicated ('What did you do?'). Two groups,

representing two people, can hold a conversation. Again the object is not to push or dominate but to sense what everyone wants to say.

Enjoyment and acceptance of warm-ups This is an integral part of the work, extremely important for the later rehearsal period. People can visibly see and feel for themselves how they are relaxed by warm-ups. Older actors and experienced amateurs often resent the idea of warm-ups before rehearsal (they seem daft and silly), but if you have a body of people who have already been through three months of workshops, they will accept the need for warm-ups through rehearsal and before performance.

Beginning to introduce rehearsal practice: getting attention One important way of gaining silence – being still oneself – has already been mentioned and it's the best way, particularly with an excitable group, but it may not be very quick. It's a good idea to establish an agreed signal. I do this at the first workshop, but not right at the beginning: people should first be allowed to become aware that energy and time will be wasted if we don't have such signals. I generally ask the group to agree that we are all silent if I first clap my hands then raise them above my head (a visual signal reinforces an audible one). This is then used throughout the whole process. It saves my voice, it's not authoritarian and it's usually quite enough. Those nearest may 'ssh' to any who may have missed the signal. Occasionally, in cases where it's difficult to be seen or heard, I may ask someone with a huge voice to yell for silence. This is generally in actual performance venues which may be full of scaffolding and stages. It is seldom needed in workshops.

I have also used toy hooters and various whistles to gain attention. I'm not too keen on whistles, because they have associations with schools and policemen, but they are effective, especially with large numbers, so long as your relationship with the group is such that they understand that you are not being bossy. You are asking for silence on behalf of everyone and for everyone's benefit.

Blocking and accepting In the very first workshop, I begin to introduce the concept of not blocking other people's ideas. This is really a way of life: an acting technique which can be carried over into the real world. I explain that people 'block' because they are afraid of the future and want to control it. Someone makes an 'offer' in an improvisation: 'Let's get on the bus'; and the blocker will say, 'I'm sitting in a shop.'

Or an offer is made: 'Shall we have a picnic here?'; and the blocker will say, 'Here's a piano.' In both cases, the blocker has refused the offer and tried to control the scene, instead of going with it. The effect on the person who made the offer is extremely deadening and depressing. They have exposed themselves and been repulsed. Not blocking, on the other hand, is very cheery:

> 'This looks like a good hotel.'
> 'Right! You carry the bags.'
> 'There's one missing.'
> 'What!'
> 'The blue holdall.'
> 'That's the one with the money/bomb/blood samples!'

In this dialogue, each partner is accepting and supporting the other and the scene can take off in any direction. Blocking and accepting is a huge area. What constitutes a block and how, with experienced improvisers, blocking may be creative, is an enormous subject which we can hardly begin to touch on in workshops. It is vitally important for people to perceive the difference between blocking and not blocking: to learn to be open, supportive and unafraid of the future, because the person they are working with will not let them down, but will consciously try and support them. Just as the group learns that the ability to trust depends on the ability to be responsible, so they also learn that not blocking depends upon supportiveness. If you can learn to support other people and not block their ideas, then you can have the trust not to be afraid of the future, because if you make an offer, it will be supported. This will develop confidence which will allow you to make discoveries and experiments, so that your work and imagination will be enriched.

The director should always try not to block, to be open to other people. This doesn't mean that everyone's ideas are automatically accepted and acted upon. It's not always desirable, or possible, to test out every new idea. The pressure of time and people is sometimes too great. We can, however, welcome the act of contributing, accept with enthusiasm that someone has come forward, has opened themselves to the process. If their ideas are welcome, even if they are not acted upon, then people gain confidence to think for themselves about their work, to bring their own ideas to it. It is very important that we try and practice what we preach.

It's absolutely impossible to work fruitfully with a habitual blocker who closes up, rejects ideas, and won't support other people. The principle of not blocking is really an attitude of mind. Once an actor has grasped and accepted the concept it can be developed and will produce lively short improvisations which will appear skilful and relevant. (Longer improvisations demand form which needs other skills.) We need people with this skill and attitude because we constantly use improvisation in workshops, rehearsals and performance, and because this concept of supportiveness will colour the whole work.

Respect for other people's work From the very beginning, people have to learn to focus on other people's work, not to talk, whisper, move about, or interrupt. At the first workshop, I may set up a simple piece of mime, individually acted out (e.g. carrying a mimed object across a space in various ways as if it were something horribly smelly, or a bomb, etc.) All start at the same time, but some will finish more quickly than the others. I set an example by maintaining absolute stillness and focus until the last person has finished. I will then reinforce, by explaining what's happened, how important it is to help other people's work by sensitively supporting and watching it. This is an attitude which carries right on through rehearsal and becomes a positive force in performance, when the actors amongst the promenading audience, become the ideal audience, positively focusing on the action and reacting to it. They also learn technically to avoid moving at all through other people's scenes, unless the action demands it.

Improvisation Having started with a period of physical and vocal warm-ups, games and exercises, people have very little difficulty in sliding into improvisation. Improvisation is a useful tool, because tiny situations can be quickly set up and used for experiments and demonstrations. We are aiming to learn certain basic skills and attitudes, and improvisation is one of our chief means.

Having introduced the concept of not blocking, I am hoping to encourage a particular approach to improvisation which will affect future work. In most workshops, improvisation is discussed beforehand: 'I come in here and say how much I like the room. You can spill the milk on the carpet . . .' In my opinion, this has several results:

1 There is a confused discussion and argument, in which several people keep quiet, or are simply told what to do.

2 It's investing in the future. If a group ignores or rejects someone's ideas, that person will feel badly let down and resentful.

3 It limits freedom and experiment, because the scene is too defined before people start.

4 The discussion is exhausting and dissipates energy.

I try and encourage people, at first in small groups, to get up and try out a scene with little discussion beforehand, and see what happens. It's an extension of the not-blocking attitude. Whatever offers are made, they accept them and see where it leads. Having improvised the scene in this way, they can then discuss what happened: what were they trying to do?; what should they keep, reject, follow up?; how could they improve the focus, the staging, etc? Then they try again, still being aware and open to offers, which may change the course of the scene.

It's hard to teach this attitude. There are always people who want to control the future and tell everyone else what to do. If you can get over the idea of not over-organising ahead, of letting things emerge, you'll find it releases a tremendous freedom and exhilaration. It will also be a preparation for a freer approach to rehearsal.

Structure of workshops

Each workshop will last 2–2½ hours without interval, as I find that to break dissipates energy. We may have a series of 10–12 workshops, of which I will take 6–8 myself. The first two will be devoted to laying down the basic attitudes as outlined above. I will probably then take the next one or two workshops which, after warm-ups, will be devoted to some particular skill, e.g. learning to focus, experiencing the difficulties of a scene in which everyone tries to talk at once, facing the problem of how to direct an audience's attention within a scene so that the action can be followed clearly. Another workshop might explore *resistances* (which are the stuff of theatre); what happens when we say one thing but think another. For example, A is a dentist filling Bs teeth but all the time is saying to him/herself, 'I love you! I love you!' or 'I hate you! I hate you!'

After I have taken three or four workshops and the group is beginning to cohere and develop basic skills, I will invite outsiders to come and take workshops. These tutors are either skilled local people (e.g. drama teachers) or professional theatre people from London or elsewhere. It's really useful and politically wise to use local people. It develops their standing in the community, which bodes well for the future, and it forms a useful bridge to working with complete strangers. A drama teacher is usually extremely well informed and, in Devon at least, enjoys a great deal of support from the excellent

County Drama Services. Locals will probably give a really sound workshop with a solid background, such as beginning to consider how to create a character.

When the group has had four or five workshops from myself and locals then they will be ready for some fireworks. I may invite a tutor for his known skills. Mike Alfreds, for example, gave a workshop on story-telling and Tessa Marwick gave workshops on voice and movement based on the Alexander Technique. Otherwise, I rely on the talent and sensitivity of the person concerned. William Gaskill will always give a brilliant, idiosyncratic, experimental workshop, which will be different each time. Keith Johnstone will be continuously developing and exploring his seminal and creative ideas. One of the outside workshops will be on music and singing, taken by the musical director of the community play. All these people work with the utmost enthusiasm and dedication. The groups will now have sufficient coherence and experience to see what is happening. They are ready to understand and appreciate a good outside tutor and are excited and impressed to be working with the very best people available. It gives an assurance of the standards we are aiming for and what we think is possible.

From now on, I alternate my workshops with visiting tutors. Quite late in the series, when increasing skills mean that the group can tackle quite complicated exercises, I will certainly have a workshop exploring *status*, since I find that extremely useful in rehearsal. I will also hope to have at least two workshops exploring themes in the play itself, so that we begin to reach forward to rehearsal. I myself will take the last workshop, which will be quite an ambitious affair, possibly with some technical uplift, such as stage lighting, a dressing-up wardrobe and some music. This workshop will undertake some large improvisation which will probably be related to the story of the play and it will give hopefully a sense of climax and achievement to the whole series.

Handling large workshops

Assistants When you have to work with a great number of people, it helps enormously to have one or two assistants who may well be professional, or semi-professional trainees. This could be the time when assistants start working with you towards the final production. A young, enthusiastic assistant, who understands the principle of not blocking, can quicken up a whole workshop, giving example and tone, by responding to suggestions, moving quickly to form the circle,

being eager to have a go. 'Oh, splendid!', 'Good!' are extremely
heartening, if genuinely and spontaneously voiced. Assistants can also
work with the slow and shy and so give them extra encouragement and
support. This is a time when assistants are beginning to learn how to
do their work and how to work as a team. The unconstrained
atmosphere of a workshop is a really effective way of testing each other
out, making small mistakes, preparing for the more intense and
demanding period of rehearsal. With visiting tutors, I myself always
join in as one of the group in a workshop, and since I am always
extremely enthusiastic and interested in what is going on, I probably
act as one of the enablers for the tutor.

Everybody works all the time I prefer workshops where everyone is
active and experiencing for themselves most of the time, rather than
the kind of demonstration workshop where a few volunteers come and
try something watched by all the rest (though this is sometimes
necessary). If everyone is doing something even the shy ones will have
a go and everyone is so occupied they have no chance to be critical of
anyone else. There is really no problem with numbers. You simply
divide people up in small groups of two or six or whatever size is
appropriate and get on with it. There are all sorts of dividing and
counting games which will mix people up and prevent them always
working with the same people. You can ask 70 people to go into
groups of ten and number off, you then ask all the ones, twos, threes
and so on to go into new groups and you will have ten mixed groups of
seven people. Or ask everyone who was born in July to go to one
corner of the room and everyone who was born in September to go
somewhere else, etc.

   You will find that a few experienced adults will set the tone, the
rest, having volunteered and, indeed, paid to come, will want to work
and will quickly find that the tasks set are within their range and are
enjoyable. Provided there are not too many young children they will
take their tone from the adults. If girls or boys are forming in giggly
groups, don't get impatient or single them out: open up the whole
workshop and play a game which will break the group up. Once they
are amongst people with more concentration they too will begin to
concentrate.

   Once these groups are working on creating a small scene or action
together they blot everything else out. As far as they are concerned
they are the only people in the room. People quickly realise that since
they are not watching other people, others are not watching them, and

this relieves part of the strain. This doesn't mean that we don't ask some or all of the groups to show us what they have achieved when they have taken it to a certain point, but it's the difference between rehearsal, when actors are very vulnerable, and performance, where you have to armour yourself. For some reason, even with perhaps twenty small groups in the same hall, the noise level doesn't usually get too high.

I frequently finish a workshop with a big group-improvisation. It gives a sense of achievement, of having got somewhere. If you divide the workshop into four or five large groups and give each a section or scene of the story, each group can work on its scene and, then they can be performed in sequence with the others watching. Incidentally, it can be curiously unnerving for inexperienced actors to be asked to perform their scene in a different part of the room to where they rehearsed it. They may work in 'their' corner and go to pieces if asked to come out into the middle. Let them show their scenes on the spot where they rehearsed until they become more confident about relating to other actors and to the space. This may require some foresight in arranging the space before you start. I always encourage applause for work shown.

Finally, with large numbers I generally work from the centre of the room and from here move around all over the space, making eye contact looking for reactions and checking that everyone is happy and absorbed.

Entrance fee We now charge £1 to adults and 50p to children and the unemployed. With luck and care, these door fees will balance out the cost of travel and remuneration to the outside tutors.

Arranging lifts Workshops give you a chance to spot who may be in trouble with transport before rehearsals start. You can find out who lives where and who will help with lifts.

Workshops are the basis of the whole rehearsal process. They introduce good practice and ways of working. I try to make workshops really entertaining and exciting and set the tone for the whole process of the play.

INTRODUCING THE SCRIPT TO THE COMMUNITY

Once the final script is delivered it may be tactful to show it to certain people immediately. The Rector of Dorchester was under considerable pressure, as indeed was the sponsor, in case the play should offend anyone and it was important to put their minds at rest as soon as possible. Beyond this you have to be careful: if certain people are allowed to see the script and not others there can be trouble and resentment.

Reproducing the script
Duplicated scripts are very cheap, as is photolitho. Try and buy the paper through the school. They can get it through a consortium at one third of the usual price. Collating is a tedious job: use lots of people and make it a party. Schoolchildren are an alternative: try and see they are not exploited and that they have some fun.

Binding scripts
We find punched holes with a treasury tag at the top left-hand corner is satisfactory and lasts quite well. Slide binders are more expensive. Scripts should be bound so that things can be added later, e.g. detailed rehearsal schedules, future rewrites.

Every script should have bound into it:
Outline Rehearsal Schedule A day-by-day outline from start to finish of rehearsal, listing every general rehearsal and including dates of technical and dress rehearsals, and performance dates. People fill in their individual calls in their diary. They check their next call with an assistant at the end of every rehearsal.

Detailed rehearsal schedule★ for the first three or four weeks.

Numbered list of scenes

Cast list With phone numbers.

Cost
We charge for scripts at cost. Amateurs are used to paying for scripts, do not resent it, and may be the more careful not to lose them. Ask everyone to name their script as soon as they have it.

Play-reading

With our first few productions, we made it a practice to deposit about 30 numbered scripts in the local library. People borrowed them, leaving names and addresses and a deposit and were asked to return them to the library and not pass them on to a friend. We lost some scripts but fewer than by any other method. However, this process takes time and it may be 3 or 4 weeks before everyone has been able to read a script. Also, to the inexperienced, it's as hard to visualise a play from reading a script as it is for most of us to hear music from reading a score.

We have found that the most successful way to help people to get to know a play is for the author to give a play-reading. The first time we did this, it was forced upon us: the text of *The Western Women* was very late because I had had to rewrite it at relatively short notice and the only way we could show people the script quickly was by my reading it. This was such a success that we adopted the idea in Ottery and Dorchester. It has a particular advantage that everyone hears the script at once under good conditions.

There seems to be a correlation between good writing and good reading. Certainly I remember from the old days of the Royal Court Theatre's is writers' workshops that the best writers were also the best actors, and both Sheila and David gave really excellent, moving and exciting readings. The play read by the author makes for an event which is important, curiously touching and celebratory. The writer is very vulnerable ('What will they think?') and there is a sense that s/he is giving the play, or handing it over to the town and that the town is receiving it. Sheila Yeger said of her experience:

> It was a very powerful occasion for me. I'd never done anything like it before. I didn't really know what the occasion would mean, but as I began to read, just to turn over the pages, and as I began to watch the reaction of the people who were hearing it, I suddenly knew what was true and wasn't true in the play. I knew . . . and by true, I meant that it had its own integrity. It is all absolutely laid open. Why? Because one would feel that an audience or the recipients were coming without the usual preconceptions and paraphernalia of the sort of theatre situation and that meant that they – I felt very strongly – would not make the usual allowances. Perhaps they wouldn't be critical in other ways, but nor would they make allowances for things which didn't have that ring of truth about them and that made me very

fearful. But it also made me feel very strong. Eventually I felt that if I can actually hold this audience, if I can hold this company of people, then I am writing. If I can't, then I've got to think again.

Timing

Don't be nervous if the play reading appears to take a very long time. No matter how fast the author seems to be reading, they are always far slower than performance. This is because the reader has to make infinitesimal pauses to differentiate between speakers, apart from feeling the need to read names, stage directions, etc. The most accurate approximation to true running time can be taken at the first read through by the cast.

Scripts available for sale Scripts can be available for sale at the reading which will also be an opportunity for booking audition times. See that the Press attend and take photographs.

CASTING

You will have a very fair idea of people's capacity and commitment from the workshops, but it's amazing how late and chancy spotting talent can be, even over a number of workshops. You suddenly notice someone, it may be that they suddenly lose self-consciousness and let fly. This was how we spotted the woman who was to play the female lead in the Dorchester play. She had never done any acting but was very enthusiastic at the workshops, while not appearing to be very talented. All the time she was gaining confidence, then suddenly, quite late in the series, she suddenly did something very interesting and allowed a glimpse of an extrovert, quirky quality. This is the most satisfactory way to cast.

Not everyone who comes to auditions will have been to the workshops. Some will have been drawn in by the play-reading, or publicity; some may even have avoided the workshops for all sorts of reasons. Amateurs are used to auditions and feel that justice is being seen to be done, everyone has their chance, etc. I loathe auditions, but I also loathe casting. I'm very afraid of making mistakes so I take all the help and advice I can. Good casting is 60 per cent of the success of a production: cast well and the work is more than half done, cast badly and you're working against the grain and have to carry your mistake. It's like driving water uphill, as my mother used to say.

It might be possible to cast the play through workshops and group discussion. This method, which throws great onus on the cast, would take a great deal of time and confidence-building. It might well be successful with a second or third community play where people knew what to expect and did not need so much reassurance.

Auditions

We audition very carefully, seeing an average of eight people an hour, recalling them if necessary. It's important that the author is involved in casting. S/he may not be able to be present all the time but should try to be there for the main roles and recalls.

I look for (1) talent (2) the capacity to change and develop (3) enthusiasm. This last quality is so valuable I'm not sure it shouldn't be placed first. Failing strong natural talent I try and work in great detail over a line or two to discover if an actor can change. If they have the capacity to develop, their potential may be large. Many older actors, often perhaps experienced amateurs, can look very good if cast according to type – and this is what they often prefer. Even people of limited talent can look convincing if cast near their own age and background. Bear in mind that many historical plays have characters which are remarkably near to present-day people (part of the charm of appearing in an historical play may be discovering how close we are to people of another era). It's often important with plays of this cast size that people are instantly recognisable as types. With 150 people there is hardly time to establish character in the audience's mind except in the larger parts. This does not mean that the actors do not regard their characters as individuals. It's a question of focus: the audience cannot take in all that number of people all the time. There is something to be said for type casting.

Obviously if you want to get the best out of people at casting you work very hard to create an atmosphere which is warm and encouraging. You are sympathetic and aware of stresses – which you do your best to minimise.

Everyone has a part

We stress that everyone who wants to be in the play will have a part. The 'all in' rule means that the playwright must either write too many parts, provide 'baskets', or be prepared to create more parts as required. S/he may have to face a mixture of all three since there may well be too many men's parts and not enough men, and a few actresses who won't fit into a 'basket'. It's quite common to find yourself short

of men. If so you have the following alternatives: (1) look around for
more men (2) double up the men's parts (3) consider rewriting men's
parts for women.

The only observation I can offer on the imbalance between men and
women is that many men who take part do so with a different attitude
to women. Men often appear to participate either because they have a
strong natural talent (when looking round for an *ad hoc* group to read a
play it's far easier to find really good men than women,) or conversely
because they are aware of vocal or physical inadequacy and are
perhaps hoping to change themselves. The range of talent in women is
less dramatic: there are indeed some very talented women, but fewer
than men yet, at the same time, there seem to be fewer 'non-actors'
among women.

Availability slips*

Vital for preparing rehearsal schedules. Duplicated slips with space
for name, address, telephone number, age if under 21, school or
organisation (e.g. dramatic society). For boys and girls it's often
helpful to have their height – you need to check these measurements
since children's heights are always changing, and some boys think
they're taller than they really are. This information will be useful in
casting children away from their own age and in relation to other
people.

The availability slip also lists all possible times of rehearsal. People
are asked to indicate if they cannot manage a certain day or time on a
regular basis (e.g. if they have evening classes every Tuesday at 7.00
p.m.). They are also asked to list odd dates when they won't be able to
attend rehearsal (e.g. business commitments or seats booked for the
ballet). There is then the understanding that they are free to be called
for rehearsal at times which are clear.

Ask people to fill these in at audition. It is wise to check them
through there and then, especially with children. There are frequent
misunderstandings. With some people you may find that though they
have filled up every Wednesday it's really only one in three, or that
even if they have a weekly booking they can sometimes get out of it.
You may need to explain that if people leave lots of time free it does
not mean that they will be called for more rehearsal – you simply need
the maximum flexibility from everyone in order to draw up the
rehearsal schedules.

Pay great attention to availability slips. It's no use casting people in
key roles if they can't make a reasonable number of rehearsals. The

more flexible a person's time the more easily s/he will fit into rehearsal.
Following a play, I had this useful comment:

> It's very important that folk intending to take part in a com-
> munity play should realise the extent of the commitment and
> that they should discuss this with their families, in some way to
> try and communicate your enthusiasm without being a bore! It
> is impossible to imagine just what is involved in being in a
> community play especially if, as for me, it's a whole new 'ball
> game'. In retrospect I would say that the commitment aspect
> cannot be overemphasised . . . The point of every link in the
> play-chain being equally important is so true.

I would answer that it is indeed a heavy commitment – but really
only towards the end of rehearsal. At the start we say that people will
be needed for an average of two evenings a week plus four hours some
Saturdays and Sundays, until the last two or three weeks when things
may get more hectic. People playing large parts (and the writer was
playing a lead) must be prepared for more. I would be scared to place
huge emphasis on commitment before we started – there are plenty of
other reasons why people may be reluctant to join in.

Identification

Auditioning 150 people it is easy to get confused. We take a standard
photo (contact print) of everyone, simply setting up a chair in a good
light, x feet from a camera on a tripod so that head and shoulders fill
the viewfinder. Keep a strict track of names. The photos are attached
to the availability slips. We have used video with the last three plays.
It doesn't seem to add much to the general stress. We set up the
camera in the corner of the room where it stays. There is someone in
charge who operates when they think fit, getting something of
everyone. Video is an enormous help and certainly cuts down on the
need for recalls: you can watch it time and again and it's particularly
useful in making comparisons.

Political casting

It's great fun to have vicars playing vicars, doctors acting doctors, etc.
More dodgily you may need to bring in representatives of various
groups and in some cases reward long effort and support. In the early
days, under pressure from professional assistants who were longing to
act, I used to allow myself to be swayed and give them fairly big parts.
I quickly saw that this was robbing the amateurs who were just as

talented. Members of the team may still act but usually in thankless parts.

We have never had any comment about using actors from out of town but if we have a few 'outsiders' taking part we sometimes try and cast them appropriately if there is an opportunity (e.g. in *The Western Women* some non-Lyme actors were cast as the invading Royalists; in the play set up by the Dorchester churches, which was about the Passion, good actors who appeared not to be practising Christians were cast as Romans).

PREPARING REHEARSAL SCHEDULES

The *outline rehearsal schedule* warns people of the overall pattern, particularly of the last week or so before performance. But *detailed schedules* covering the first three or four weeks should ideally be in everyone's hands a month before the first rehearsal. There are generally three/four sets of detailed rehearsal schedules over an eleven-week period:

1 Weeks 1, 2, 3, 4 available one month before rehearsals start.
2 Weeks 5, 6, 7 issued week 3.
3 Weeks 7, 8 issued week 6.

Thereafter, with production so near, notice will be relatively short and everyone should be warned of this.

Preparing rehearsal schedules is an incredibly difficult, complicated job and I make the following list and analyses.

1 Chart on squared paper: list of scenes across; list of characters down left hand side: mark off in crosses and thus you can see at a glance who is in which scene.
2 A written list of scenes and who appears in them.
3 Actors to parts/parts to actors – cross reference in alphabetical order.
4 Using the availability slips, make a chart on squared paper: days and times of rehearsal schedules across the top; actors' names down the side. Mark off the days when people are not available regularly. Use a column on the right-hand side for irregular comments (e.g. 'away 14–31 Jan'). Thus, where you see an open column, there is a possibility of rehearsal.

At some time I transfer all this data into my own director's copy, since we are always having to re-arrange or change rehearsals.

Now begin to prepare the first rehearsal schedule. You won't be able to go in sequence because you'll have to find a day when all the people in one particular scene can come together. However, this is the worst rehearsal schedule you'll have to prepare; from now on, you will have a pattern.

Try and aim not to keep people waiting. Don't have great big rehearsals unless it's a great big scene: take them in small groups for an hour or so, and then let them go. You want to try and give a sense that you will start rehearsals promptly and that if people come to rehearsal they will be used all the time.

Try and organise the schedules bearing in mind the demands of people's lives. Obviously, you will plan your big general rehearsals reasonably far apart and will not make too-great demands on people who have small parts, bunching all their rehearsals together. The retired, mothers and unemployed can work during the day and, if scenes allow, this is a very useful time although it may mean you can't rehearse at the school. Try and set up children's rehearsals early, directly after school, and certainly don't plan to use large numbers of children late at night. You can sometimes arrange for the release of individual children or small groups at school during lunch break. The biggest rehearsals will clearly take place between 7.00 p.m. and 9.00 p.m. or at weekends. If you are going to hold late rehearsals, they should be for as few people as possible.

In order to give people sufficient notice and allow time for duplicating and distribution, you will have to start plotting the second rehearsal schedule about fourteen days after the first read-through. This is just enough time to have some idea which scenes may need more attention.

When issuing the schedules ask people to check all their calls, let someone know immediately if there is a mistake, and fill in their rehearsal diary. After each rehearsal they check their diary with an assistant, not only because the actor may be vague but the rehearsal may have been changed.

Computerisation

In Crediton the rehearsal schedules were computerised (the programme planner had to take a week or so of his holiday to do it). Since I did not direct the Crediton play I have no real experience of how computerisation worked. In a sense, although drawing up rehearsal schedules is an awful job, in the end you have a feeling for individuals and their life-pattern which is useful right the way through rehearsal.

Music rehearsals

People are rather bad about attending music rehearsals as such. They tend to think, 'I'm only one of hundreds – I won't really be missed.' I now slip music rehearsals into big general rehearsals, or make arrangements with the musical director that he has a group of people for a certain period, or double-rehearses them while I have another group. I don't isolate music rehearsals on the schedule until people have fully understood that they have each an individual responsibility to go to them.

Inform key people

See that various people whom the schedules may affect get a copy of the rehearsal schedule (e.g. headteacher, deputy head, caretaker, designer, etc.).

Keep a record

These plays are generally composed of a very large number of small scenes. I make a chart on squared paper, listing each scene and when it is scheduled. I check the scene off when the rehearsal actually takes place, thus I can see if any particular scene has been neglected.

The sheer detail, size and complexity of rehearsal schedules will help people to realise the scale of the undertaking and the amount of work which is being put into it.

REHEARSALS

The director must first of all be thoroughly experienced and good at his/her job. S/he must have all the necessary directorial skills plus a feeling for caring and teaching. S/he must be flexible and patient.

Directing a community play differs from directing any other play only in the following factors:

1 Size of cast.

2 A great mix of talent, age and background, including many people who will have no previous experience of acting at all.

3 You are working with people who have full-time commitments and families.

4 A relatively long rehearsal period of 11–12 weeks with an absolute maximum of $5\frac{1}{2}$ hours rehearsal a day for the director (less for actors), except weekend rehearsals which may be longer.

Commitment, enthusiasm, energy, confidence and supportiveness

These are the qualities which will bring the play to a successful production. All the skills of author, director and others will have little effect, and may indeed be negative, if you don't nurture and encourage enthusiasm and supportiveness. A significant part of the director's job is encouraging these qualities and nothing should ever be allowed to check or discourage them. The directors must themselves be enthusiastic and energetic otherwise it will be impossible to create an atmosphere in which these qualities can truly flourish. In putting on these enormous productions, will and skill are vital but of themselves they are not enough to free and inspire actors to amazing things.

Talent is a gift, and of course one wants a talented actor who is also committed, enthusiastic and supportive; but talent without these positive qualities can be destructive, especially amongst inexperienced actors who must be confident to give of their best. Talent is glorious, but talent which is selfish and self-centred can wreak such damage in a community play that given a choice I think it would be a close thing whether I would not prefer enthusiasm and commitment to talent which was selfish, self-centred and destructive.

Before you start rehearsals, you will have a core of actors who have already been to workshops and who know and trust each other and you, and with whom you have already established working methods and discipline. If you are lucky, you will also have people who have worked in other shows, who may have to travel quite long distances to be in this one. Their loyalty, skill, enthusiasm, and experience will be a great support to you and an example to the rest of the cast.

Rehearsals demand more than workshops

There are basic differences between workshops and rehearsals which actors must understand. A rehearsal is much more demanding than a workshop: actors have to get on with it; a certain amount of work must be got through at each rehearsal; there has to be a structure which builds to the climax of production. The show must be ready on time. This puts a certain strain on actors but, provided you are aware of it and control the pressure, they enjoy it. It's an experience of commitment which is planned to last for a definite time; to have a shape and lead to the final achievement of performance, and as such it's very exciting. Over the relatively short period of time, people can organise their lives around it.

General rehearsal practice
Punctuality

It's not necessary for everyone to attend each and every workshop, or even to be particularly prompt. In rehearsal, however, it can be damaging if people turn up late or not at all.

People have chosen to be in the play, and they want to be in it, but they may need to be taught how important it is that every individual called for rehearsal is on time. It's possible to think of this as being linked with demonstrating the importance of each single person: asking for punctuality shows that you are serious and take their efforts seriously, that they are needed. This helps trust and commitment.

It's so easy for people to think, 'Oh, I'm not doing much; an assistant or someone can read me in'; but everyone has their own timing, approach, weight; performances are built by actors working together and matching themselves exactly. Working with a substitute is not the same as the real thing. You especially need to know who is present in a big rehearsal. People may be missed and you need to demonstrate that it matters. We try not to read a register – that would take too long and seem like school. Instead, we invent various games. The simplest is perhaps to have a list of surnames under each letter of the alphabet. Everyone goes into a group under their own letter; they all check who is present; first group to finish is the winner. We have a namecheck list at the beginning of every big rehearsal.

People have to learn that a definite amount of work has to be achieved with each rehearsal. If they don't come, not only will this tax other people's patience and energy, but the work will have to be done at some later date and may possibly rob time from other scenes.

Most rehearsals are in small groups where it is easy to check. You will be fortunate if you can manage a dozen huge rehearsals with everyone present. Sometimes it seems a miracle to me that everyone is there for the production.

You can make it easier for people to be punctual by always starting rehearsals on time. If a previous rehearsal is over-running try and arrange for an assistant or co-director to start the next rehearsal. (This is one reason why you need more than one rehearsal room.) Try and finish big rehearsals promptly, unless there are exceptional circumstances when you have also obtained the agreement of the cast. At the end of each rehearsal, check the date of the next rehearsal of that scene not only generally but with individual diaries.

If someone is late for rehearsal and doesn't turn up, an assistant should always telephone: the manner should be warm and friendly, but clear and firm. Ask people to give notice if they can't come to rehearsal. This allows time to find a substitute or to rearrange a rehearsal; it also makes the position of someone who doesn't turn up without notice much weaker.

If someone is persistently late, try and understand why. It's no use adopting a blustering or nagging tone; you'll only put people's backs up. Examine the difficulty together and be objective (i.e. get them to understand the problem from other people's point of view); don't try and pull non-existent authority. Say, 'What do you think? How should we tackle this?' If there is a real difficulty then of course you will try and work round it. If someone is always late or doesn't turn up, you have a choice of working round them or of issuing warnings, and then either threatening to put them in a smaller role and being ready to do so (this often works like a charm with children), or chucking them out, which is drastic, but serves as an example that you are serious. You may have people leave the play through this problem, because they simply do not understand the degree of commitment needed to achieve the standard towards which you are all working.

Punctuality and the need to be present become more clearly understood when the actors realise that rehearsal time is being totally and positively used: that each period of rehearsal as far as possible is working towards a defined goal and ends with a sense of achievement.

Warm-ups

Rehearsal warm-ups are slightly different to workshop warm-ups. There are no preconceptions about workshops which, in a sense, are one long warm-up. The structure of a workshop is so free that you can set up games and exercises and no one will question them; joining in is a form of commitment, a demonstration of willingness to let go and try something new. People who are afraid of this sort of thing will stay away.

In rehearsals there may well be older people including perhaps amateur actors who are defensive and stiff. They certainly need warm-ups but you have to lead them gently. It's irritating to have people stand aloof at the side, but I think it's better to put up with it than have a fuss, so I encourage people to join in warm-ups, but I don't insist. By this time the majority of the cast will recognise the value of warm-ups and those who are not joining in may feel a little outside. This in itself is a situation that has to be watched: you don't want to isolate people. Some people who can't face physical warm-ups may join in vocal warm-ups and that is a start.

Children

We haven't always been consistent with our over-14 rule. In Axminster we were strongly influenced by the drama teacher, who was co-director: she had a number of pupils of 11 years old. In Dorchester there was a family who desperately wanted their young children to be in the show and once we had let one or two families in, in fairness we had to allow everyone, and ended up with over 30 of them between the ages of 2½ and 14. Actually, I found it easier to cope with this group, whose parents were in the show, than with the far higher number of young teenagers we used in Sherborne, where there were 80 youngsters between 11 and 16, amongst a cast of 180 (a very large proportion). The young people were so exuberant they perhaps overbalanced the show.

This balance between young and old is extremely important. If you get it right the older people are leavened and enlivened by the spirit of the youngsters, while the youngsters learn maturity and self-discipline from older people. There is, too, a good spin-off in that, working together, the generations come to have sympathy with one another. Children, of course, differ profoundly according to their age group: 6–10-year-olds are different in interest, maturity, self-discipline from 14-year-olds, and boys are different to girls. There are very seldom more than one or two extremely young children (i.e. 2/3 year-olds) who will of course be brought to rehearsal when they are needed and taken away immediately afterwards. With children aged 5–8 the problem is usually one of concentration. They are often part of a family who are also in the play and their mothers may or may not keep an eye on them. Mothers are, as a rule, delighted that their children are in what is essentially a vast play area and that they are apparently enjoying themselves. A situation which may need careful handling.

The problem of boys of 10–14 is usually rowdiness. They gang up with a leader and can be troublesome. The old rule applies: break up the group and send them to different parts of the hall. Girls of this age are usually no trouble. Conversely, girls of 14–15 are more difficult than boys of the same age, who in my experience are for some reason fairly docile in rehearsal. Girls are maturing faster at this time and testing themselves in all sorts of situations and it can make them appear cocky and careless. The answer is to work them hard in rehearsal and then send them away. As soon as you can, give them some visibly demanding, responsible, technical task and they usually rise to the challenge.

Sustenance for children We generally have a stock of Mars Bars, barley sugar and/or boiled sweets. The children may be coming to rehearsal straight after a long day at school and may have had nothing to eat since 12.30 p.m. They really need a bit of sugar to keep them going. We sell Mars Bars at cost (get them from a cash and carry through a friendly sweet shop if you can; this makes them cheaper), or give them a boiled sweet free. For obvious reasons adults have to pay 1p per sweet. In Dorchester the children never got their sustenance because at the committee meeting where the matter was brought up someone objected on health grounds: sugar/teeth, etc. This is a valid point but unfortunately I wasn't present and the point was not made that someone has to (a) find out what the children want which is healthy and (b) provide it and, if it's perishable, replenish stocks. No one filled in the 'Action' column (see p. 68). The issue had become a bit complicated and we never managed to face it again.

After rehearsal Children who live in outlying villages may have to be collected after rehearsal; they should not be left to wait alone in the cold and dark if rehearsal ends before their lift arrives.

Promenade performances: particular needs in rehearsal

Promenade performances are an immensely exciting form of theatre, as far away from television as it is possible to go. Promenading has another advantage: it gives people lots to do. In all the plays, we have almost the entire cast in the audience throughout the performance: they never stop acting and relating to the action; they are always to some degree in character. Actors in rehearsal are always tempted to bunch around a stage where the action is taking place. Unless the scene demands it, they have to learn and rehearse, allowing the audience to be nearest to the action, while the actors themselves are dispersed right through the hall. The excitement of theatre is intensified by physical proximity: if we stand near to someone, we influence them emotionally and thus mentally. The role of the actors in focusing on the action and reacting to it becomes a vital element in these intensely exciting performances.

The promenading actors have a very demanding and subtle role which has to be learned and rehearsed. In a specially written historical play about a precise community, the audience (i.e. the town itself), is the chief character in the play, and the actors, themselves townspeople, form a special bridge between action and audience. They must know when to talk, improvise and take part in the action;

when to emotionally identify and be part of the action yet remain silent; when to focus attention as the 'ideal audience'. In big scenes they will be in character, part of the action, e.g. listening, quietly or not as may be, to a speech by the mayor in huge composite scenes, e.g. a race-meeting they may be building the action by a series of small improvisations all over the hall and in small 'private' scenes; e.g. a mother talks to her daughters while they make a pie, the actors will form the 'ideal audience', focusing on the scene and reacting to it as an audience, and yet be still in character.

The actors also have to learn how the promenading audience will behave and how to control it. Given space, the audience will tend to shuffle from stage to stage following the action, and audiences are very quick to learn to watch the lights as a clue to what next will be happening where. Actors have to learn to grab the audience's attention, to say, in effect, 'Over here!' and to play very hard at the beginning of scenes to overcome the sound and distraction of an audience moving. They also learn how to make audiences give way for movement through the auditorium. The actors have to be taught how distracting uncontrolled movement can be. It's a fundamental law of theatre that the eye is quicker than the ear: if someone moves through an important speech, that speech can be missed. This is a big problem given such large casts in promenade performances. The particular skills must be learned and perfected throughout rehearsal.

Improvisation

We use improvisation a great deal. It vividly helps people, especially children, to see around the character, to get beyond the bare works of the text and illuminate the character. Many of the cast will be very relaxed with improvisation, having done it in the workshops, and will set an example to the others.

We also positively use improvisation in building the action. People are relating to each other the whole time in character and improvisation is an excellent way of setting up small episodes and scenes. These are, in fact, usually rehearsed improvisations by the time we come to production, but there is nothing to prevent spontaneous improvisation taking place. Many people find themselves with extra lines, which cheers them up a great deal. The audience love overhearing these small snatches of dialogue and it is a delight to see people committed and totally part of the action although no one especially may be watching them. Thus, at a race meeting, a man pushes past you, saying, 'Where's the beer tent?' and a vicar in a side aisle fulminates against the evils of strong drink. In *The Western Women* there was a large scene, taking place all over the hall, when the exhausted men, defending Lyme during the siege, for the first time accepted that they could not carry on and allowed the women to take over their posts and their guns. The whole atmosphere was very quiet, indeed tender: all over the hall tiny improvised scenes were taking place, each one watched perhaps by a dozen people, and yet the total effect was intensely, even shatteringly, moving. Incidentally, while audiences love to overhear improvisation, they rarely enjoy being put into the position of having to take part: it makes them self-conscious. Actors have to learn to speak 'past' the audience unless there is a specific need to do otherwise.

Praise
The general rule
It's rare indeed that I don't give praise after every single piece of work, however small. I try never to praise dishonestly – if only for the meanest of reasons (others will observe and not trust me when I praise them) – but also because I try and make truth the basis of the work. Praise can always be given for trying: 'Good. I could see you were really concentrating. Well done! And you were speaking up much better too. But I don't think it's quite there yet, do you? You see this bit here: what do you think she means when she's saying this?'

It can be dangerous to pick out some small success which is not relevant to the main part of the scene just because you're desperate to find something to praise ('I love the way you pick up the cup and wipe it'). The actor may be so delighted by the praise that the irrelevant action becomes the focal point of the scene for them and it will be hard to get them to give it up.

Exceptions to the praise rule: 'difficult actors'
You are sometimes faced with an actor who is messing about showing how clever s/he is, indicating that s/he is much bigger than the production, and generally being a pest. There is usually one person in the cast who elects him/herself to this role. Such people are not generally very talented because lack of confidence is part of their difficulty. In a way I don't altogether resent their appearance: they seem to draw the poison and mischief from everywhere else upon themselves, to become a kind of scapegoat. However, they have to be coped with otherwise they will waste time and undermine people's concentration and their confidence in the director. First try to build

up the difficult actor's confidence. If this has no effect you may perhaps feel it right to be firm and say clearly, 'It's not good enough.' The degree of pressure you use must be related to what you think the situation requires. It's no use praising work which is clearly meant to challenge the director and disrupt the rehearsal process. Point out what is happening: 'You really haven't bothered to learn your lines have you?' and (if you really want to isolate them): 'It means that we're all being held up.' Everyone watching will see what's happening and, if there is basic trust between you, you will find that you have the support of the rest of the cast. You don't want their vocal support since you want to control the degree of the difficult actor's isolation very carefully, but you want to remove the idea of the difficult actor challenging you, and show that s/he is really challenging the rest of the cast. You won't altogether stop him/her being difficult because that's his/her self-elected role, and because of pride, but s/he will stop being bloody difficult.

Another awkward type is the attention-seeker who may quite well be moderately talented because acting is one of the means s/he employs to make people notice him/her. Don't reinforce this attention-seeking. I find the best course is a firm supportiveness, but if s/he insists on wasting everybody's time, then refer him/her to an assistant: 'Could you ask Bill, I'm sure he'll be able to help you', and pass on to something else.

A much more difficult case is the really talented actor who sometimes causes trouble through temperament. In point of fact, amateur actors are much less prone to really destructive temperament than professionals because professional star actors have been spoiled by playing big parts where the play depends on them, so they take advantage of their power. At the same time the responsibility of the huge burden they carry for the success of the play means anxiety throws them off balance. These particular circumstances almost never apply in community plays. However, you may meet them and should be prepared. Again you will find that the cast knows very well what is going on and you will need to demonstrate that you can cope. I find it best, faced with this sort of problem, to be supportive, warm, reinforce 'good' behaviour and be very exact in praise. Actors are 'temperamental' because they are unsure, because the particular effort and energy required to support and display talent has as its reverse nature the negative quality of restlessness and perhaps the wish to demonstrate this power by making life difficult for others. You must control the worst aspects by protecting those members of the cast who may be most affected by the temperamental actor. Best of all is to be objective, yet supportive, to refuse to fight in any circumstances. The actor is really testing out whether s/he can trust and respect you. If you can demonstrate that s/he cannot rattle you and that you really know your job, you will find that s/he calms down and works very positively. If you allow yourself to become subjective when faced with a talented but temperamental actor, there is a danger that s/he will start to gain an ascendancy and then be really destructive. Your confidence will bleed away and with it your creative energy.

The purpose of all this praise and encouragement is to invite actors to experiment and let go, to convince them of the value (and sometimes even the possibility) of their own creativity.

EARLY STAGES OF REHEARSAL

We usually have a large, general rehearsal on a Sunday afternoon to read through the play. I am aiming to give a sense of coherence, to stress the value of each and every member of the cast, to establish working methods and to start a support organisation.

Many members of the cast will never have met before. There are so many of them at the first rehearsal that the size of the undertaking is perhaps comforting: you are just one of a crowd.

Hopefully, the professional team are all present. The designer has brought the model and will explain it and has probably pinned up drawings around the hall. The musical director may play some of the music. The rest of the professional team are introduced. The stage manager, or an assistant, is asked to time the reading.

It's fairly standard practice to read through the play at the first rehearsal. It gives people a sense of 'We're off!' There is also a small taste of the essential excitement and challenge of performance. At this first rehearsal I re-establish the principle of protecting people and of assuring them that they won't be made to look foolish. Just as I would at the start of any professional production I point out that a read-through is not a performance but simply a way of having a look at the play as a whole before we begin to break it up into small parts. If some people feel inspired and let fly during the read-through that is fine, but the point is to protect those who are bad readers. They are not necessarily bad actors and even if they are, it doesn't matter: they are going to get better. Everyone understands and is supportive.

Starting support organisation/tea, etc.

The tea break is an opportunity for people to get up and stretch themselves and to start relating to each other. They now have something to talk about. The big weekend rehearsals last four hours or more and we always have tea, squash, biscuits, etc. It's possible to ask people to bring their own thermos flasks, but some will forget, especially children, and it's a good idea to get the rhythm going at the first rehearsal. The support organisation is a way of involving yet more people (they may later turn into the Fair Committee). A tea break is a good time to make general announcements, take orders for sweat-shirts, souvenirs, etc.

A sense of identity

After the tea break, it's time to make people realise that each one of them has a responsibility in bringing the play to performance. I always emphasise that the play is about the town and the people, not just the principals (as it should be). This is probably the only rehearsal at which everybody will meet together for some time. To help give a sense of identity in such an enormous production I almost always organise people into their relative play families and we use these small groups as a base for improvisation and working relationships right through rehearsals and performance. Thus, as in life, everyone has various people whom they can relate to closely. They begin to build up a rich, strong relationship within these groups. For example, in *The Western Women* a 14-year-old boy who played the Town Clerk's assistant was also a member of the Somers family, but naturally enough got together with other boys in the town. Throughout the play he related in character to these and other groups; his basic relationship to the others was established at the first rehearsal.

Changes in the script

A new text is an exciting adventure: a world première is a very different process to working on a printed text from Samuel French.

It is very important at the first rehearsal that you describe the process which must take place in shaping a new play. A playwright cannot totally foresee what will work. Testing a play in rehearsal will reveal sections that are too long or simply not working. You need to make clear to the cast at the first rehearsal, while they are all together, and before the process begins, that if there are cuts and rewrites it won't be because they are bad actors. On the contrary, the better the acting the easier it becomes to detect flaws in the writing. Try and define your common goal: that the play should be brought to a successful performance and that everyone has a great time. Will you achieve your goal with a flawed play which will bore and confuse the audience but where the actors' parts remain totally unchanged and intact? The play is the basis of all. When it is tight and clear it allows the acting to be forceful, exciting and exact.

Try and do as many rewrites as possible before you go into rehearsal. We all hate losing lines but in a community play, consisting of over 100 small parts, cuts may mean that half someone's part has gone and you may have to make a very damaging decision as to whether to sacrifice the play or the actor. In my experience, amateurs are less vociferous about this than professionals and by and large very modest and disciplined. If you have to cut and rewrite, make sure the actors concerned know exactly why and what is gained by the cut. You will probably cut because the writing is too lax and not earning its place in the story, or because it's not clear (in the general phrase, 'not working'). It's very seldom that you need to cut a scene because the actor can't do his job. There are other methods to cope with this (see below).

If you are careful to analyse the text, so that everyone understands why a scene is not working, the actor whose part is cut is demonstrably sacrificing something for the good of the play and s/he gets credit for it. Of course, you will try and make it up to the actor in some other way but that is not always possible. It's far easier to make and accept cuts and rewrites if there is an atmosphere of warmth, trust and security at rehearsal.

Taking the play to bits

Once we have got over the first big general rehearsal, it's usually a question of a succession of small rehearsals with a few people tackling their scenes probably for the first time. In the early stages we are trying to find out what the scene demands and also to discover character. Discussion would seem to be the obvious way of uncovering the author's intentions, and of course discussion is very valuable and has its place but, with inexperienced actors, I prefer going into a scene, discovering things, surprising ourselves, making mistakes. Your whole persona, physical and mental, then enters into the discovery. You find out things not only through your brain but through what your voice and body suggest. All the time, physically, vocally and intellectually, you're uncovering ideas, material and attitudes. The doing becomes discovery. This is not mindless, but neither is it intellectual. The actor thinks and feels his way into a part, rather than intellectualising about it. This is particularly good for actors who are physically bound (and most amateurs are). Moving about frees them and makes them less self-conscious. The body begins to suggest things to the mind and vice versa.

I don't encourage too much sitting around beforehand, discussing the text in minute detail. We just read the scene through and, with hardly any discussion or direction, start walking it. Watching the actors very closely suggests to me all sorts of ideas which we might explore. The ideas come from what the actors do, plus our perception of what the text requires. Once the actors understand this method, they realise that the scene is being created in terms of their personalities: in a sense they are creating it. We then start again, this time stopping frequently for discussion and improvisation, etc. We are aiming for understanding what the script needs and what the characters are. At this point, we work very slowly, questioning every line and indeed every word, in terms of character, its place and purpose in the play. I almost never slide over a point in the early stages, unless I sense someone has had enough. Knowing when to press on and when to stop is very important in a director. At the same time, I have a timescale in my mind and never let the work fall too far behind.

Many years ago I would plot the moves of a play from start to finish, but now I find freedom and risk are truly creative. You don't know what will happen but something will and it's up to you to recognise and use it. The method is an obvious extension of the no-blocking/ trust attitude. The ideas become a creative flow. It's tremendously exciting, like skiing or windsurfing, but it does rely on the director's talent and experience. If, for some reason, the ideas fail to come, then experience takes over. While I encourage great freedom in rehearsal, I know that I can retrieve the situation whatever happens. No scene ever totally fails in rehearsal because there is always something to be learned and you can always find something positive. If I make a mistake, I tell them what has happened and why, and this helps their understanding of the scene and paradoxically increases their confidence in me. I try to leave everyone at the end of rehearsal with a positive sense of achievement.

Learning lines

I do not encourage people to learn their parts too early. The first few weeks of rehearsal are an experimental, fluid period. As the actor senses out the character and needs of the scene, s/he will begin to half learn the lines and they will be linked to the imaginative and physical experience, so becoming part of the whole organic process of creating a character and telling the story. As the ideas are still unformed, so are the inflections and thoughts behind the lines. Conversely, lines learnt mechanically too early may become a hard shell which actually distorts the developing performance. An inflection once learnt is hard to change. Early rote learning is especially characteristic of older, experienced amateurs, who are used to turning in a 'professional' performance in a style which may be many years out of date. It's hard to change such people. They are very useful in a team because they are 'strong', and know how to focus, but it's a way of acting that draws attention to itself and can appear superficial.

Respect for the text

Amateurs are used to working with printed texts. They don't usually think of the author very much and seldom appreciate that the author is perhaps chiefly responsible for the final production. (A director can easily mess up a good play but it's very hard indeed to do more than slightly improve a bad one.) The play is a totality which begins with the writer, a creative artist, and the work must not be altered without the writer's consent. The author's contract will contain a clause to this effect, and it's a right which is jealously guarded.

I demonstrate absolute respect for the writer's text. Even if I cannot wholly respect the work, I am still very guarded about changing it. A text is a compass and every artistic decision is taken with reference to it. If you monkey about with the text you destroy your faith in the compass and the play may begin to drift. A fine, skilful writer composes exactly to the smallest preposition and the most insignificant comma and everything leads to the final dramatic statement.

The chief difficulty comes with bad learners: some actors are bad at learning, some are careless. You have to decide yourself where you will draw the line. You cannot finally win in the contest with a 'difficult' actor who will never take the trouble to learn lines properly and who thinks it smart to mug his/her way through. I never encourage actors to think it's a good idea to rearrange the dialogue without a good deal of discussion. The actor may be right, but s/he has to convince us.

Background study

While you don't ask actors to learn by rote, you have to teach amateurs who may never have acted before how to study their parts outside rehearsal. How to go over the text rethinking the discussions that took place, the thoughts behind a move and why it was made at such and such a point, to think about character and background and to research them. This is particularly important, as a scene may not be scheduled for rehearsal for another two to three weeks in the early stages.

MIDDLE STAGES OF REHEARSAL

It may take three or four weeks to get through the whole play because we are working so slowly to begin with. Now things move a little faster. We are concerning ourselves at this middle stage very much with developing the individual actor. By the end of the period we will hope to have found how each character contributes with the others to build a scene. What is the point of the scene? How does it take the action forward? How fast we go depends very much on the skill, confidence and emotional state of the actors. You try and analyse the problem that confronts them and then break it down into separate parts sufficiently small and understandable so that, when you present it to the actor, they can successfully surmount each stage like a flight of steps. Some people need more steps than others. We reduce the play to very small sections and even the director may have little sense of the whole; but s/he must never lose their overriding sense of time-pattern. The production must reach a certain stage by a given date. This is a messy, chaotic, creative stage. You are in a sense retracing the dramatist's steps and recreating them in terms of the living actors. Only the text remains of a piece and is your guide back to cohesion.

Now is the time when you push to build up the confidence of the weaker actors and really begin to make demands on the stronger ones. At the same time, you may begin to notice a quality emerging which you now seek to maintain while bringing up the performance to a near professional level in other ways. Almost all inexperienced actors have a freshness, an occasional awkwardness, which is very attractive. It's an energy, vitality and feeling of real life. It is literally charming and quite different from the pleasure we get from skilled professionals. Appreciate this and don't perhaps seek to cover it up.

Artistic truth

Your goal with actors is to help them understand artistic truth, the integrity of an artistic statement or idea: its power and focus. I sometimes think this is the artist's chief task: to know when they are close to artistic truth or sliding away from it. Artistic truth has a simplicity which comes not from first ideas but through refining and selecting a vast chaotic mass. Within this mass the artist has to learn how to sense if s/he is close to the core of what s/he is trying to reveal. One of the tasks of the director is to help the actor begin to sense the artistic truth of what the character and scene demand. I think that this is finally a sensing and not necessarily an intellectualising process. Having been through all the stages of feeling out the character, discussing it, analysing it, the actor goes back to the rehearsal process and tries to express the message, power, emotion, statement or whatever. You are hoping and working for the moment when the actor will say, 'Yes, I could feel that I was nearly there', or 'No, I didn't quite get it'. When the actors themselves can feel that they are getting near to artistic truth or diverging from it, then a vast step forward has been taken. Actors then develop quickly in power and sensitivity because they begin to be confident that they can rely on their own sense of what is happening and that they themselves can search around till they recognise that they are near the core of what they are trying to express.

Saying 'No'

By the time you are a few weeks into rehearsal, when there is sufficient trust and confidence, it's safe to be negative, to say simply to some actors, 'No, it wasn't right.' (Even so it is always wise to praise something a little.) The actor must be capable of understanding that by saying 'No' you are actually paying them the compliment of offering a stimulation because you consider they are strong enough to face up to thinking things out for themselves. You are inviting the actors to find out the solution. When I know the atmosphere is strong enough, I can allow myself to say truthfully, 'I know something's wrong but I don't know what to do' and see what the actors suggest. I know that I can always retrieve the situation because I can cast around until I find something, but it's great if the actors are carrying a share of the rehearsal. I would never end the rehearsal on a negative note. With any actor, no matter how strong and talented, I always point out what has been achieved, praise and thank them for hard work and perhaps suggest a broad goal for the next rehearsal.

Focus

Amateur actors often find it difficult to focus quickly, whereas a professional focuses almost instantly and will turn power into a narrow beam exactly on target. Most amateurs have to wander around a little in rehearsal until they find out how to do it, how to project themselves emotionally at the right pressure at a precise point. It's a skill that comes with confidence, a clear understanding of what is required, and practice/experience.

Direction by actors

In the early stages of rehearsal, once I have established the principle of trying things out on our feet, there is an enormous amount of discussion. Everyone throws in ideas. Later in rehearsal you sometimes find one or two people who want to tell others what to do. It's always the actors who are least sensitive to other people who do this and it will be irritating to the other actors who feel they are having to put up with someone else's personality problems. The actor's ideas may be useful, well-timed, carefully expressed, or they may not; but an inexperienced amateur may well be confused by the direction and embarrassed as to how to react to it. If an actor starts giving direct instructions to another I head them off and open up the discussion. This is in fact educative, for the most acceptable way to suggest ideas is for the actors to do so generally and possibly indirectly, i.e. through the director. If an actor feels it's a dodgy situation but wants to make a suggestion he or she should have a word aside with the director.

'Poor' actors

There are, alas, bad actors: people who are so bound and, apparently, so unimaginative, so lacking in energy, that no matter what devices you employ, you seem not to be helping them much. They will improve. It is your responsibility that the actor should never feel that s/he has failed.

The actor's job is to appreciate what the situation and story require, command the vocal strength and flexibility to reveal it, and focus their energy to get the line and thought over to the audience. Actors may be 'poor' because they lack confidence, or they don't understand what the scene/character/story requires, or their imagination is bound, or their voices and bodies are not sufficiently flexible (or a combination of all these).

Actors don't have a chance to be good if they don't understand what is wanted. One of the chief tasks through the first six or seven weeks of rehearsal is to help people understand the meaning of what they say and what is needed to tell the story. I often ask people to put a speech into their own words so that they have to think it out freshly. Improvisation is another tool which will help reveal and clear up confusion and misunderstanding. Sheer lack of knowledge of historical conditions often makes an actor look dull. Once you are sure that the actor really is clear about basic understanding and this is still not giving their imagination sufficient lift, you can seek out other ways of helping them.

Vocal problems

If you listen to inexperienced actors speaking, it's quite common that the line lacks force and conviction. The voice is not 'anchored'. At the same time the voice is not flexible or strong enough to make an exact point.

This is how many people speak in real life. Their voices are neither particularly strong nor flexible because they don't actually have the need to communicate fresh ideas or convince with new opinions and so have never developed the vocal capacity, etc. They seldom need to be much more expressive than 'Put your coat on before you go out'. In the theatre, the actor may have to communicate all sort of nuances on this line.

To some degree it's a problem of under-used imagination, body and voice. I tackle this at several levels: build confidence so that they will dare to venture out of the safety and reassurance of habit; imaginatively, so that they have some idea where they want to go; by means of warm-ups and exercises I actually try and free voice and body physically.

Technical help

Anchoring the voice It is possible to give people the experience of 'anchoring' the voice as opposed to having the inflections wandering vaguely and never hitting the spot. In an exercise (shown us in a workshop by Glyn MacDonald), you imagine something small on the ground before you – a dog? a small child? (exactly what it is is left to your imagination: Glyn never talks in her workshops, she leads by suggestion). You then admonish and control the puppy, raising a finger, making eye contact and saying 'Uh Huh!' with energy and conviction: you have to be definite or the puppy won't do what you want.

Are they taking in enough breath? Inaudible actors are sometimes simply not taking in enough air to support the voice.

Singing the scene It sometimes frees people and gives them fresh energy if they sing the scene, they can also try large extravagant gestures if they like.

Picking out key words An inexperienced actor may not know quite how to get a speech across – how to do so with sufficient energy. It helps if s/he selects the key words, those words which are actually carrying the meaning of the speech, and emphasises them, giving the others less weight. There is a tendency to emphasise unimportant adverbs, like 'very', and such words may actually hold the speech back. What really drives a speech along are verbs.

Blocks In helping to release people who may not have acted before, there is a difficulty and responsibility. As a director you very quickly realise that some people have difficulty in releasing themselves imaginatively and artistically because they are blocked by their own psychology. I take the view that this is an extremely sensitive area and I have neither the skills, training nor right to interfere. It is a great responsibility to make someone face their problems unless that is the point of the work and you are qualified to do it. I simply try and help the actor in terms of the part, to release through imagination, improvisation and exercises, at however superficial a level. Nevertheless, by releasing even to a small degree, inner problems may begin to surface. I have not infrequently known people considerably moved by something in their part which relates to their own life, and it's obvious that the release brings comfort and insight to them. I have never known this release to be destructive. It very rarely happens publicly, but the person themselves or someone near them will tell you of it. Sometimes this inner block is clearly so huge and so painful that the actors will never approach it and I can only hope that the part has been cast so that we can work around the block. Sometimes, indeed, the block provides an inner tension, which generates energy and talent. The whole area is one of which the director must be aware and towards which they must be careful and sensitive.

Hiding a 'poor' actor

If there is really no way the actor is ever going to succeed with the problem as it stands, then you must alter the problem. For example, if someone has a vocal disability, you must give them lines or shouts against a storm or loud music. If they are simply incapable of speaking loudly enough, you don't deprive them of the line, but get someone else to repeat it. If they are simply boring, there may be several reasons: the lines may be boring, or the speech may be making too great technical demands. Sometimes actors appear so placid that no amount of breaking up a speech into pitch, pace, intensity, ever seems to make them more lively. It's extremely unlikely that they will be in a large part, as you will have spotted the real weaklings during casting, so you are unlikely to have a disaster on your hands. Stick with the problem, don't abandon such actors. Try not to single them out and make it obvious that you think they are hopeless. Don't make them feel foolish and insecure. Support them with confidence and praise whenever you can, even if only for trying. If all else fails, distract attention from the actor: have something else going on at the same time. Better still, use the distraction positively, so that the two simultaneous events compete or blend to raise the temperature. It helps to give a poor actor a very strong goal (e.g. s/he must reach a certain point fast and loud). Remember that it's a long rehearsal period and there is plenty of time for actors to grow in confidence and also to take their tone from other people. It's possible for other actors to 'carry' the poor ones: sometimes poor actors simply get picked up by enthusiasm. This can easily begin to happen in performance; when you look back you may well be amazed at what the actor has achieved.

I don't think I have ever recast an actor because s/he was 'bad'. I once had to swap someone round because of a confusion of names in casting, where by some ghastly mischance, I found I had cast an 80-year-old to play the sexually demanding husband of a young woman. This could reasonably have been an interesting scene, but in the particular case, it was destroying the point required by the script. We explained honestly and tactfully, being concerned to maintain the actor's confidence and he appeared to accept the situation with considerable humour.

Difficulties with dance and movement

Dance is the one area where I have found it impossible to help an amateur dancer look as good as a professional. We are, most of us, physically bound and by contrast the movements of a trained dancer are amazingly controlled yet free. Maybe a movement specialist would have more success. For this reason I avoid having amateur actors (or for that matter professionals) dancing in a situation where they should look very good.

Beginning to run scenes: shifting the goals

If we repeat a scene several times, we do so step by step, raising the target a little each time. I praise what's been done, even if I only say, 'Very good! Splendid!' without being specific. I am praising for endeavour amongst other things. I may say, 'Now, let's try it again, and this time, see if you can pick up the cues faster' (or perhaps with specific suggestions to individual actors). When they have finished, I praise again: 'I think there could be even more energy. You see this line here . . . We might just try it by words alone.' When they have done it, I praise again. I suggest that we repeat the scene: 'Keep the pace going, but bring up the sound level.' I am seldom sure when we begin to go through a scene what it is going to require in order to grow, or how a goal may be reached. As the actors do the scene they show me how it can be improved next time. In a sense, I go step by step just as they do. I would never ask actors to mechanically repeat a scene without giving them a fresh reason to do so. A director must also know when to stop: when the actors have had enough, and to go on would be counter-productive.

Helping to animate big crowd scenes

Sometimes (it varies from play to play) you may find that, in a crowd, the actors seem inhibited or are mistiming their reactions. There can be several reasons which you can explore: maybe they don't quite understand what's required, or the scene has lost its freshness, or indeed they may be over-eager. It's the sort of thing which you will want to put right fairly late in rehearsal. One short-cut I have found useful is to divide the crowd into groups (probably geographically because nearness to each other is important) with about twelve people to each group, and ask one particularly bright person to be leader and bring her group (it's generally a woman) in with whatever the scene wants. It's often simply a question of energy and you will find this develops enormously in performance.

Seven-week sag

Given a fairly long rehearsal period of 10 or 11 weeks, there is a section in the middle, possibly around half-term, when you are quite a long way from the start of rehearsal but pressure and excitement have not yet really begun to build up for the actual production. This can be a dangerous time, particularly if you have done your work so well that you can take a break at half-term. This lulls people and they may get careless about turning up. It's also the moment when someone unsure will choose to drop out: they feel there's time to get a replacement. We often have to make a special effort at this time to remind people to be punctual and supportive and to point out that the production is much closer than they think. This can take the form of a talk at a general rehearsal, or a letter* sent round to everyone, sometimes both. The tone of the address is in no way nagging, but seeks to remind people of the uniqueness, excitement, idealism of the project and to point out that production week is actually only a very short period away.

LATE REHEARSAL PERIOD

This starts three or four weeks before production and is concerned with putting the play together and obviously giving extra rehearsal to those scenes which need it. This is straightforward rehearsal practice, but bear in mind that most amateurs need considerably more time to absorb an idea than professionals and also may not be able to sustain a development as strongly as professionals. They need to run scenes more frequently.

We are now asking, 'How does each scene form part of a phrase within the play? How does the form of the play shape towards the climax? What is the play finally trying to say?' From being chaotic and dispersed, the production begins to come together so as to reveal the form and build the story of the play. It is important that everyone is part of this process, that they all share responsibility in the performance.

A few weeks before production, we start to put the play together. I try always to go with the rhythm of the play and put the scenes in natural consecutive sections. I explain what I am doing, so that the actors can get used to working towards the shape of the whole. Just as we first asked, 'What is the point of this moment?', then 'this scene?' now we start thinking of the play in large sections. Around this time, I may well make a careful analysis of the play: what it is about. What does the author want the audience to know/feel? I try and demonstrate how each character and each scene is part of a large phrase within the main structure. Each phrase builds up to a larger section and the sections towards totality. I may read this analysis out, carefully explaining; sometimes it's written up on a wall for reference.

Late surge

There is a point, which may be quite late in rehearsal, when the best way to finally impel the actor into performance may be by raising the imaginative temperature, so that having built on a firm basis of exploring the play and the character, and having gained confidence, the actor has an experience of excitement of breaking down the barriers of reserve and self-consciousness. By raising the temperature of rehearsal – encouragement, excitement, praise, enthusiasm, will, pressure – and building on the trust you have already created over many months, you can encourage the actors to dare; to let go and launch themselves into imagination and so, hopefully, release themselves physically and vocally.

With inexperienced actors it may be best to leave this surge of excitement till fairly late in rehearsal, actually till within the last two or three weeks before production, so that the release and momentum is not lost. Inexperienced actors often cannot maintain developments: they regress; they are not used to committing themselves imaginatively and they may slide back.

When to time their artistic 'push' is something the director must sense and decide. If you can maintain the actor's release and build on it until production, the excitement of performance will ensure that the actor won't slide back except insofar as any performance will go up and down.

Super-objectives

Stanislavski is perhaps a little old-fashioned today, but I find discussing his concept of objectives and super-objectives helps some actors a great deal.† It's almost impossible to give 120–150 actors individual super-objectives in the sort of detail that Stanislavski requires, and if you get a super-objective wrong, it's like being on a wrong compass bearing. Nonetheless, we sometimes have discussed super-objectives in general terms. A few individuals may grab the idea and possibly work them out for themselves, but, mainly, this discussion has the effect of fixing everyone's mind on the totality of the play and it makes each of them feel an important responsibility for presenting the play to the audience.

Moving into a larger space

The production will shortly be moving into the performance venue. You may had had to rehearse some scenes in relatively small rooms; going into the larger venue can be traumatic for inexperienced actors

---

† See Stanislavski, Constantin, *An Actor Prepares* (Methuen London, 1980).

who will be thrown by having to project into a much bigger space. Once you get into the venue be very cautious about going back to rehearse in smaller spaces: if it's necessary then make sure people keep their levels up.

'Assembling' for a scene

With a promenade production the actors have to learn to move around the hall with the least possible distraction, so as to be in the right place at the right time. There is a whole sub-action proceeding in parallel with the main play, as people move around and organise themselves. This is very carefully rehearsed in the later stages of production. The actors learn how to finish a big movement from a previous scene, so that they end up where they will want to be later. How to 'seep' discreetly through a part of the hall furthest away from the action; how to assemble on a particular stage, whilst the focus is elsewhere during, for instance, a noisy, busy scene which is grabbing attention at the other end of the hall. Once assembled, the actors have to learn to hold absolutely still until they feel the lights coming up.

A few technical tips for late in rehearsal

I have a few fairly rough methods which I would not use until very late in the rehearsal period, until the imagination was really lively and the sense of identity in the role thoroughly built up by improvisation, supported by discussion and research. Imaginative re-creation is by far the best way to help someone build the performance, allied with physical and vocal exercises as part of the warm-ups from the very start of the rehearsal period.

Inaudibility This can be a problem, especially with children. I use two fairly mechanical methods here:

1 Place the actors as far apart as you possibly can (a football pitch is not too small a distance) and make them shout the lines to each other. This breaks the barrier of 'not feeling right' when they speak up. They continue to maintain a good deal of volume after the exercise is over.

2 A tip from my days at the Central School of Speech and Drama is to use half a cork (about half an inch high) propped between the teeth to hold the jaw open. Warm up with a few nursery rhymes and then say some of the lines. The prop does two things: it forces you to use your tongue and lips very hard and it brings the voice right forward to the front of the mouth.

Speaking to the end of a line Many writers write to the end of the line, with a small climax of music or meaning. Young actors, particularly, tend to fade at the end of the line. The combination of teaching them to maintain energy and volume at the end of their line, and 'cue biting' help a scene enormously.

Picking up cues Fairly late in rehearsal, a vigorous period of working on cues will enormously improve the look of inexperienced actors. You can take as much as ten minutes off the running time of a play in this way and it is all made up of meaningless, infinitesimal pauses which drag at the pace. You need to explain the difference between speed and pace: between picking up cues fast but speaking the actual lines at the pace they have been rehearsed. Teach 'cue-biting' where appropriate: start the line on the last syllable of the cue, not just after it. Cue-biting is far more difficult than it sounds and people will be thoroughly thrown the first few times they do it. Take it in small sections and let them gradually get used to it. Encourage them to go through it themselves – indeed they will have to, you won't have time to take them right through.

   If you have a really good play whose subject appeals to the town and involves genuine and powerful emotions, if it exploits our capacity for imaginative excitement and identification, doesn't make too great technical demands (as does Shakespearian verse-speaking), if most of the parts can be cast not too far from life, if the director and the rest of the professional team know their job, then an inexperienced acting company can look not merely good, but brilliant. The excitement and pride of a whole community celebrating together can lift their performances to a point of ecstasy.

8

To performance

BOX OFFICE

The box-office manager has a responsible and heavy job, but there are always people who like doing it. You need someone clearheaded, good with figures, unflappable and reasonably good at handling people. It's important that the box-office manager is very clear as to what his/her responsibilities are and we now issue detailed notes* for guidance. We stress that these notes are a basis for discussion since everyone will want to organise the work in a slightly different way; but the notes mean that important points are less likely to be overlooked.

Sub-box-offices – direct selling

We generally open booking to the cast and helpers five weeks before the production opens and to the general public one week later. Local shops will always sell tickets: it's good for their image and it draws people into the shop – so don't think that the virtue is all on their side. You'll obviously try and use shops at key points in the town. It's quite common to have a rather embarrassing number of offers and since you don't want to make things too complicated you have to tactfully turn some down: bookshops are natural points of sale; men's outfitters less so; general stores are very good for the image. Since the Box-office manager will need to check constantly how tickets are selling you need co-operative shopkeepers who won't mind this kind of regular query. Agree on a suitable time to phone. As the booking proceeds you may want the totals daily. Some shopkeepers are very helpful about giving information as needed, others have their own little ways. Try and find out beforehand. If the catchment area is large we sometimes have sub-booking-offices in other towns or villages; tickets can also usually be sold at the school during lunchtime; a good way of involving sixth formers.

Telephone bookings

This job can be arduous since you clearly need someone there all the time to take calls. In Dorchester, even when the play was sold out, the phone still kept on ringing with scarcely 48 seconds between calls. An answering machine would have been welcome.

Direct-mail advertising (see Publicity p. 98)

Postal Bookings

Sometimes the Box-office manager handles all postal and telephone bookings; sometimes, as in Dorchester, they are done from different addresses. Send out a handbill and a postal booking form with your direct-mail advertising. The standardised form greatly helps administration.

Previews and Civic Night

Unlike London, the first night is never necessarily full. In the country people wait until they hear how things are. For this reason we start with two very low priced 'previews' which are sure to spread the word and to give the less well-off a chance to see the play. In the past we had to 'paper' the first one or two nights and have done so gladly because word of mouth is so important. If we foresaw the need to 'paper', we would wait until the last possible moment, i.e. the end of the Sunday dress-rehearsal, and then make an announcement with suitably optimistic reassuring noises that any member of the cast or their family could have free tickets for the Monday, on presenting themselves at the box office first thing Monday morning (we warned the box-office manager). This ensured a really good, enthusiastic send-off for the play and it meant that those likely to be most interested had a chance to see the play twice. Happily, it's no longer necessary. We can now get perfectly good houses on the first two nights and we don't worry if they are not absolutely full – it gives the cast time to get used to moving amongst people on the floor.

We have a Civic Night on the third performance, which stands in place of a London first night, and assemble as many mayors, ladies and gold chains as possible. The local headteacher and/or mayor generally give a small drinks party beforehand. Perhaps the party is played into the hall with a fanfare. Amongst other things, it's very useful to be able to invite the leading citizens of a 'target' town. Frequently the mayor of your 'target' will say, 'We must have a community play in our town. Will you come and talk to us?'

FAIR

Before each performance of the play we have a fair which lasts for half an hour. This is organised by the Fair Committee. Each night a different charity, club or group sells any goods it chooses and keeps the money. The fair sellers dress up as elaborately as they like in sympathy with the period of the play. There is usually some grumbling about dressing up but it makes an important difference to the atmosphere. We generally offer to help with mob caps and aprons; the fair sellers themselves provide long skirts, shawls, etc. The fair is useful because:

1 It makes a great start to a promenade performance. The audience comes into a glamorous exciting party atmosphere and it takes people's minds off their feet.

2 More people can become involved. We aim for 20–25 sellers a night.

3 It may raise more money. This is problematical. The charities themselves, given a captive audience of say 350, can raise £80–£100 a night, depending on how much energy they put into selling. Sometimes a charity has spontaneously given us a cheque to express their appreciation. We have tried levying a percentage on sales, but some people get very mean at this point and it can make for bad blood. If you do decide to make a levy do it through the Fair Committee. Sometimes the cast takes over the fair for an evening to help raise money for the play.

Structure of the fair

Music

This is probably provided by the band who are performing in the play itself, but sometimes a group will come along and sing (e.g. the Yetties at Sherborne), or people will play guitars etc. in odd corners.

A centre-piece

This is some small performance to give the fair shape. The centre-piece may be morris dancers, a puppet show, dancing, gymnastics, judo displays, small mummers' plays or scenes, such as Quack Doctors and Strong Men, etc. You are unlikely to get heavy-weight groups (e.g. morris dancers), to come every night, but you might get them at 2 out of 11 performances. A special feature, developed over the last three shows, has been mini-circus performances by young children trained in circus skills as an alternative to taking part in the play itself. It helps to dress the thing up a little. Have a good ringmaster.

Craft people

Any craft is fascinating to watch. Down here in the south-west we are
strong on spinning, buttonmaking, weaving, thatching, etc. It is
unlikely that craft people attend more than 2 evenings out of 11 as they
may have to come quite a distance.

What to sell?

A good sales person can sell anything, but people love fruit: tangerines
sell by the box-load. Anything savoury: sausage rolls, small pasties,
but not hulking great sandwiches; sausages (preferably hot); patties
and pies, mincepies, homemade biscuits, gingerbread, shortbread,
small cakes or pieces of cake, sweets, particularly homemade ones,
cheese straws, fudge, meringues with real cream (butter cream is too
sickly). People get very thirsty and it's a good idea to provide fruit
cup, or some other non-alcoholic drink, but don't encourage the sale
of drink by the fair during the interval because this conflicts with your
sale of coffee. It's delightful to carry small posies of flowers or herbs
through the evening or lavender bags, peg dolls, small gifts; but not
gift-wrapping paper or potatoes, both of which I have seen on sale at
fairs.

Everything sold should be portable

Have trays, not stalls. The hall will get very crowded, especially with
space needed for mini-performances: stalls will get in the way. Tray-
sellers can go up onto the stands and involve those who are sitting.
Finally a tray-seller can leave quickly and discreetly without having to
pack up. *Crafts* will need a base to set things up. Put them up on stages
where they will be seen and out of the crush, unless, like my daughter
who spins and weaves, they prefer to be at floor-level. She says that if
she is set high up people don't talk to her about the work.

Visual impact

Try to go for height: things that will stand above people's heads. We
sometimes have a great Cross of Lorraine, perhaps 12 feet high, with
programmes stapled on to it, and this stands on the floor and is turned
by somebody so that it catches the light. Have arches of flowers or
garlands. In *The Western Women* the designer decorated 12-foot
cardboard rolls, as used for rolling carpets. They were light and easily
carried in and out and were controlled by 10- and 11-year-olds
(another way of involving younger children). We also stick bunches of
ribbons on sticks: anything which makes the scene fun as soon as you

Entertaining Strangers. A father names his young son who has died of cholera.

The Western Women. ▲ Rehearsal: some of the actors are not yet fully engaged while others display a rather empty vehemence with their hands; a common gesture with amateur actors and usually a sign that the actor feels excited but unsure and is compensating physically.

▼ Performance: the same scene: the actors now fully understand the scene and have also been given a physical task, shifting barrels, in which all must co-operate; their energy flows into making the point of the scene, all are engaged and bodies are used unselfconsciously.

The Western Women.

▶ Rehearsal: on guard at the town perimeter women begin to suspect that the enemy may have gone. Facing the actresses will be rows of banked seating.

▼ Performance. The same scene: note the actors in the audience not strictly part of the scene but identifying with the action. (See pp.215–216.)

▲ *Today of All Days*. Set in 1936 and one of the few plays we have attempted with a near contemporary theme.
▼ *Colyford Matters*. While the audience attention is on the current scene three actresses, have quietly taken up their places for the next scene. (See p.233.)

The Poor Man's Friend.

Two examples of the audience perching. (See p.248.)

▲ *The Tide.*

▼ *The Ballad of Tilly Hake.*

▲ *The Garden*. To help failing memories the parts were written out on slates.
▼ *The Poor Man's Friend*. Complicated courtroom scene which spread through the whole venue and audience.

Possession, imagination, excitement. ▲ *The Western Women* Women of Lyme demand the right to help defend their town.
▼ *Entertaining Strangers* People of Dorchester greet their Vicar in his hour of triumph.

enter the hall. Light is very important: the fair should not be lit flatly, but with stage lighting. No balloons, they look very pretty, but they may be held by children and burst during the performance.

Organisation

The Fair Committee sets up and organises everything except what the participating groups may sell and the actual running of the fair itself on the night. The Fair Committee will decide who to invite to take part in the fair (some small organisations may like to hold joint nights) and which group takes which night.

The Fair Committee is also responsible for finding all the other events, performances, crafts people, etc.

The Fair Committee issues very clear, written instructions* and has meetings with all the representatives of all those taking part well ahead of time. At the performance, the stage manager is in charge of the fair and should meet all the fair-people before they go into the hall. We don't open the door to the audience until the fair is in position so that things start with a bang. This may mean that quite a crowd of the audience is waiting outside the door. Make sure that the fair-people enter by a separate entrance and don't have to force their way through the waiting audience. The fair-people need somewhere they can lay out their goods, collect themselves together, listen to the stage manager's instructions and get themselves into the hall about three minutes before the fair is due to start. At the end of the fair, according to the style of production, they should be called out section by section, so that the audience is not aware that they have gone. So, two minutes before the start of the play, withdraw half the sellers, including crafts people who may be encumbered; at one minute withdraw a quarter: at half a minute withdraw the last quarter. Make sure that there is music and a few people who can juggle remaining, so that there is no deathly hush, unless that's what you want.

Fair-people should then be able to go back to their collecting point, and either deposit their stuff if they are staying for the performance or the interval, or leave the building.

We do not issue free tickets to fair-sellers The Committee should explain that the production simply cannot afford to subsidise 20–25 people a night. The fair-people are getting a captive market and a free venue. The one exception is crafts people, who may have come quite a distance and who have to be tempted. Very discreetly, we allow crafts people to stay and watch the performance free.

Distracting costume It can look odd if sellers who have helped in the fair are promenading during performance in costume: they are not in character and yet they look like part of the show. They may detract from the production because they are not focusing like the cast. Not a big problem but it needs watching: we find the best solution is to ask fair-people to remove any light-coloured caps, etc. which might catch light and so draw the eye.

Cast Encourage the cast to join in the fair after they are dressed. It adds enormously to the fun and atmosphere.

Hot potatoes Occasionally organisations have sold baked potatoes and butter to the audience as they leave the auditorium after the play. These are also very popular with the cast on a cold night.

PRODUCTION WEEK (see also Stage Manager's job description, pp. 155–157)

One week is just enough to set up the community play for a production, but two weeks is better. If the performance is to take place in a school, you can usually only get one week to set up; with a public hall, you are limited by financial considerations. At St Mary's Church, Dorchester, we had two weeks to set up the production so it was slightly less frenetic. Extra time was badly needed because until the scaffolding and stages were erected and carpeted the acoustics were very bad. We needed as long a space as possible during those two weeks to 'tune' the play and bring the levels up.

Scaffolding for seating and stage

With our first show it seemed so easy. I produced a scale drawing: a parent was agent for a local scaffolding firm and, interpreting my design, put up three banks of scaffolding with no fuss, charging £80 for the lot. I didn't even think about bearing and loads. I quickly found out how lucky I had been. With the next play, *The Tide*, a local firm lent the poles free, but they did so by clearing all the rubbish out of their yard and dumping it on the town-hall floor. Fortunately we had covered the floor with an old carpet (which I had spotted a nearby hotel throwing out) and we had an extremely experienced stage manager who regarded any challenge as a personal problem. This man simply taught himself scaffolding, mobilised a team of amateurs, sorted out the poles and got on with it. However, when the scaffolding was up, the caretaker (see p. 70) called in the county surveyor. The surveyor said the load was not sufficiently distributed, and demanded that all 11 tons of 2 banks of scaffolding be jacked up 2 inches or he would not allow the production to take place. The stage manager borrowed an industrial jack and the job was done in a day. This sounds simple, but it was really an enormous crisis and, with our limited resources, could have been disaster. An essential part of Paul's pride in his job was that he took it all on himself. He didn't tell me of the surveyor's demands: I found out and I was extremely worried. With considerable self-control I kept out of the way while he solved the problem.

It was only in Bridport that the full horror of scaffolding hit me. Again I persuaded a local firm to lend us materials free and this time, wanting to avoid the previous trouble, we also hired two of their fitters; but there was no one like Paul Roylance who actually enjoyed laying his neck on the line and taking responsibility for the design, and perhaps, to be fair, we were more aware of risks. The school hall was relatively long and narrow, so we planned an enormous bank of scaffolding to take up one end and seat about 120 people. The very large structure was built by a team which included a local civil engineer and two professional riggers. But no one would take responsibility for its design and so for its final safety, and the scaffolding began to be taken apart and put together again daily to try and satisfy everyone. Men with long faces came and shook their heads. Finally, it just remained up.

In Sherborne, we were on a sprung floor which could not take the load and I was happy to do without scaffolding for once; but raised banks of seating embracing the play and the production suffered. Thee were some chairs on low platforms which ran round the edges of the room but this wasn't enough.

When we came back to Lyme Regis for the second time with *The Western Women*, things seemed even worse. This time I gritted my teeth and found a local contractor who was just starting. He undertook to hire us scaffolding and to erect it at a cut rate out of good feeling and the promise of publicity in the programme. We were only charged £122 for two large banks of seating and a raised stage. I nearly threw up: what horror might have been avoided in the past! However, in Newbury in 1983, the year previously, the community play had had to pay £1,200 for a simple scaffolding structure which was also their lighting grid and at the same time a skeleton around which they built the tent. This did not include the banked seating which was separate and loaned free of charge. So scaffolding is an area where you have to keep your wits about you. Hiring can be expensive: poles @ *xp* per foot for *y* weeks, plus a supply of connectors, etc., plus professionals to help put it up. Given the right tools, amateurs can *dismantle* scaffolding in a few hours. A professional engineer should certify its safety, then you can get the scaffolding insured and you will feel a great deal happier.

Lighting

The cost of hiring probably means that you won't have the lamps until the week before opening, although many firms will let you take them away at the beginning of the weekend, instead of on the Monday. Remember that unless you have a very good blackout, you will have to light the show late in the evening, i.e. after the main rehearsals are over, and directors should bear this in mind in pacing themselves. It is no fun working during the day, rehearsing from 5.0 p.m. to 10.0 p.m. and then going straight on to light till 2.0 a.m. You must aim to spare your amateur cast. Rough-time all the lighting cues beforehand and only fine-time them at the technical rehearsal. If you cannot manage to plot all the cues before the technical, don't try and do this slow and boring work with the actors standing around. Have the lighting person busk their way through, send the cast away at the agreed time and work afterwards, fining up the cues through the dress rehearsals.

Timetable

As soon as you get sole use of the hall, clear it and start erecting stages and scaffolding. You'll need the stages for the actors to rehearse on and you'll probably need to use the scaffolding for hanging lamps (we run extra tall poles at the back with cross poles and use this as part of the lighting grid).

Alternatively, you take the technical rehearsal over two evenings (Thursday and Friday: P – 4/3) and have two dress rehearsals on Saturday and Sunday (P – 2/1).

It is very important not to tire the cast. You must warn the cast of rehearsal times, particularly stopping times, and try and stick to them. If you have to do extra work, always try and confine it to the least possible numbers and send the rest away. You must also pace yourself, not merely so that you remain alert, but in order that you will not become so tired that you lose patience.

Timetable for production week (Table 5)

This timetable is, of course, only meant as a guide.

(P − 10 = Performance minus 10 days)

Fri. evening	(P – 10)	Lights collected; hall cleared; rehearsal in venue
Sat.	(P – 9)	*Scaffolding takes precedence*: start as early as possible and hopefully it may well be up by evening or earlier; stages set up; start hanging lights that evening and the following day; stage manager can probably work at the same time as they are hanging lights
Sun. morning	(P – 8)	Morning: continue hanging and cabling the lights; stage manager works in hall Afternoon: *rehearsal takes precedence*: you will probably want a run-through; you may need to plan for smaller extra rehearsals in the evening elsewhere Evening: lights are hung; stage manager works
Mon.	(P – 7)	Stage management works during the day Evening: costume parade elsewhere; in hall lights are focused; stage management probably unable to work in hall since lights need blackout
Tues.	(P – 6)	As above, plus second half of costume parade
Wed.	(P – 5)	Evening: run-through in hall; from 10.0 p.m. onwards, light cues plotted with stand-ins
Thurs.	(P – 4)	Rehearsal; lighting after 10.0 p.m. as above
Fri.	(P – 3)	Run-through; lighting person may like to try out cues through this rehearsal
Sat.	(P – 2)	Technical rehearsal
Sun.	(P – 1)	Morning: unallocated time allowed for coping with trouble Afternoon or evening: dress rehearsal, although I prefer to have an afternoon dress rehearsal in order to save the actors; this may be impossible because lighting cues needing blackout, etc.

The golden rule always is to work ahead and get as much out of the way as possible. It is very tempting to say, 'We can do it at the tech', but remember, you will be dealing with amateurs who have jobs and families. You have to let them get some rest and pay some attention to their homes.

Costume parades

These should take place four or five days before the technical to allow
time for alteration. They are organised by the designer. The director
attends to make comments, etc. Have a third person to take notes. To
some extent, use the dressers, so that they learn their way about. Have
two stage lights on stands, so that the costumes can be seen under
proper conditions, but let the costume parade take place away from
the hall, so as to give the stage management and lighting people a free
hand to be getting on with their job. Call people in small groups, to be
ready dressed by the time indicated, and try and keep to the timetable.
The director must be careful not to be too pernickety and ask for great
changes, there should have been close enough contact earlier on to
spot any gross misunderstandings. Design is an enormous undertaking with such a big cast and you must be considerate.

Dressing-rooms and costumes A school has plenty of space. Otherwise
you may have to adapt (see Venues, p. 70). If you come under the
Children and Young Persons Act 1963, you will have to have separate
dressing-rooms for boys and girls, plus chaperons (see p. 88). You will
need a few dressers each night and it's very useful if you can have one
or two people who will help right through the run and know their way
around. The younger professional designers have always helped
superintend the dressing-rooms. The older and more experienced
designers generally have jobs which draw them quickly away.

Washing costumes Arrange for washing socks, shirts, aprons, etc. at
least once during the run. Everyone does their own and helps others in
case of need. At the end of the run, arrange for the cast to wash
everything possible. Give a date by which costumes must be returned
otherwise they will dribble in for ever. Heavier things should be dry
cleaned: you want to build up your wardrobe and this means that
costumes must be stored clean.

Respect for costumes The cast needs to be taught: don't eat messy food
or go to the pub in costume; treat costumes with great care; hang them
up and put them away; don't drop them on the floor. Children need
particular help and reminding.

Two-stage management teams

The stage manager generally organises two teams to run the production: one for each end of the hall. Each team is solely responsible for its

own end and they share the middle. This cuts down the amount of movement through the hall and makes for much greater efficiency. Each team consists of 4–6 people, one is led by the stage manager, the other by the ASM. The teams are very carefully rehearsed.

Set and furniture changes
There is a special technique for changing settings in promenade performances which is so neat that changes are almost unnoticed and the audience sees a fresh scene with grateful surprise.

The principle is that sets are only changed when there is a distraction elsewhere in the hall (we 'assemble' actors in the same way). The director and stage manager make a careful list of all changes and work out exactly when they will be best carried through. The stage hands, who all wear black with soft shoes during the performance, are carefully rehearsed so that sets are changed exactly on cue with greatest possible speed, discretion and economy. If they get it right it gives the show a really satisfying polish.

Technical rehearsal
The technical rehearsal is for putting everything together and finding technical holes and faults. It's also for rehearsing any big cues, including lights, music and cast which, by their nature, you cannot do earlier. For example, at the end of *Entertaining Strangers* we had to co-ordinate: putting a movable stage into position; actors moving from stage to stage in the dark; an electric kettle producing steam (and safeguarding the cable); at the same time all the cast, singing, had to take up positions all over the hall as the lights came up. This was a reasonable cue to put together at the technical but the component parts were rehearsed separately beforehand.

The purpose of the technical rehearsal needs explaining to the cast in advance, I tell them it is a stopping rehearsal *in full costume* (this needs emphasising). Time will be used to discover and clear up any points. Anyone can halt the rehearsal at any time if they have a problem; either it will be solved on the spot, or a note made to deal with it later. The technical is *not* for rehearsing particular scenes or actors. I generally allow 3 × running time, i.e. starting around 10.30 a.m. and ending about 5.0 or 6.0 p.m.

This doesn't allow much time for refining lighting cues to perfection. Better to concentrate on cues which must be done with the cast as a whole. Don't let the cast go home for lunch if you can help it: since they are in full costume this would take too much time (but warn them to bring food/refreshments). If everyone is psychologically prepared for a long day and you stop when you say you will, technical rehearsals can be good fun. Warn people not to put too much into their acting: they may be stopped within 30 seconds; indeed, this is the point of the rehearsal. Time may force you to jump from cue to cue, but I always regret this – something is missed. Warn the actors that small groups and individuals may have to be kept on for futher, detailed technical work, but try not to have to do it.

Photographs We don't allow flash photographs during dress rehearsals and performances. (Nor would I want the actors to take any sort of photo when they were supposed to be in character.) So we encourage people to take their flash photos at the technical. Since we're stopping all the time it's not distracting, and the cast are in full costume.

Checking in With such a large cast you have to be sure that everyone has arrived, and be able to take measures if they have not. We generally have a huge list, ruled in columns and displayed in a prominent place: people must tick themselves off by an agreed time, or warn us if they will be late checking in. Watch out for those who inadvertently, or otherwise, tick themselves off ahead. Have someone list those who have not checked in and read the list out at an appropriate time, i.e. during warm-ups before performance. This impresses everybody that you mean it seriously. Start the check-in at the technical and continue it through the dress rehearsals, so that everyone is familiar with the procedure by the time they reach performance.

Dress rehearsals
Usually we have one dress rehearsal. With *Entertaining Strangers* we had two, since the show, by our standards, was very large and complicated. For the second dress rehearsal we had an audience: friends of the cast, etc. We didn't announce the fact that we would have a public dress rehearsal until about 24 hours beforehand, hoping by this means not to affect ticket sales.

As is usual practice, we treat the dress rehearsal as a performance, but without the fair. Try and organise notes so that you can let children go first and then release people progressively. Try not to give too many people too many notes yourself. See that other people don't tire the cast with long, protracted notes. Be very firm, positive and optimistic at the end of the last dress rehearsal.

Previews
These are in all respects full performances, plus fair. Remember that front of house will be getting into its stride as well.

HOUSE MANAGER

The house manager is responsible for those areas of the auditorium and audience not covered by the stage manager or the box-office manager; thus s/he works closely with both.

The house manager sees to:

Approach to the hall
People may have to spend quite a long time waiting or queueing. You should have a suitable space and create one if you have to. This is seldom necessary in a school, but in Dorchester, in a church, we built a foyer with screens in a side aisle which we moved just before the performance. You should make this space as interesting and attractive as possible: people have a lot of time to read quite detailed notices. Your main sponsor or anyone sponsoring a particular performance may well like to use it.

Stewards
Stewards are recruited, briefed and controlled by the house manager. The fire officer may well demand a certain number per night to help evacuate the building in case of emergencies. Stewarding jobs include: tearing off ticket counterfoils at the door; organising seating on scaffolding and checking seating tickets. Manning the side-doors to prevent free entry; you have to be very strict about this since, such is the demand for tickets, that people try to sneak in. It's useful to have a member of the cast helping: they are more confident about challenging and won't be fobbed of by 'I'm Jenny's grandma and I'm helping to dress, etc.' Once the performance starts, the fire officer will probably require that stewards stand by the exit doors, holding hand torches in case of power failure, to get the audience out quickly.

Fire
The director, house manager, stage manager, box-office manager and lighting person should agree on a code word to be used in case of fire.

This will be a signal to bring up the house lights, open all exit doors and get the audience out. Discuss how you would do this. A code word is important since, to minimise the risk of panic *the word 'fire' is never to be used*.

Entrances for actors and fair

The house manager will need to lock the doors which the public will use at least 45 minutes before the start of the fair, otherwise people will come in before you are ready and sit around watching the actors warming up, etc. Have a separate entrance for actors and fair people. Waiting audience, not allowed in until 7 o'clock, will get miffed if apparently 'privileged' people push through.

Cloakrooms

Try and have somewhere secure and attended where people can leave coats, etc. In a promenade performance they don't want to carry stuff around – also they take up more space in bulky coats. School halls can get very hot indeed.

Promenade productions

Seating If you are doing a promenade production you must announce it on all your publicity. We say something like, 'Promenade performance with some limited unreserved seating' (if no charge is to be made) or 'Promenade production: some guaranteed seating, supplementary fee 50p' on all posters, handbills, press advertising (where feasible) and tickets.

People tend to be rather careless about how much space they take up. To some degree we overcome this problem by placing a strip of marking tape right across the seat every 18 inches. We have a couple of stewards on each stand (strong-minded sixth formers or heavyweight cast are good) to check tickets and organise people to fill the stands from the back corners to the middle, and so down. They act not unlike the old gallery pushers at filling up the spaces. Unless this is done, the back seats may not be properly filled and it sometimes happens that entire rows are empty. It needs a good deal of strength of will to say, 'Madam, would you mind going up one row?' – and getting them to do it.

Perching There is always plenty of space to perch in a promenade production; people sit everywhere. I like this. It's a form of audience involvement and its very theatrical. Theatre is about the tension between imagination and reality and the actual presence of the audience in a scene (or having to move them aside to get there) intensifies this theatricality.

Seats for critics and other VIPs

The house manager and the director should have a nightly list of people for whom they wish to reserve seats, and should go round together planning where to put them. It's important that the director is involved because they know which seats are best for viewing, which are too near the band, etc. Try not to put a block of like-minded people together: they will influence each other too much. It's bad enough having such a collection of elderly people on the stand.

Since we are very clear that we don't actually have numbered reserved seats, there is sometimes some resentment at seeing seats with 'reserved' notices on them; it's wise to tape such notices to the seats otherwise they may disappear. The most effective way to reserve seats is to put children from the cast on them if they will agree to do it. I am always torn in my mind as to whether it's best to pamper critics and give them a seat or make them promenade. Promenading is a far more exciting, involving experience. Some do both, coming down off the stands at half-time. By and large I think we get the best notices from promenaders.

Extra seats

Whether we have reserved seats or not, we always keep a space free for wheelchairs (the fire officer will require this anyway, and you must also have a ramp for wheelchairs to be brought up from floor-level).

Since scaffolding is such an unknown quantity, even given accurate measurements, you can't be sure exactly how many seats will be available. The lighting person who perches on the top of the scaffolding may take up more room than you thought, or the construction may mean that certain seats are unusable. For this reason we never budget to sell all possible seats on the scaffolding. Further, if the space for wheelchairs is not filled (and generally it is not) it is useful to have a secret stock of chairs to bring out as required.

Thus it almost always happens that at the start of the evening you will have some seats available and, you need to fill them because usually the floor is so crowded and you want as much space as possible. It is useful to have spare seats: some people always fail to notice that it is a promenade production and are either infirm, carrying very young children or peevish. The house manager should

offer the seats to members of the audience who look as if they need/
would appreciate them. It is surprising how many decline. Be careful
not to give a seat right in the front to someone who may be restless,
e.g. a young child. The audience is very visible.

Interval refreshments
The house manager times sellers in and out.

VIPs
The house manager should pamper mayors, nobs, sponsors and their
guests, etc., showing them to their seats, arranging for coffee, bidding
them farewell and so on.

Cash
Decide who is to be responsible for programmes and merchandising,
including safekeeping sellers' floats, cash security, etc. (This apart
from the fair-sellers who are a different group of people and will
organise their own money.) Parcels of money must be kept separate:
the play earns a royalty from the publisher if you are selling published
texts and you need to know your programme/mugs/sweatshirt/raffle
profit. Above all keep box office separate from everything else since
the author is owed a percentage of ticket money.

PERFORMANCE

We want the actors to do warm-ups and usually the only place large
enough for them all to work in comfort is the performance venue. Also
we want them to take part in the fair, possibly helping with stewarding
and selling programmes. So the call is at least an hour before the
performance starts.

A Director's role
As director of the play and of Colway Theatre Trust, I generally saw to
it that I had absolutely no formal jobs to do during the performance. I
attend all performances of my own productions; with somebody else's
production I would occasionally miss an evening, but rarely. Not
having a job left me free to greet people and cope with any chore or
crisis. These have ranged from quelling a tame sheep bleating outside
because it wanted to join in the fun; children being sick in the middle
of the hall, having eaten too much in the fair; and someone having a
heart attack. Something or other needs your attention every night. In

Entertaining Strangers we seemed to be particularly unlucky with minor bumps and ailments. Luckily, we had two doctors in the cast and one or both was needed almost every night. You need to know where you will find key people in the hall during a performance: it was a great help that I always knew that Dr Clark would be found in his favourite position beside the south door of the church.

Timetable of performance (Table 6)

5.30 p.m.	Stage manager starts preparing hall; actors arrive and dress when they please
6.30 p.m.	Actors must have checked in by this time
6.35 p.m.	Warm-ups, including musical warm-ups Warm-ups are taken by co-director, or other, to leave the director free to liaise with house manager, etc. Notices Check-in list omissions
6.40 p.m. or earlier	House manager and box-office manager arrive and with director go through reservations as necessary Stewards arrive
6.45 p.m.	Fair assembles away from hall
6.55 p.m.	Warm-up ends; fair-sellers come into hall; stage manager calls the half hour
7.00 p.m.	Doors open for the audience
7.10 p.m.	Stage manager calls the quarter hour in the Green Room and dressing-rooms
7.20 p.m.	Stage manager calls beginners in the Green Room and dressing-rooms
7.28 p.m.	Stage manager signals half fair-sellers to leave
7.20 p.m.	Stage manager signals quarter fair-sellers to leave
7.29½ p.m.	Stage manager signals the last quarter of the fair to leave.
7.30 p.m.	Stage manager, having checked with lights, music and beginners, signals the show to start

Cast going in and out of the hall during performance

The cast has to learn a very rigorous discipline. They are already aware that they mustn't move during people's quiet scenes. If it becomes too great a strain, actors can go out into the Green Room where, hopefully, they can make a noise and let off steam; but in order to go in and out they may let light into the hall and make a noise. They have to learn how to move quietly and smoothly and keep out of the light. They should only go in and out of the hall between scenes or during noisy bits. Watch for and control excitement and forgetfulness and noise after a scene is over and tension is released. Young children

are particularly restless and all the cast should be encouraged to take
responsibility for children and to gently remind and control them.

Young children can become very good indeed about movement
discipline but their concentration is stretched over two hours.
However, everyone's bad points are also their good points and the
reverse of the restlessness of young children is an excitement, sparkle
and sense of sheer enjoyment that no adult can ever display.

Interval

We try for 15 minutes or less. Coffee and squash is served to the
audience in the hall, usually on 3 trollies to get through the process as
quickly as possible. Coffee is also served to the cast in the Green Room
at cost with free squash for children. We now use in-cup drinks which
require little effort as they only need added hot water and there is no
washing-up. We get them from J. Bolton & Son, Wessex House,
Uplyme Road, Lyme Regis, Dorset DT7 3LP. They supply a range of
drinks from coffee and chocolate to soup; you can still make a
reasonable profit. Have people with large plastic sacks for the empties
otherwise there will be a line of plastic cups along the edge of stages.

After performance

Hall, Green Rooms and dressing-rooms need to be swept and tidied
after the show. This is quite a big job and shouldn't be left entirely to
the stage-management team, who deserve their evening drink as
much as anybody else. We now make a rosta of about 10 people per
night to help clear up. Usually, nobody needs to do it more than once.
We include everyone except young children and the most aged. The
stage management is still responsible overall for leaving the hall in
good order. This tidying is of course particularly important if you are
working in a school or church hall: it's all part of the community
image.

Notes

Notes are generally needed after the preview and first night. Don't
give them in front of the audience or friends. Keep them brief.

The pub

Try and end the performance in time to allow everyone who wants to,
to go to the pub. This is an extremely important part of the evening:
people love to wind down, celebrate, discuss the performance
together.

Through the run: keeping things steady

As people realise what they have achieved, they begin to glow with satisfaction; but performances go up and down and you have to know when to speak to the cast, encouraging them, or pulling them up. Amateurs may get bewildered and a sort of mild hysteria can sometimes run through the cast, a kind of a miserable excitement which seems almost infectious: people begin to be 'off' or 'dry' or have minor accidents. At such a time I am prepared to be very firm: to give them a lead and confidence that there is a structure they can rely on.

The actors are eager and willing, longing to do well, thrilled by the success and sometimes there is an over-confidence which masks great insecurity. They need a certain amount of help and guidance. They are not sufficiently experienced to know that a performance may be down because they were dropping their cues, or playing heavily and slowly, or lacking in energy. They need to be told about the dangers of 'second-night drop' or of going over the top because they are over-excited. Performances need to be continuously monitored and the information fed back. Don't try their patience by continuous nagging with a constant stream of negative information. When things are going well they will be aware of it, just as they know when they are going badly – but they may not know why. Try and tell them what is making tonight's performance different from last night's. In everything you say, however negative, always try and end on a positive and encouraging note.

Mid-run break

We do not perform on the middle Sunday and Monday. This is very important in that it gives people a rest after two weeks of very hard work and, when they come back, they are confident that they are on to something very significant and they savour every minute. Watch out for the last performance: warn them that it is as important as any other; the excitement is tremendous and people need steadying. Warn the stage manager to look out for real booze in any drinking scenes: it is a great temptation to amateurs and others.

Prompting

We usually never have a formal prompter. People can almost always get themselves out of trouble, with less fuss and distraction than in taking a prompt. Amateurs won't usually believe this, but sometimes we have tried both ways at a dress rehearsal and preview and then taken a vote. There are two exceptions to this rule: some actors are genuinely troubled in case they will forget certain speeches and in such cases I arrange for a prompter (in most cases I do it myself because everybody else has a job by that time). If someone has to cover for an absent actor, then they obviously need prompting.

Reactions and comments
The second week of production is the time to ask people for comments and reactions. We have sometimes invited them to fill in a form and the notes and statistics are always useful and may provide guidance or ammunition for the future. See Peter Hamilton's Dorchester Analysis.*

AFTER THE LAST PERFORMANCE

Cleaning up
This is organised by the stage manager but everyone helps, so it's a party as well as being quick and efficient. You need to do it on a Sunday when most help will be available. After the production there will be appalling mess and chaos in the hall but, given the enormous amount of help and goodwill, the hall will be clean and back to normal in one day. Clearing up becomes, almost touchingly, an expression of community effort and mutual support: people take satisfaction in doing the job together. Everyone appreciates the need to return the school or church to its former quiet, clean state: it's a way of saying 'thank you'. The filth under the scaffolding will probably make you glad of an industrial vacuum cleaner if you can borrow one but, after that, everyone brings cleaning things and then it's hot water, muscle and good feeling.

SM and Design teams will need three days to sort out, clean/wash and return all borrowed items. Ask the cast to wash as many items of their own costumes as possible. (You need to stress promptness.) A decision will be required as to the future of any costumes made for the show; they are valuable, try not to let them moulder in some damp hole. CTT will usually add any costumes to the CTT wardrobe so that while each production benefits from the one preceding they add to the store for plays which follow.

PARTY
Everyone always wants a party. Nobody wants the play to end. This is virtually the first time that everyone is together in a more or less

unstructured situation and its interesting to see in what way people seem different and to have changed: who has emerged during the production and now takes a lead, who has grown more confident, as well as, less nobly, who sits in a corner holding hands with whom. It is fascinating for those who have been through the whole process to contemplate the new group dynamics.

It will not be lost on anyone that, unless they do something about it, the party will be the last time everyone will all meet together. This is when announcements are made about future plans and it's important to strike while things are still roaring along. The Organising Committee will need little encouragement to organise something definite: the formation of a society/committee meeting/workshops/another party. Best of all is if it can be announced, as during the Dorchester party, that there will be another community play.

9

What happens afterwards

Every play has concrete results and some are described in the first section of this book. They include, amongst others, the Dorchester Community Plays' Association, the revival of Crediton Town Band, Playwriting groups, Arts Festivals, further community plays, improvisation groups, village plays, Sherborne Arts and Crafts Association, the development of school promenade productions with greater town and parental involvement, Ottery Community Theatre etc. Always there is general artistic composting of the area, growing awareness of arts potential, improved community feeling. What actually happens and what form it will take depends on the people of the particular town. What do they expect? What do they want? This work is by and about people: individuals and groups. What happens will be because of the people who get it going and what they want.

But the high profile activities are not the only results of a community play. Every single individual who has taken part is changed and affected in some way. To me these personal developments are as important as the big show-case products. People change.

Here are some notes from Margaret Ansell of Dorchester who, when the play was over, gave some perceptive comments.

Married lady – mid 50's – husband not involved. Before play – general housekeeping, helping husband in small business, doing books etc. Social outings mostly with husband.

Came to pre-play workshops and suprised to find how much these were enjoyed, confidence grew, more extrovert, new friends; different backgrounds. Helped with costumes, admin, took part in play and was thoroughly engrossed. Through having been involved in C.P. another side of personality 'blossomed' and confidence grew, as in many cases, an extra awareness of the world outside of marriage. In this case the husband was happy and pleased for his wife.

In some cases resentment was felt, even deeply, by partners and members of the family not involved with C.P. Perhaps a

non-participatory family ought to be encouraged to attend and
watch a rehearsal, towards the end especially, and perhaps not
then feel so cut out. The plays are very time consuming and it is
possible to become selfish when involved in the C.P., going
along to a rehearsal or two could well help to understand the
enthusiasm and commitment of those involved. Helping with
refreshments at last two weeks of rehearsal threw a whole new
light on my point of view for my husband.

A new lease of life was given to some young families. Several
couples SHARED a great experience. Outside confines of home
– young children – routine – jogging along, managing to find
child minders somehow, making a great effort to go out together
and becoming closer. Not just odd evenings out but culminating
in an exciting shared experince.

Whole families – husbands, wives, children all taking part. In
many cases one parent with children/child. Sharing with –
experiencing with – own family seeing one another in a new
light.

Some participants have felt discontent etc. with their home
situation since play and one couple – wife involved, husband not
– have split up – no other person involved.

There is no doubt that for many people being in a C.P. can be
most disturbing, it reaches the parts other activities can't reach!
It is up to the individual how they cope.

My priorities have changed – I am more relaxed about the
housework – used to clean from top to bottom if visitors
expected – always looked forward to having visitors but much
less uptight and tired now when they come. Having let things go
somewhat during C.P. now realise they didn't matter anyway.
Am much more 'laid back' now and speaking to others find they
feel the same.

Close relationships built up with hitherto strangers. Lots of
new friends and acquaintances. Still greet each other in the
street, I suspect each thinking of a wonderful shared experience
– bonds are formed.

Lasting friendships formed, often close.

Mixing with people from all walks of life on equal terms.

Discovering unknown skills in ourselves.

Although giving in so many senses, time, energy etc., receiving so much more.

This letter is one of many, particularly vivid perhaps because the writer has so much natural vitality. In addition numbers of letters were written to South West Arts, in protest at the cut, by people who had taken part in community plays. They provide a view, as it were, for the benefit of a third party. Here are some typical examples:

From Peggy Topsfield of Ottery St. Mary:

> I have watched teenagers, otherwise unoccupied, who flippantly approached the workshops or rehearsals, develop into interested, concerned, and 100% co-operative mmbers: I have talked to ladies (even older than myself) that have thrived on the involvement and the opportunity to relieve their loneliness and become a needed part of a team; I have seen very young children from the age of six upwards became attentive, disciplined and thrilled to be taking part. I have experienced complete camaraderie between a cast of all ages.

From Gwyneth Chaney of Lyme:

> It is difficult to explain the spirit of community that it engendered. . . it is claimed that everyone can take part and have their horizons enlarged and I write as someone who has been wheelchair bound for many years. . .

From Gillian Perrow of Lyme:

> I am a single parent with two small children and I found out that I had such a good support system amongst my friends; all those rehearsals and performances. There were 11 performances and only one person was off sick during all that time; what other organisation can boast of such a feat? I still have contact with a lot of people around Lyme a year later and a special knowing that we shared something very unusual and wonderful. We were all dedicated without our political beliefs etc. being in the way. I had a strong feeling of a world in peace, the overall feeling that we all supported each other for the performance to be better and better, totally. Never have I experienced such support from so many different types and ages of people in my life.

From Doris Neahey of Crediton:

> We were a motley collection of people – from a window cleaner to a University lecturer, from factory workers and unemployed to top professionals in various fields, from schoolchildren to

ancient people (I was the oldest member!). As a result of this, new friendships were formed, old ones renewed, history was relived, there were new interests, a fresh sense of comradeship, of belonging, of achievement and an acceptance of us 'furriners' by the original Kirtonions. In fact Crediton really came alive. It is a wonderful feeling to walk down our High Street and be hailed as a friend by so many people, young and old.

At the time of our third production *The Poor Man's Friend* someone who helped CTT when it first started became alienated as we grew more stable and apparently successful. Speaking to *The Guardian* (December 1st 1981) he tried to do us a small injury saying of CTT: 'When the circus has moved on nothing remains.' Although this comment is manifestly untrue it bothered me for a while for it begs the question as to whether the professional team should remain in a town when the play is over. But with our tenuous funding situation we were forced to justify our grant aid by constantly setting up fresh high profile productions, we had to produce a play a year and our tiny resources simply could not allow us to maintain a presence and do much follow-up work. But now it seems to me entirely right that the professionals should clear off and the town take over. The town itself should harness the energy the play has generated, should face the new possibilities which have been demonstrated. The townspeople should meet this challenge by themselves and in their own way.

Sally-Anne Lomas wrote to me:

'The Circus comes to town' – words used in a bitter critique by one doubter, but let us think about that phrase and the tradition it refers to:– The Circus – what did it mean to isolated rural towns: excitement, adventure, stimulation, the world of imagination, an event looked forward to with enormous joy, which added immensely to the life of the town for the weeks it was there, brought with it a whiff of the cosmopolitan, of the world beyond the confines of everyday life. What town would turn away a circus? A bitter, repressive, stagnant town. Yes, then the CTT is a circus, how brilliant! But it is a circus people created for themselves, it is the town's own circus, one which they have experienced not just as audience but as creators, it has changed these people, it is the circus and more.

Billie Browne later played a large part in setting up the Dorchester Play and is still a force in the Dorchester Community Plays Association which organises many events in the town, issues its own newsletter and is beginning to set up a community play for 1989. Billie saw the Bridport play and read the comment. She wrote to me at the time:

> . . . . nothing remains – So what if only intangibles remain? I should have thought it worth doing if only for the memory of having been part of something so tremendous.

This last point perhaps deserves particular thought. When people ask me what happens after community plays, I tell them. But I am often tempted to say: So what? Perhaps the play, and what it does to people socially, personally and in terms of art is justification enough. The doing is sufficient. It is fashionable, received practice to demand that something happen next: to justify the present in terms of the future. It is really a kind of greediness, of grabbing. Thus we find ourselves in flight from what is happening now. We are in a constant state of stampeding towards the always receding what-comes-next, creating endless restlessness of spirit and unappeasable thirst. This never ending stress on the future, on building, on progress, on productivity, on achieving, destroys inner peace, spirituality and art. The richness, serenity and fullness of life is now.

Perhaps those who take part should have the final word. Here are two letters written a year after the experience:

From Jill Pope of Dorchester:

> The play and everything surrounding it is as clear and sharp still as if it was still in production. It brought such a richness to our lives which we couldn't have achieved in any other way. . . Colway offers a community a deeper wider and richer experience at first hand, something few other theatres can even begin to offer. Professional 'proscenium' theatre seems very flat in comparison.

From Brenda Croydon of Dorchester:

> You'd be pleased and heartened, I think at the rapturous greeting of other community play people that goes on in the streets, shops, shows etc. . . . That pleasure at seeing each other again and sense that only we really know what a great experience the work of *Entertaining Strangers* was is something important, that continues, whether or not the events that the Newsletter describes get full support or only that of the few. Roll on 1989.

Appendix

1 Guide notes for first meeting with Head.
2 Sponsorship proposal.
3 Play leaflet.
4 & 5 Sheila Yeger invites Ottergians to help write their play.
6 What is an Acting Workshop?
7 Handbill for workshops.
8 Newsletter.
9 & 10 Appeal for Materials.
11 Rehearsal Availability Form.
12 Detailed Rehearsal Schedule.
13 Encouragement during 'Seven Week Sag'.
14 Fair details as distributed to interested groups.
15 Notes as basis for discussion with Box Office Manager.
16 Questionnaire following the Dorchester Play.
17 Analysis of 'User Hours' in Dorchester.
18 Bridport Analysis of Money coming into the Town.
19 Workshop Booklist.

C O L W A Y   T H E A T R E   T R U S T

<u>FIRST MEETING WITH SCHOOL</u>

Date
Name of School
Address
Telephone No.
School Secretary
<u>THOSE PRESENT</u> :

Head   Home Phone

Deputy Head (s)   Home Phone

Heads of Depts.   Home Phone

Others   Home Phone

GOVERNORS

Councillors

Special influence

Remarks on School

OTHER SCHOOLS TO BE APPROACHED
Name of School
Address
Phone No.
Head

Name of School
Address
Phone No.
Head

Name of School
Address
Phone No.
Head

1 Guide notes for first meeting with Head. *Page one*.

COLWAY   THEATRE   TRUST

QUESTIONS TO BE CONSIDERED AT THE FIRST TALK WITH A SCHOOL

1. SPACE FOR PERFORMANCE

    Hall :   Size

                Availability

                Fire regulations, numbers

                Any rostra, steps, etc.

2. WARDROBE & COSTUME MAKING

                Workshops

                Store

                Rails, coathangers, machine?

                Cooperation from Sewing Dept.?

3. OFFICE

                Use of phone

                Duplicating

4. LIAISON & COOPERATION

                Relationship of school and town

                Relationship Amateurs

                Feeling amongst teachers

                Governors, are they supportive?

                May I talk to: teachers, Governors, School, PTA?

                Deputy Heads

                Caretaker

                Who does Drama? Teachers, years? How much?
                Involvement not just of English/Drama Dept.
                but also:

                Music, Art, History

                Technical - is there any particular teacher
                interested in the technical side?

5. WORKSHOPS before starting? Help from staff

6. CASTING

Guide notes. *Page two*.

7. REHEARSAL / PERFORMANCES

        Calls upon Hall

        Secondary rehearsal space in school

                         outside (Amateurs?)

        Amount of time for rehearsal

        HOW MANY PERFORMANCES?

        T.V.

8. FUNDING

   No expense falls upon the school except :

        School to provide rehearsal space, hall, heat, power, etc.

        School to absorb small costs, e.g. bits of wire, nails, screws, paint, thread, small pieces of wood, card, paper

9. GENERAL

        Amateurs - Dramatic, Operatic

        General Talent - art, music, energy, etc.

        Other bodies, e.g. British Legion, Rotarians, etc.
        How to involve them? Speakers?

        KEY PEOPLE IN TOWN

        Mayor?

        Ward Councillors

Guide notes. *Page three.*

To be written by   27th June, 1984

D A V I D   E D G A R
_____

PRODUCTION: November 18, 19, 20, 21, 22, 23 & 26, 27, 28, 29, 30   1985

St. Mary's Church, Dorchester

C O M M U N I T Y   P L A Y S - L O C A L   I N V O L V E M E N T
_____

A COMMUNITY PLAY seeks to involve as many people as possible, from
2 to 92 years and of every skill and background. Not only as actors, but
helping with publicity, stage management, costumes, hospitality, transport,
etc. etc. Built around a small core of professionals, experienced in guiding,
helping and enthusing amateur talent.

Past experience shows that at least 4,500 people will be directly involved,
either as actors, helpers, or members of the audience, but literally nobody
in the community will remain unaware, given the care, time scale, and
virtually guaranteed success of the project. These shows sell out: people
come from all over the country to see them.

During the period up to November, 1985, we shall be working continuously
in the town, raising enthusiasm and commitment for the play, holding
workshops, low level community projects, leading up to rehearsal in
September '85 and the production itself, in November '85 (see attached
notes for detail).

2 Sponsorship proposal. *Page one.*

SPONSORSHIP - WHAT WE CAN OFFER

COMMUNITY IDENTIFICATION

Identification with the Community over a long period (18 months).

During this time we shall be working carefully, deeply, imaginatively and energetically, relating to the community and raising interest and enthusiasm for the Play. A great deal of this work will be done by the Dorchester people themselves.

National Identity:

Colway Theatre Trust productions are reviewed by National critics and receive National editorial publicity, and in the past, National TV coverage.

MEDIA

NATIONAL TV AND RADIO

Channel Four wish to make a programme about the work of the Colway Theatre Trust and we are discussing now ideas as to how the programme may be built around the Dorchester Community Play. In the past, our plays have been featured nationally on BBC 2 Arena, Newsnight, etc.

LOCAL TV   Coverage is virtually guaranteed.

BBC RADIO   Has featured our work: Kaleidoscope, Woman's Hour, Down Your Way,etc.

LOCAL RADIO   Wide coverage. 2 Counties Radio plans to continuously feature the play
                 and to mount a major programme to coincide with the production.

        Possible TV Advertising in South & West (part paid by Sponsor)
        This was used in the Lyme Regis Play and is surprisingly cheap.

        Press Advertising   Local press advertising.

We will make every effort to see that our Sponsor's name and logo is featured in media coverage and it will of course appear in all Press & TV Advertising.

Sponsorship proposal. *Page two*.

WE CAN ALSO OFFER

PUBLICITY MATERIAL PRINTED BY US:

Featuring Sponsor's name and logo. Handbills and posters.
We shall be distributing about 15,000 handbills and 500 posters.

NEWSLETTER

We shall shortly be starting a Newsletter (probably quite simply produced)
to keep in touch with all those who have already expressed interest and
to gather more interest. This will appear about every 2 months.

PROGRAMME

Our programmes are beautifully produced, souvenir items. No paid
advertisements appear in them. We know that they are cherished as a
mementoe long after the play is over. Our Sponsor's name and logo will
of course be prominently featured.

DISPLAYS

A display featuring the Sponsor's name, logo and product at the entrance
to the Community Play and at low key projects, where practical: also
at the Public Meeting/Press Launch.

SPONSOR'S GUESTS: Tickets & Concessions

An agreed number of complimentary tickets per night, preferential booking
and concessions.

HOSPITALITY

Should the Sponsor wish to invite guests, we can assist at a small reception
afterwards, if necessary.

Sponsorship proposal. *Page three*.

EVENTS LEADING UP TO COMMUNITY PLAY

THE WRITER: DAVID EDGAR

David Edgar is a writer of world standing, author of over 40 immensely
successful plays. He adapted "Nicholas Nickleby" for the Royal Shakespeare
Company, which was a smash hit in London and New York. His most recent
play, "Maydays", was recently produced by the RSC at the Barbican. The
Dorchester Community Play will be David Edgar's first new play following
"Maydays" and this alone will guarantee maximum National coverage.

David Edgar will spend a considerable time in Dorchester, relating to the
community and gathering material, e.g. he plans to visit Schools and the
Library; he may set up a table in a Supermarket; visit Old People's Homes,
etc. The arrangements for his visit are now under discussion.

PLAY OFFICER

Building on our experience in Ottery St. Mary, the Play Officer will be
the chief liaison between the hundreds of different groups and individuals
as they become progressively involved in the play: s/he will service the
various Committees and will look for "gate openers" with a view to
gaining their co-operation. The Play Officer will hope to draw in those
who might not normally be associated with such a venture, i.e. the young
unemployed, mothers with young children, older people, the socially disadvantaged, etc. S/he will advise and help the Author during his stay in
the town and will also help him with practicalities, e.g. fixing up a table
in the Library/Schools/Supermarket, arranging meetings, finding the Writer
accommodation, etc. The Play Officer will also help initiate, guide and
advise low-key community projects and consult with Teachers regarding
School activities/Play Packs, etc.

PUBLIC MEETING

The Public/Press Launch will be held around late April/May, 1985. We shall periodically release material to the Press and may also consider further "Press Parties".

COMMITTEES

We already have an Organisation Committee and they are at present forming a Projects Committee to organise and initiate low-key community projects.

We shall also have the following Committees: Fair, Finance, Publicity, Hospitality, Production.

WORKSHOPS

These will be held from March - July, 1985. They are designed to be both entertaining and instructive: Theatre Games, Improvisations, etc. and teach not only basic acting skills, but are designed to draw in those who would not normally join in amateur groups. They also teach quickness of reaction, group feeling and sensitivity. There will also be Workshops in Speech, Movement, Mime, Masks.

FAIR

Each night before the Play begins, there is a Fair, when different Charities/Organisations in the town dress up and may sell tempting food, etc. and keep the proceeds. The Fair is built also round crafts and a big, central section, such as Morris Dancers.

REHEARSALS

Will start early September, '85. Rehearsals will take place on 4 evenings a week, plus Saturday and Sunday. Most individuals will be needed not more than 6 to 8 hours a week.

Sponsorship proposal. *Page five.*

PRODUCTION

Eleven performances spread over 14 days, which allows for rest in between. It must not be forgotten that we are working with people who are already themselves in full-time jobs. Such is the popularity of these productions that they sell out almost as soon as they open. We could do more performances, but we think it would place too much strain on our amateur actors. Alternatively, could we find larger venues, we could sell more tickets.

FOLLOW-UP

It is our experience that the stimulating and enriching effects of a Community Play are felt long after the play itself is over. Specifically, in Sherborne, the man who administered the play, went on to found the Sherborne Association of Crafts and Arts. In Bridport, we discovered/ trained/encouraged a Theatre Worker who has since set up "The Improvisational Theatre Co." involving Bridport people in a wide range of theatre activities. In Crediton, the Arts Festival and New Plays Festival (plays by local writers) have been built up around the impulse of the Community Play. Following "The Western Women," Lyme Regis produced its own large Community Play to commemorate the 300th Anniversary of the Monmouth Rebellion. But beyond these, there is an enormous amount of bridge-building. To put it more simply, people make many more friends: the young and old learn to like and understand each other; the Community Play nurtures a sense of sharing and co-operation.

OUTLINE BUDGET

EXPENDITURE

Cost of Play	£24,000

INCOME

Ticket Sales	£ 8,000
Marketing & Programme Profits	£ 1,000

Grant Aid

South West Arts: Project Support	£ 2,000
Writer (help with commission)	£ 1,000
Composer/Musical Director	£ 1,000
Arts Council of Gt. Britain (help with writing commission)	£ 1,000
Television South	£ 1,800
	£15,800
To be raised	£ 8,200

Sponsorship proposal. *Page seven.*

9. Fund Raising
Fund raising is in essence a community activity. Virtually all the money raised by the town will come straight back into the town, and a great deal more money will be attracted into Dorchester by the Play, both in terms of outside grant and aid and ticket sales. We shall have much satisfaction in working together to raise funds and give the town a very entertaining play. All kinds of help and ideas are needed. Would anyone offer a large house for a social occasion? Would you be prepared to help with food for fund raising occasions? How about concerts, jumble sales, sponsored events? If you have ideas, please let us know.

10. Scripts
Help will be needed with duplicating, collating, binding.

11. Tea
During rehearsal breaks in the big weekend rehearsals we need people to be responsible for bringing materials, making tea, washing up, collecting the small charge we shall make to cover costs.

12. Transport
Some children will need lifts home at night. We may need to offer lifts to the elderly on the evenings of performances. Would you be a driver? We may also need help with transporting goods, materials, properties, etc. Do you have a large car/van/lorry you would be willing to lend for a few hours?

13. During Performances
We shall need Stewards for the Hall (6 each night); Programme sellers (4 each night); Dressers (6 each night); COFFEE MAKERS to organise and make coffee during the interval.

14. Fair Preceding The Play
Every performance is preceded by a Fair — we will find a "centre piece" — e.g. Morris Dancing, or a Punch and Judy Show, etc. and there will be plenty of music, colour and glamorous lighting. Each evening a different organisation is invited to dress up and sell tempting food, fruit, wine, arts and crafts, etc. They keep the proceeds, and could it raise around £100 per night. Would your Group like to consider running one? Later on we shall form a Fair Committee. In the meantime please fill in the form overleaf.

15. Baby Sitting
Families may get together and help each other, but may need assistance if they are all at rehearsal/performance together.

16. Secretarial
Could you give a few hours secretarial help a week?

17. Helping Talk to People and Manning the Production Office Phone
We need help with making people welcome when they come to the Costume Workshop and with answering the phone. Could you give a few hours a week from September 1985 onwards?

18. Accommodation
Cheap Flats will be needed by the Play Officer and members of the MSC and Production Teams from October, 1984 to December, 1985. Also a Getaway Workshop, a large room with water facilities, electricity, etc., ideally near the centre of town, so that people can drop in easily, have a cup of coffee and exchange news, work, etc.

Sponsored by
Huntsman Ales
Eldridge Pope
ELDRIDGE POPE & COMPANY p.l.c.

Financial Support also Includes

South West Arts

Arts Council OF GREAT BRITAIN

TVS Television South;

TSW Television South West;

Designed by GWP Dorchester
Typeset by Shaun Ryan Typesetting (Dorchester)

DORCHESTER Community Play

Views of Dorchester specially drawn for the Community Play by Michael Bowman

Join us in making a new play for Dorchester about Dorchester

PATRONS
Dame Peggy Ashcroft DBE, Lord Coleridge, John Fowles Esq., Mrs. Clare Glazebrook, Councillor H. W. Haward JP, Chairman WDDC, Mr. & Mrs. John Hubbard, The Mayor of Dorchester, Sir Colin K. H. Sanderson Kt. CB, CRE, DL, Chairman DCC, Lord Olivier OM, Roger Peers Esq., Curator Dorset County Museum, Christopher Pope Esq., The Bishop of Salisbury, Tom Sharpe Esq., Mrs. J. Edward Steff.

3 Play leaflet with two folds. This is side A.

I would like to take part in the

Dorchester Community Play

NAME..

ADDRESS...

....

TELEPHONE...

AGE (if under 18)....................................

I am a member of CLUB/SOCIETY/ORGANISATION (if applicable)

....

HERE'S HOW YOU CAN JOIN IN!

(You will not be under any obligation, but if you are interested in one or more of the activities below, please tick the appropriate box).

Detach this section and return to Mrs. Jackie Byrne, Librarian, Dorchester County Library, or at the Community Play Office.

1. Acting ☐
There will be workshops through the Summer of 1985. Auditions will start in July. Rehearsals start September, 1985. Maximum for any individual – two rehearsals of about two hours a week and some Saturday or Sunday afternoons, unless playing a very large part.

2. Music ☐
We will need an orchestra for the play – also a bandmaster to help the Musical Director rehearse during the week.
I play instrument(s).................

3. Technical ☐
Help with carpentry etc – preparing the venue – erecting scaffolding – stapling carpet over it – setting up stages and seating, stripping scenery, painting.

4. Stage Management ☐
Gathering materials and properties, etc. – Would you like to be part of the S.M. Team? – Helping run the show.

5. Electrics ☐
Would you like to help with rigging the lights etc?

6. Costumes ☐
Seamstresses would need to be made at every level of skills and varying amounts of time, from giving a few hours or taking more work, to hemming a skirt or making a complete costume – unpicking and dyeing of materials – help with laundering and pressing.

7. Committees ☐
We are forming committees to cope with all aspects of the production! organising, fund-raising, projects, hospitality, production, publicity, technical, etc. Would you like to actively serve on one of these committees? If so, we would like to hear from you.
I would like to serve on................Committee

8. Publicity ☐
Office to display posters, distribute handbills, slip handbills into newspapers. Publicity ideas and opportunities are always welcome.
Why not invite one of our Speakers to your Meeting?

What is a Community Play?

A Community Play involves as many people as possible from a particular town, who aim to create a work of art of the highest standard. People of every talent, age and background may join in and become part of an exciting and challenging effort, which will express and celebrate their community.

The Writer

Our play will be especially written for us, with our help, by *DAVID EDGAR*, one of the finest playwrights in the world today. David's play, "*Maydays*" was recently performed by the Royal Shakespeare Company at the Barbican. He also adapted "*Nicholas Nickleby*" for the RSC. David has already visited Dorchester several times, and finds us all enormously interesting. He will talk with us, hear our ideas and voices, and generally absorb the atmosphere of the town. A number of Dorchester people are already actively researching with David into the history of the town and he would like to meet as many people as possible while he is here.

What will the Play be about?

David Edgar says, "Although we don't know if they ever met, the 'contest' between Henry Moule and Sarah Eldridge for the soul of mid-Nineteenth Century Dorchester is a very exciting one. On the one hand, you have a committed Minister, who struggled all his life for the improvement of the conditions of life of his Fordington parishioners, but who must have appeared a killjoy to the taverners and booksellers and indeed gentry of the town; on the other a warm, good woman who fought to create a new kind of business operation in the teeth of prejudice and vested interest. I am very keen to tap people's memories of anything they have heard about either the Moules or the Eldridges – and indeed I am trying to build up a total picture of Dorchester in the mid-19th century, focussing particularly around the great cholera outbreak of 1854".

Music

The music will be especially exciting, being composed for the play by Andrew Dickson, one of the most inventive and original composers of music for the theatre in the country.

How big will it be?

There will be probably be a cast of around 120, but many more people will be involved backstage, making costumes, publicity, etc. (see opposite). Theatre can use any number of skills and interests.

Can I join in if I have never acted?

Yes! It's your play! There will be Workshops from May, 1985 onwards, and these will be run by ANN JELLICOE, Director of the Colway Theatre Trust, together with professional tutors from London and elsewhere. These Workshops will be designed to get people working together in a friendly and informal way with theatre games and improvisation. Come and see what it is all about, no-one will press you to join in. There will be a small entrance fee to help cover expenses. (*We regret, only people of 14 years and over may attend these Workshops*).

It sounds a Very Big Undertaking

How will we get it on? By careful organisation and many willing hands. The Colway Theatre Trust now has great experience in mounting these plays. Besides Lyme Regis, they have helped mount plays in the Axe Valley, Bridport, Sherborne and Crediton, together with smaller Village Productions. Our play will have a small core of full-time professional theatre workers: Director, Designer, Stage Manager.

What Will it Cost?

A very exciting sponsorship of the Community Play has just been announced by ELDRIDGE POPE & COMPANY, who wish to demonstrate their commitment to the community of Dorchester and to foster the whole enterprise. Recognising that fund-raising is itself a community activity, Eldridge Pope are offering to sponsor £2.50 for every £1.00 raised by Dorchester, to a limit of £5,000. This is an extremely important sponsorship, and we are thrilled and encouraged by the generosity of Eldridge Pope; TVS *Television South* and TSW *Television South West* are also generously supporting us, together with South West Arts and the Arts Council of Great Britain. The previous plays have all paid for themselves and incidently brought a lot of outside money into the town.

Play Office – Dorchester 66024

The Town Council fully support the Community Play and have lent us a PLAY OFFICE in some rooms at the rear of the Corn Exchange. We have appointed a Play Office who will be helping to organise all the events leading up to the play, and we are also setting up a small MSC Scheme with Craft and Music Specialists, who will work particularly with various groups in the town at community level. We have in mind "*Reminiscence Theatre*" involving older people and *Circus Arts* for children of 11 to 14. If you know of groups of people with whom the MSC Team might work, please let us know. We are looking for groups of age 11 and upwards who would be interested in joining in some form of theatre work, providing entertainment, stimulation and relaxation. The phone number of the Play Office will shortly be announced, but in the meantime, messages can be left at the LIBRARY or at the COMMUNITY PLAY OFFICE at the rear of the CORN EXCHANGE

Rehearsals start:
September 1985

Performances:
November 18th, 19th, 20th, 21st, 22nd, 23rd and 26th, 27th, 28th, 29th, 30th, 1985

Play leaflet. Side B.

I might have been there ----

I might have been there .....

I might have been there ....

I M I G H T H A V E B E E N T H E R E ....

A SERIES OF 5 LIVELY AND INFORMAL MEETINGS WITH WRITER,<u>SHEILA YEGER</u>,
IN WHICH YOU ARE INVITED TO HELP CREATE THE MAIN EVENTS OF THE
OTTERY ST.MARY AND DISTRICT COMMUNITY PLAY.

D I S C U S S I O N S , G A M E S , I M P R O V I S A T I O N S -
C O M E T O O N E - C O M E T O A L L .

EVERYONE OVER 14 WELCOME. NO EXPERIENCE NECESSARY. WEAR CASUAL
CLOTHES. BRING A CUSHION!

VENUE: OUR ROOM UPSTAIRS AT THE TOWN COUNCIL OFFICE BUILDING,
          THE FLEXTON,OTTERY ST.MARY

1. Tuesday 7th August,8.00pm: <u>THE GREAT FIRE</u>
                              The Fire started in Jesu Street and spread
                              rapidly,stopping just short of Otter Mill. Over
                              100 homes were destroyed. One of them could have
                              been yours!

2. Wednesday 8th August,8.00pm: <u>HAVING A GOOD TIME</u>
                              Picnics,Fairs,Musical evenings. No TV. No radio.
                              Perhaps making your own entertainment was often
                              hard work. Bring musical instruments if you like.

3. Thursday 9th August,2.30pm: <u>THE ANGEL IN THE HEARTH</u>
                              The Victorian Lady - demure,ladylike - the Angel
                              in the Hearth? But was she really so different
                              from women today?

4. Thursday 9th August,8.00pm: <u>JOHNNY'S GONE TO BE A SOLDIER</u>
                              1854 - The Crimean War. Men from Ottery and District
                              went off to fight. Your husband,brother,son or
                              <u>you</u>!

5. Friday 10th August,8.00pm: <u>HARVEST HOME</u>
                              Harvest - a time for hard work and reflection
                              also celebration. Bring your stories of the farming
                              year,recipes recitations and songs.

4 & 5 Sheila Yeger invites Ottergians to help write their play.

OTTERY ST.MARY AND DISTRICT COMMUNITY PLAY

H O W   Y O U   C A N   H E L P   T O   W R I T E   I T !

Our play will be set in Victorian Ottery between 1850 and 1866.
1850 was the year Ottery St.Mary celebrated the renovation of the Church
by local craftsmen. While in 1866 the town was devastated by the Great
Fire which wiped out over 100 homes. Between these two momentous events
were others, some of local and some of national, even international
signoficance.

None of the events will be within living memory. Yet it is possible that
many people living in Ottery and the surrounding villages will have
heard stories about them passed on by grandparents or even great-
grandparents. Sheila would love to hear these stories however small they
may seem. She would particularly welcome information and especially
photographs, or though they will be rare, about the following events and
activities:-

  - celebrations in the restoration of the Church 15th May 1850
  - celebrations at the send-off of soldiers going to fight in the
    Crimean War 1854-6
  - any details about local men who fought, who were wounded or killed in
    the Crimea
  - the founding of the Cricket Club 1858
  - the attempt to stop the Tar Barrel Ceremony when Police were sent
    in from Exeter 1858
  - the coming of the railway
  - the cholera epidemics of 1855 and 1856
  - the day gas-lighting was installed 1865
  - the Great Fire 25th May 1866
  - the collapse of a chimney killing 8 people 2nd September 1866
  - any information regarding the Mill, producing silk, at this period
  - any details of old traditions at harvest time around Ottery,
    especially corn dollies
  - details of old Christmas time traditions in and around Ottery
  - any information about Fairs. Market days, Glee Clubs, Handbell Ringing
    Picnics and so on.

And if you know anything else at all relating to this period in Ottery and its
District which has not been mentioned Sheila would be glad to hear about that
to. MESSAGES CAN BE LEFT IN THE LIBRARY IN THE OLD TOWN HALL, OTTERY, OR AT
THE PLAY OFFICE ON THE FIRST FLOOR OF THE TOWN COUNCIL OFFICES.

OTTERY ST MARY & District Community Play

3 Sept 1984

WHAT IS AN ACTING WORKSHOP ?

The first of a series of acting workshops for the Ottery St.Mary and District
Community Play is next week - on Tuesday 11th at 7.00pm at the Primary School,
Longdogs Lane,Ottery. What will the workshops be like?

They will be fun,informal and very worthwhile. As ANN JELLICOE,the Director
of the Colway Theatre Trust,said:

' You will learn about aspects of acting and theatre; you will get to
know people who will be in the Community Play which SHEILA YEGER is
currently writing,and we hope you will start to see how creativity
is in everyone and how we can learn to release it in ourselves.'

The workshops will be led and organised by ANN JELLICOE,who has taught at
the Royal Academy of Dramatic Art,the Central School of Speech and Drama,
and Dartington College of Arts,in addition to her professional work as a
Theatre Director. To quote ANN again:

' The first two Workshops will be spent getting to know one another
and in exploring what happens when we improvise. There will be lots
of games and practical help to make us feel easy and confident. This
theme of practical help,good fun and building confidence are what
the workshops are about and will be progressively developed right
through the series. In no way are we out to embarrass people or
to put them on the spot.'

Later Tuesday Workshops will be either with specific aspects of the Play,
e.g. the Workshops led by JOAN MILLS,Director of the Community Play and
NICK BRACE,Musical Director,or will take advantage of the talents of gifted
teachers.'For instance,BEN BENISON is brilliant at helping people to be
free and inventive. KEITH PALMER is extremely talented at encouraging the
inexperienced,so these two will come fairly early in the series. WILLIAM
GASKILL and MIKE ALFREDS are Directors of international standing and we
will be more ready for the privilege of working with them nearer the end
of the Course.' - ANN JELLICOE

6 What is an Acting Workshop?

SPECIAL WEEKEND WORKSHOPS

There are also 3 special Weekend workshops when ANN says:

' We shall be able to really get down into the subject of our Play
and gain correspondingly greater insight,enjoyment and reward.
Again the structure of the Workshops will be games,exercises and
improvisations,which will help us release our creativity and
discover our talent. But,since there will be more time and a
relaxed atmosphere,we shall be able to go deeper into the subject.
These Weekend Workshops will be particularly valuable and present
an exceptional opportunity. You'll have a really great experience.'

So put on something comfortable and go along to the Primary School for
7.00pm. Entrance to each workshop is 75p for adults,50p for the unemployed
and students. For children under 14 years of age your chance will come
during Spring Term,1985, when a series of workshops is planned with a view
to performance in the Fair before the Play.

Sherborne Community Play

Acting Workshops

Getting together in a friendly and informal way with professional
theatre people to do improvisations, theatre games, story telling etc.
Its fun, interesting and rewarding.

Amongst those leading the Workshops; *Mike Alfreds (Shared Experience Theatre
Company), Chris Bradwell (Theatre and Dance Officer, SWA), Richard Howard
(Joint Stock Theatre Company), Ann Jellicoe (Director, Colway Theatre Trust),
and Linda Watson (Drama Teacher, Exmouth School).*

ACTING WORKSHOPS on Wednesdays, May 5th, 12th, 19th, 28th,
and June 9th, 16th, 23rd, 30th, and July 7th and 14th at 7.00 p.m.

Movement Workshops

Even if you have little or no experience of dance you will find
these Workshops really exciting.   They will help you to begin to
move freely and expressively.   In particular the Workshops will
be looking at ways we can use movement to express ideas.

Running the Workshops will be; *DANCE TALES - South West resident dance company -
the first dance company to receive a revenue grant from SWA.   There are four
dancers, who, as well as performing to a very high standard, are known for their
immensely exciting Workshops.*

TWO WEEKEND DANCE MOVEMENT WORKSHOPS

Saturday May 22nd, 2.30 to 5.30   Saturday July 3rd, 2.30 to 5.30
Sunday May 23rd, 2.30 to 5.30   Sunday July 4th, 2.30 to 5.30

*You can attend all these Workshops or any
combination of the four.   There will be a
tea break (bring a thermos).*

ALL WORKSHOPS AT FOSTER'S SCHOOL HALL, TINNEY'S LANE

Entrance: Adults 50p   Schoolchildren and unemployed 25p.

All Welcome

The Workshops are designed to lead up to rehearsals for the Community Play.

7 Handbill for workshops.

OTTERY ST.MARY AND DISTRICT COMMUNITY PLAY.......NEWSLETTER ONE 16.7.84

Dear,

Welcome to the COMMUNITY PLAY TEAM.

Thank you for your interest and enthusiasm. We can assure you that
the months ahead will be full of fun and hard work. But you're not
alone. There are more than 100 of us already with more joining in all
the time.

GETTING IN TOUCH: The information you gave on the tear-off slip from
the handout has been noted and filed! In some cases,for example if
you ticked costumes or the Fair it will be some time before we need
your help and we may not be in direct touch with you for a while. In
the meantime we will be sending you details of events,gatherings,
workshops,etc.

WHAT'S THE PLAY ABOUT?: The subject of our Play is of the greatest
interest to us all.Havingmet and talked with many Ottregians and researched widely,writer Sheila Yeger has chosen from the short list
named at the Public Meeting to take the period 1850 to 1870. This
period includes the Great Fire;the coming of the railway and the re-
dedication of the Church.

SEE YOU IN THE SQUARE: The stall in the Square on Tuesday 10th July was a
tremendous success. Sheila,Ann and I met and chatted with shoppers and passers-
by. Now we plan a repeat. We'll be there again on Saturday 21st July. Come and
meet us! Find out more details of our Play. We hope to have information available
describing the acting,speech,music and movement workshops starting in September.
Now we know what the play is going to be about Sheila is longing to hear from
you with stories anecdotes and information as well as detailed accounts relating
to the period of the Play.

PLAY OFFICE AND COSTUME WORKSHOP: We already have a Play Office on the first
floor of the Town Council Building and a telephone will shortly be installed.
We've been hunting for a large room in the centre of Ottery for us to use as
the costume workshop. The Town Council have very kindly offered us the use of
another room in the Town Council Offices. It's a marvellous central location.
Many thanks to the Town Council and their very real support for this Community
venture.

That's it for now. We'll keep in touch with all developments. If you'd
like to contact me,Andrew Pastor,just leave a note in the Library or in
the Play Office.

SEE YOU THIS SATURDAY AT THE STALL!

ANDREW PASTOR
Community Play Officer

8 Newsletter.

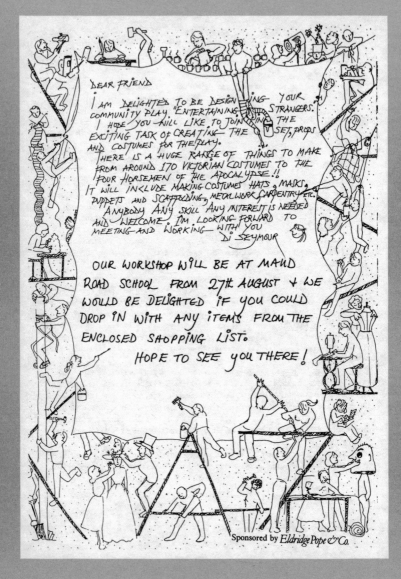

DEAR FRIEND

I AM DELIGHTED TO BE DESIGNING YOUR
COMMUNITY PLAY 'ENTERTAINING STRANGERS'.
I HOPE YOU WILL LIKE TO JOIN IN THE
EXCITING TASK OF CREATING THE SET, PROPS
AND COSTUMES FOR THE PLAY.
THERE IS A HUGE RANGE OF THINGS TO MAKE
FROM AROUND 170 VICTORIAN COSTUMES TO THE
FOUR HORSEMEN OF THE APOCALYPSE!!
IT WILL INCLUDE MAKING COSTUME HATS, MASKS,
PUPPETS AND SCAFFOLDING, METALWORK CARPENTRY ETC.
ANYBODY ANY SKILL ANY INTEREST IS NEEDED
AND WELCOME. I'M LOOKING FORWARD TO
MEETING AND WORKING WITH YOU
Di SEYMOUR

OUR WORKSHOP WILL BE AT MAUD
ROAD SCHOOL FROM 27th AUGUST & WE
WOULD BE DELIGHTED IF YOU COULD
DROP IN WITH ANY ITEMS FROM THE
ENCLOSED SHOPPING LIST.
HOPE TO SEE YOU THERE!

Sponsored by *Eldridge Pope & Co.*

9 & 10 Appeal for Materials. (Drawn by Di Seymour.)

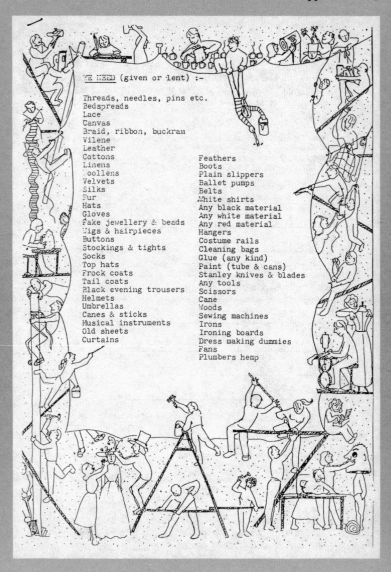

WE NEED (given or lent) :-

Threads, needles, pins etc.
Bedspreads
Lace
Canvas
Braid, ribbon, buckram
Vilene
Leather
Cottons
Linens
Woollens
Velvets
Silks
Fur
Hats
Gloves
Fake jewellery & beads
Wigs & hairpieces
Buttons
Stockings & tights
Socks
Top hats
Frock coats
Tail coats
Black evening trousers
Helmets
Umbrellas
Canes & sticks
Musical instruments
Old sheets
Curtains

Feathers
Boots
Plain slippers
Ballet pumps
Belts
White shirts
Any black material
Any white material
Any red material
Hangers
Costume rails
Cleaning bags
Glue (any kind)
Paint (tube & cans)
Stanley knives & blades
Any tools
Scissors
Cane
Woods
Sewing machines
Irons
Ironing boards
Dress making dummies
Fans
Plumbers hemp

REHEARSAL AVAILABILITY FORM

Please be as flexible as possible

Name (please print) SIMON. BLACKSELL
Address: ...HARNERS. MEAD. DALWOOD..
.......E. DEVON........................
Tel: Number....STOCKLAND. 561......
If none, where to contact:..........
....

I have a regular commitment on the following days/times and
would be unable to attend rehearsals.

PLEASE INDICATE IN RELEVANT BOX TIMES UNABLE TO ATTEND. LEAVE
ALL OTHER BOXES BLANK.

1)   WEEK

Time:	4 – 5.30pm	5.30 – 7.0pm	7.0 – 9.30pm
Mon.	School meeting		
Tues.	school meeting		
Wed.	School meeting		
Thurs.	school meeting		
Frid.	school meeting		

                          WEEKEND

Time:	2.00 – 6.30pm	7.30 – 9.0pm
Sat.		
Sun.		

2) Odd dates that I am unable to attend rehearsals: (please
                                                       list)
        Feb 18 — 26

3) I shall be away for a period of time (over 4 days) during
                                                     rehearsals

4) I am fully committed to taking part in "THE WESTERN WOMEN"
    and will attend rehearsals as scheduled.

Mon. & Tues. I always leave meetings 4 — 5.30.
Weds, Thurs, Fri I sometimes leave meetings.
In any case I have to leave school   Signed Simon Blacksell.
real early. but if needs be I could get away.

11 Rehearsal Availability Form.

4.1.84.

REHEARSAL SCHEDULE

Please make absolutely sure of your Scene Number and where you are wanted. We hope we have made no mistakes over availability, but we are only human. Please double check, if in doubt, and ring Sally-Anne Lomas or Nick Moseley at Lyme Regis 2821 if there are any problems.

All rehearsals in Woodroffe School Hall unless otherwise stated.

This detailed day by day Schedule goes up to the beginning of the School Half Term, but General Weekend Rehearsals are covered for the whole period. Barring disasters, there will be no rehearsals from February 20th - 24th. New day by day schedules will be issued just before February 20th.

PLEASE MAKE EVERY EFFORT TO ATTEND AND BE PROMPT AT REHEARSALS. If you are late, you waste other people's time, patience and nervous energy. If you cannot attend rehearsals for any reason, please telephone Sally-Anne Lomas or Nick Moseley at Lyme Regis 2821 so that we can arrange to cover the gap.

Tea: We have arranged for tea to be made at the General Rehearsals, but need mugs. If everyone would "donate" a mug when they come to the big General Read Through on January 15th, they can reclaim them at the end of rehearsal period.

REHEARSALS:

Wed. Jan. 11th

4.15	All Blake Boys scenes, including Blake, Marshall (Lanzon), Gaitch (Thistlethwaite), William Davey (Glen Carlyon), Frank Hassard (Nick Pridden), Giles Newall (Philip Moseley), John Davey (Steve Postles) Richard Coram (Simon Pettit)
	Boys: Jack Weekes (David Hibberd, Jun.), George Bagster (Julian O'Kelly), Sam Bagster (Sam Perlo), Dick Gaitch (Tom Mayne), Nick Guppy (Jerome Shapland) Tom Loveridge (Paul Blow)
	N.B. PLUS: Alice Oliver (Sarah Hibberd), Rose Somers (Sarah Woodbridge).
	NOTE: Following Boys Scenes to be arranged:
	4.15 Wed. Jan. 18th.
	4.15 Wed. Jan. 25th.
	4.15 Wed. Feb. 8th.
5.30	Scenes 19 & 44: Blake, Bazeley only
7.00	Scene 1: Seeleys (no baby)

Thur. Jan. 12th

4.4.15	Scene 6: Fishwives (Geare not required)
5.15	Scene 33: Cannonade
6.00	Scene 38: Women want to fights
8.00 - 9.30	Scenes 11, 14: Moxeidges, Johanna, Rebecca plus Symon Boddie.

Fri. Jan. 13th

4.15	Scene 3: Town Clerk
4.15(double)	Scene 39 (v) in B 12
4.45	Scene 4: Belots
4.45(double)	Scene 39 (vi) in B 12
5.30	Scene 24: "Guards are being Changed"
7.00 - 7.30	Scene 25: Royalists
7.00(double)	Scene 39 (i) in B 12
7.45	Scene 39 (iv) in B 12

12 Detailed Rehearsal Schedule.

Tel: Dorchester 66024
(0305)

Community Play Office,
Maud Road School,
Dorchester.

Dear

A Community Play is not merely a play, it's an expression of our relationship with each other and indeed if "Entertaining Strangers" is about anything it is about helping and supporting each other: "it's our Jerusalem".

I am writing this letter to you all because while most people are wonderfully committed to coming to rehearsal, a number of you are either not coming to small rehearsals or more subtly feeling they need not come to the big General Rehearsals. What I think must be happening is that some people are saying to themselves: "They can get on without me. My part is pretty small. It won't matter. I have to go to such and such ... or I would rather so and so ..." whatever personal concern they may have. Of course on occasions some of us cannot manage to come to rehearsal and are very good indeed about letting us know.

But not turning up makes the rehearsal less valuable since the work has to be done again and the energy and enthusiasm revitalised. Even more important: it breaks the chain of commitment.

However small a part may be, every single person has a vital role to play, not only as an actor, but in demonstrating faith in the idea of a Community Play. Helping, giving, sharing, all of us reaching towards a goal: an expression of commitment to positive things, to energy, enthusiasm, idealism.

What we are doing with this play in a small way is celebrating, bearing witness to our belief in the goodness and faith of people. Many of you are coming to rehearsals with extraordinary dedication, commitment and enthusiasm. I'm beginning to feel that amazing feeling of trust, friendliness, warmth and supportiveness, which always happens with these plays and which maybe, we hope, spills out into life.

I do beg you not to betray this capacity in yourself: to open yourselves to the idea behind the Community Play. To take part in the positive forces and ideas which are shaping the play: the giving and sharing, the energy and excitement. Every single person who is not there robs us in some small way of this experience.

Opportunities to share in working towards something which celebrates and tries to achieve an idealistic aim don't come often. Please come when you are called. Take your fullest part. Sometimes I know it's impossible and then you will let us know. Please allow yourself to be part of, to support this extraordinary feeling of excitement and energy which we are all beginning to sense.

Sincerely and affectionately,

Ann Jellicoe

Sponsored by *Eldridge Pope & Co.*

13 Encouragement during 'Seven Week Sag'.

COMMUNITY PLAY

THE FAIR

Each night for ½ hour before the performance starts there will be a Fair. This serves several purposes:-

1. The play is a promenade production. This means a large proportion of the audience will be walking around and standing. We don't want them to be reminded of their feet, as they might be if they came into the usual quiet auditorium before the play starts! Rather, we want a genuine, glamorous, "party" atmosphere.

2. Helping with the organisation of the Fair more people can become involved in the Community Play.

In terms of organisation, the Fair falls into 2 parts - WE organise:-

Glamorous and exciting lighting, music, crafts, sideshows (e.g. quack doctors, "strong men", animal tamers, etc) and hopefully a big centre piece (e.g. Morris Dancers, a Mummers Play, etc.). Also, the actors will be walking around in costume to give atmosphere.

The other part we ask YOU, the organisations, to provide:-

Up to 25 people per night in simple costume, in sympathy with the period of the play (we can generally help with mob caps, possibly aprons, etc.) You can sell anything you think people might like to buy, but remember they don't want to carry too much through the evening and they don't want too much sickly food - savoury things are always popular. Things which sell well include sausage rolls and sausages (hot if possible), mince pies, homemade biscuits, gingerbread, shortbread, small cakes or pieces of cake, sweets, particularly homemade sweets. Tangerines are very popular indeed because they are refreshing. Drink (non alchoholic), though we generally don't encourage the sale of drink during the interval, because this conflicts with the sale of coffee, etc.
Goods
Anything small and pretty, particularly with Christmas in mind, e.g. lavender bags, peg dolls, posies of dried flowers, gift cards, embroidered handkerchiefs, etc. Some organisations have hired out cushions, as the benches can be very hard! If you wish, you can also sell during the interval.

Occasionally, one or more organisations have undertaken to sell baked potatoes and butter for the audience as they leave the auditorium after the play and these are very popular with the cast as well on a cold night.

The goods have to be carried around on trays. There are no stalls, as we have to clear the Fair quickly and discreetly.

The Fair Assembles at about 6.45 p.m. before the doors open at 7.0 p.m. and leaves the Hall just before the play starts at 7.30 p.m. (There will be careful briefing of details nearer the time).
We regret we can't allow free tickets for the play for people joining in the Fair. If you stay to watch the play, you must have a valid ticket for that evening.

If you are selling the right things, you can make about £100 a night for your organisation, have a jolly good time, and also be supporting the Community Play.

14 Fair details as distributed to interested groups.

COLVAY THEATRE TRUST

BOX OFFICE MANAGEMENT

Proposals for Discussion

1. <u>Tickets</u>.   400 tickets per night will be ordered by ordered
by:..(Name)............350 may be sold for each performance. More are
printed so that it will not be necessary for the BOM to personally
collect any unsold tickets on the day of performance so as to be able to
sell them at the door.

Tickets will be a different colour for each performance
bound in books of 25.   Each ticket will have a serial
number and two counterfoils, with a box to indicate Adult
or Child which should be ticked off at the point of
sale; one counterfoil is retained at the point of sale,
the stewards tear off the second counterfoil at the
entrance to the hall.

<u>Seating Tickets</u>   There will be separate tickets issued
for seating (see Note 6). These will be the only white
tickets.

2. <u>Sub Box Offices</u>   The Box Office Manager must be in
complete control and s/he is responsible for handing over
selected number of tickets to the Sub Box Offices and
recording the serial number of tickets handed over. On
days of performance, the BOM rings the SBO at an agreed
time to find out how many tickets have been sold for that
particular day.   The BOM then gives the order: "Sell
no more tickets" to the Sub Box Office and the BOM then
knows how many tickets are left for sale that evening.
All further enquiries at the Sub Box Office are then
referred to the main Box Office or to the Theatre.

3. <u>Accounts</u>   The Box Office Manager is responsible
for banking all monies. S/He should keep account of
tickets sold and monies received.   S/He should also
include monies taken at the Sub Box Office on the

15 Notes as basis for discussion with Box Office Manager. *Page one.*

accounts, so that we have an overall picture. As we get
nearer performance, we shall need to check the number of
tickets sold both for that evening's performance and in
advance, fairly frequently. We need to be able to take
measures, if necessary, to increase the audience or to
warn the cast.

4.   Collecting Money   Money will be collected from the
Sub Box Offices at regular intervals, to be agreed
between the Box Office Manager and the Sub Box Office.

5.   Advance Bookings   Telephone bookings should be paid
for within at least 3 working days after ordering,
otherwise tickets may be released for sale. Tickets
ordered by telephone on the day of performance must be paid
for by 7 o'clock, otherwise they may be sold.

  Advance Booking for Cast will open . (date)

  Advance Booking for the general public will open .(date)

  Party Bookings   Where substantial booking enquiries
are made before this date the Box Office Manager may,
at their discretion undertake to hold the tickets/seats
and confirm them after this date. We should discuss
when party bookings should be paid for.

6.   Seating   50 seats on scaffolding and 25 chairs for
OAPs only may be reserved in advance each night. There
is a possible area of trouble here: postal bookings may
ask for reserved seating when there is none left. The
form for postal booking states that if there are no
seats left, then the supplementary fee will be returned
at the door. It is important that if people cannot have

Box Office notes. *Page two.*

seats for postal bookings which they had hoped for, we
make this very clear when returning their tickets, and
we may have to work out a form which the Box Office
Manager can include with the tickets. There is no
reduction in seating for children. We specifically
want the seating to be kept for older people and wish to
discourage seating for children.

Seats for Civic Night Please note that no seats on the
scaffolding or chairs may be sold in advance at Civic
Night, as they may be needed for Civic dignitaries,
V.I.P.s etc.

7. Performance The Box Office Manager or a responsible
deputy should be present to sell tickets at least 20
minutes before the doors open. With the extra
complications of seating, we should discuss the possibility
of a second desk with someone to deal specifically with
returning money for supplementary seating and dealing
with queries, e.g. apportioning any extra seats that
may be available. The person manning this desk will be
under the control of the Box Office Manager.

8. Stewards There will be a number of stewards at each
performance who will be responsible to the House Manager
but who will closely work with the Box Office Manager.
At the start of the performance, stewards and House Manager
may help check tickets. They will control access to seats.

9. Cash Security We should have clear arrangements as to
security of cash taken on the night at the door.

10. Refunds As a general rule, no refunds should be paid.

Box Office notes. *Page three.*

11. <u>Complimentary Tickets</u>   The Director will from
time to time issue complimentary tickets, or a signed
pass (marked "Guest") to specifically invited guests.
These should be treated as tickets.   Anyone requiring
a complimentary ticket must obtain authority from the
Director.   Complimentary tickets will be issued
sparingly.   None will be given to members of the cast.

TO BE DISCUSSED:

1. Tickets to be ordered by....(Name)...

2, By what date are they to be ready?

3. When do coach parties pay?

4. Need for form to tell postal bookers that all seats are taken and
that money will be returned at the door. Form to be organised
by....(Name)....

5. Do we need a second desk? Who will man it?

6. Areas of responsibility/contact between Box Office Manager/ House
Manager/ Stage Manager/Stewards

7. Cash security..

Box Office notes. *Page four.*

A. ADDRESS

Dorchester	[40]
Within 3 miles	[5]
Within 20 miles	[13]
Within 10 miles	[22]
Over 20 miles	[1]

Male [29]
Female [38]

B. PREVIOUS EXPERIENCE

Please tick

Have you acted before
- in the last 4 years [33]
- prior to 4 years [25]
- never [24]

Are you, or have you been involved, or connected with the arts, visual, performing, music or dance? [43]

C. HOW DID YOU BECOME INVOLVED IN THE PLAY? You may tick more than one box

Through publicity, adverts, local radio, newspapers, leaflets, news items	[40]
Through friends already involved	[18]
Someone suggested you join in	[17]
Because of The Public Meeting	[7]
Through work already doing	[9]
Asked to participate	[14]
Another route in	[7]
'Persuaded'	[7]
Work-shops	[22]

D. PERCEPTIONS I would like your perceptions of the play. How you feel about it, what you think, your own view even though it may be shared. Please tick 1 = minimum/low, 5 = maximum/high

This is bound to be

	1	2	3	4	5
	1	3	14	29	32
	4	2	9	13	51
	5	13	21	28	11
	1	0	7	27	44
	7	18	29	14	8

(i) How successful do you think was The Play as a social catalyst for the group/cast?
(ii) What level of personal satisfaction did you get from being involved?
(iii) How much did being in the play develop your theatre skills?
(iv) How high do you think was the overall theatrical achievements of the cast?
(v) Do you think the Play will be a springboard for the development of theatre/the arts in the town?

E. Which for you were the best, most important or effective bits, scenes or moments in the whole play? Can you describe briefly two of these?

e.g. (i) the scene where ....

or (ii) the place where ....

over/

16 Peter Hamilton's questionnaire following the Dorchester Play. (Figures show the composite results from 80 replies.)

Can you say why you liked them particularly?

(i) ....

(ii) ....

F. If you would like to include any additional thought, comment or perception about any aspects of the play, please could write them here ...

In allowing me to reproduce his questionnaire Peter Hamilton made the following notes:

"I think the form needs modifying:

1. To include an 'age' and 'occupation' block.
2. By changing D(iii) to 'How much did being in the play develop your theatrical awareness?'
3. By changing F to the plural, ie. thoughts, comments, etc
4. To allow a space for people's own particular benefits and gains.

However, given these reservations and the limited number of returns, 79/180, there are some interesting observations. Among these are the raw, dipstick figures which show that 43% of the sample came from outside Dorchester (over 3 miles), that 30% had no acting experience and that 57% were women.

In section F where there was space for additional thoughts and comments, there were:

26 empty unfilled spaces
16 returns of unreserved, one-line praise for the achievement, the experience, the buzz, etc.
24 people went to some lengths to explain and pin down the particular nature of a very positive experience.
13 contained a blend of positive aware criticism and some doubts on the structure and nature of the play itself."

WITH MANY THANKS FOR YOUR TIME

Peter Hamilton

Peter Hamilton
20th November 1985

Questionnaire. *Page two*.

COLWAY THEATRE TRUST   DORCHESTER COMMUNITY PLAY   ANALYSIS OVER 1 YEAR OF USER HOURS/CONTACT SESSIONS

Notes:

(i) This is an attempt to list the hours/contact sessions of amateur involvement. The contact sessions are computed by multiplying the number of sessions by the number of those taking part. The length of a session is taken as an average of 3 hours.

(ii) The figures relate only to AMATEUR involvement and do NOT include any time worked by Colway Theatre Trust professionals and ignore all general, non-specific involvement and participation in consciousness and fund-raising activities, e.g. the figures do not include those watching non-stop theatrical/musical performances during the "Fun Day" and all other street events; those who participated in fund-raising activities; all Work Packs prepared for Schools and used by children in connection with the Play. Nor do they include all those who attended the Public Meeting and other Talks and Meetings addressed by Ann Jellicoe, David Edgar and others, etc. etc.

(iii) Not listed is any work in Beaminster, the next target area.

(iv) These figures are probably the nearest we can compute, but are likely to be an understatement.

(v) Interaction: A factor which should be taken into account is the way in which maturing groups begin to interact independently, e.g. the Video Group worked with Old Folks and on school work, etc. The Research Group taped old people Reminiscing and also collected material for an exhibition in the Museum which they themselves set up. They also wrote, collated, pasted up and themselves published a book: "Dorchester 1884".

ACTIVITY	NUMBER OF HOURS/PEOPLE/WEEKS	TOTAL USER HOURS	CONTACT SESSIONS
Acting Workshops	9 sessions x 2 hours x 50 people (average)	900	450
Activists	(i.e. people who filled in cards saying they wished actively to help with the show)		
150 high activists	2 hrs. per week x 24 weeks x 150 people	7,200	3,600
350 low activists	½ hr. " " x 24 sessions x 350 people	4,200	2,100
Committee Members (30 members)	2 hrs. x average 14 meetings x 30 people (8 hrs. work per month outside Committee Meetings)	2,160	420
David Edgar Research Group	David Edgar had a Research Group of 6 people who started work September, 1984. They consider that 1 of them did 500 hours work; 2 did 200 hours and 3 did 100 hours	1,200	400
*Circus Arts in Schools (Afternoons 2 hrs, Lunchtimes 1 hr.)	2 schools x 3 hrs. per week x average 20 children x 26 weeks	3,120	1,040
*General Workshops in Circus Arts Skills	2 groups x 3 Workshops x 3 hrs. x 25 people	450	150
	C/F	19,230	8,160

17 Analysis of 'User Hours' and 'Contact Sessions' in Dorchester.
Page one.

ACTIVITY	NUMBER OF HOURS/PEOPLE/WEEKS	TOTAL USER HOURS	CONTACT SESSIONS
	B/F	19,230	8,160
•Old People: Reminiscence/ Video Sessions	Average 15 people x 2 hrs. per week x 20 sessions	600	300
•Video Workshops with unemployed	2 Workshops: (i) 8 weeks x 6 people x 3 hrs. (ii) 12 " x 3 " x 3 hrs.	144 108	48 36
•Workshops with disabled	8 weeks x 4 people x 3 hrs.	96	32
•Community Service (making sessions)	For offenders who "do time" by serving the Community in their free time. Made giant puppets for the Fair, Salisbury Fields Fun Day, etc. and other events. 6 people x 7 hrs. per week x 8 weeks	336	48
Actors' Rehearsal Hours	176 actors x 7 hrs. per week x 11 weeks = 13,552 hrs. 176 actors x 25 " " x 1 " = 4,400 "	17,952	5,784
Actors' Performance	176 actors x 11 performances x 4 hrs. (dressing, warm-ups, performance)	7,744	2,581
Band (Dorchester) Band " Performances	Average 20 players x 3 hrs. x 6 rehearsals = 360 hrs. " 20 " x 3 hrs. x 11 performances = 660 "	1,020	120 220
Costume Makers	Average 86 people each giving average 30 hrs.	2,580	860
Technical Helpers (in setting up play)	90 people each giving average 20 hrs.	1,800	600
Audience (Dorchester)	5,500 people x 3 hrs.	16,500	5,500
Fair Sellers	20 people per night from a different group in the town. 2 hrs. making; ½ hr. selling x 11 performances	350	220
	TOTAL USER HOURS	68,460	24,509

Note: * Work organised by the Manpower Services Commission Team of 3 "places" also helped with the general setting up of events, etc. where they relate to the community. The MSC Team also took part in the actual production of the play on a similar basis.

Analysis. *Page two.*

COLWAY THEATRE TRUST

B R I D P O R T   C O M M U N I T Y   P L A Y

AN ANALYSIS OF THE MONEY COMING INTO THE TOWN FROM OUTSIDE

The main argument for Art is Art, not money. "The money would be better spent in some other way" (e.g. Housing for the Aged), is a common remark, but it is extremely unlikely that this money would ever be raised or spent for that pur- pose. "The Poor Man's Friend" was an event that raised community conscious- ness and enhanced the quality of life, and incidentally, by much media attention, brought Bridport valuable publicity.

The figures that follow are based on careful analysis and are a conservative assessment, remarkable though they be. The figures relate entirely to money coming into Bridport from outside. They do not include money raised or spent in Bridport itself as the result of the Community Play.

1. Grant Aid

Leche Trust	£ 500	
South West Arts	£1,118	
Arts Council of Gt. Britain	£ 500	
Silver Jubilee Trust	£ 500	
Youth Opportunities Project Scheme	£1,175	£ 3,793

2. Visitors from outside Town who came to the Community Play

From an analysis of ticket stubs, telephone bookings, etc. it is estimated that 540 people came into the Town from outside. (There would have been a further 150, but for the bad weather!).

A Questionnaire was issued to each member of the audience. 212 of those who answered came from outside the Town. Most of them said the Community Play was the chief reason for visiting Bridport. They gave a fairly detailed breakdown of their expenditure and these figures must be on the low side, because the questionnaire was generally filled in halfway through the evening, and visitors may well have stopped off for a drink, or to buy petrol, etc. before going home. From their answers, we were able to analyse that each person attending the Play spent an average of £3.98 during the Fair, on programmes, etc. or in the Town itself, in addition to the price of their ticket.

Official Observers & Critics

There were several "official" observers and critics who came into Bridport to see the Play. These included Arts Council and SWA Officers, Kaleidoscope (who spent three days recording), Newspaper Critics, pro- fessional observers from other Companies, etc. Some of these stayed in private hospitality, but most paid for their own overnight accommo- dation in Hotels, etc. The BBC and Arts Council rate for expenses is just under £30 a day.

Outside Visitors & Official Observers, etc., tickets
                    and money spent in Town .... £ 3,544

                                        C/F   £ 7,337

18 & 19 Bridport Analysis of Money coming into the Town.

B/F £ 7,337

3.   T.V.Crew

The TV who spent a good deal of time in the Town, filming the
Show, have so far spent a total of 90 nights here, in Hotel
accommodation, and of course spending through the day on meals,
petrol, cigarettes, etc. If we estimate the Crew's daily spending at the very conservative rate of £30 a day, we have a total
of £3,060.   £ 3,060

4.   Household Shopping

The Director and Co-Director did most of their shopping in the
Town over a considerable period.   Estimate   £   400

        TOTAL OF MONEY FROM OUTSIDE, COMING INTO BRIDPORT,
        AS A DIRECT RESULT OF THE COMMUNITY PLAY £10,797

JOBS CREATED

Since the professional core was recruited for various periods, probably the best
way to assess the amount of work created by the Play is to count the number of
"job weeks", e.g. the Costume Designer spent 15 weeks on the job; the Deputy
Stage Manager spent 6 weeks. In all, the Community Play created an estimated
149 professional job weeks. It also created 50 Youth Opportunities Project
job weeks.

SECONDARY FUNDING

Recent American research by the U.S. National Endowment for the Arts, December
1980, demonstrates that each dollar (or pound) subscribed in Arts Funding,
goes round eleven times before it "leaks out" from the State, in taxes, goods
and services paid out, etc. etc. It thus stimulates the economy eleven times,
and creates jobs and the demand for goods and services. In a small Town the
size of Bridport (population 6,000 plus), obviously the money will "leak out"
much sooner because the Town does not support itself in the same degree as,
e.g. the State of Louisianna. However, it is probably true that each pound
goes round two times before it "leaks out of the Town, i.e. £10,797 does the
work of £21,000 in stimulating demand for goods and services.

Workshop Book List

In planning and setting up workshops you may find the following books helpful. It's not an exhaustive list, a search in a specialist bookshop would probably yield more titles. I myself always keep a record, making notes, of other people's workshops and have built up a file of ideas.

Brandes & Philps: *The Gamester's Handbook* (Hutchinson)
Brandes, Donna: *Gamester's Handbook 2* (Hutchinson)
> Two very practical books listing and describing games according to how they may be used e.g. 'Introductory Games', 'Trust Games' etc.

Chilver, Peter: *Improvised Drama* (Batsford)
Johnstone, Keith: *Impro* (Methuen)
> The condensed thoughts and experience of one of the finest and most original teachers in the world. Explains concept of blocking, status etc. Get this if you get no other.

Morris & Evans: *Drama Resource Cards* (Longman)
> A series of cards with planned workshops and specific techniques e.g. fights. You can pick up the card you want and take it to the workshop. Aimed chiefly at schools, practical and well thought out.

O'Neill & others: *Drama Guidelines* (Heinemann Education)
Polsky, Milton E. *Let's Improvise* (Prentice Hall)
Spolin, Viola: *Improvisation for the Theatre* (Pitman)

Index